TEACHING FUNCTIONAL ACADEMICS

TEACHING FUNCTIONAL ACADEMICS:
A Curriculum Guide for Adolescents and Adults with Learning Problems

Michael Bender, Ed.D.
Director of Special Education
The John F. Kennedy Institute for Handicapped Children
and
Associate Professor
The Johns Hopkins University

Peter J. Valletutti, Ed.D.
Professor of Special Education
Coppin State College

University Park Press
Baltimore

UNIVERSITY PARK PRESS
International Publishers in Medicine and Human Services
300 North Charles Street
Baltimore, Maryland 21201

Copyright © 1982 by University Park Press
Second printing, April 1983

Composed by University Park Press Typesetting Division.
Manufactured in the United States of America
by Eastern Lithographing Corporation.

Library of Congress Cataloging in Publication Data
Bender, Michael, 1943-
Teaching functional academics.
Bibliography: p.
Includes index.
1. Handicapped—Education. 2. Handicapped—Education—Life skills. I.
Valletutti, Peter J. II. Title. LC4812.B46   371.9   81-11477
ISBN 0-8391-1662-4   AACR2

CONTENTS

PREFACE

This book has been developed as an instructional resource for those professionals working with adolescents and adult populations with learning problems. It is intended for use by educators instructing or preparing to instruct adolescents and adults in schools and other instructional settings.

Members of interdisciplinary teams, as they assist educators in facilitating functional objectives, will also be able to identify information relevant to their professional area of competency.

Parents, surrogate parents, and other advocates as well as individuals working in activity centers, workshops, group homes, apartments, and other community residences will find the information contained in this book useful in planning daily routines and schedules.

Personnel working in state and private residential centers and specialists in music, art, drama, dance, and leisure and vocational education also will find material pertinent to their respective teaching areas.

Finally, this book is designed to serve as a text for students taking courses in curriculum development, methods of teaching, and in areas involving the scope and sequence of curriculum activity in functional academics.

ACKNOWLEDGMENTS

The material for this book has been developed over a period of eight years. It is an outgrowth of many curricular ideas first presented by Drs. Bender and Valletutti in their *Teaching The Moderately and Severely Handicapped,* Volume III. The completion of this work would not have been possible without the assistance of a number of individuals. Foremost among these are: Edith Garrett, Reginald Griffin, Rochelle Hammerman, Dixie Hughlett, Ruth Matyuf, John R. Meyers, Greg Pesik, Nicolette Pesik, Shelley Post, Madelyn Russo, Kimberly Ruppersberger, Jill Schauben, Claudine Steisel, Candice Suggars, and Terri Tyler.

Special acknowledgment is given to Kay Heeter, Lorraine Richter, and Marguerite Csar for their tireless efforts in typing and retyping the manuscript.

STYLISTIC DEVICES

A number of stylistic devices are used in this book for clarity and fluency. They are:

1. The individual is referred to as male because males have significantly more learning problems than females.
2. The word "individual" is used in all cases to refer to the learner. This is to emphasize that the instructional activities are not age specific and can be used for children as well as the adolescents and adults for whom this book is primarily intended.
3. Suggested Readings and Resources have been organized purposely to reflect practical as well as theoretical information.

LIST OF FIGURES

to my mother Sally Bender for her continuing encouragement and support and to Stephen Benjamin Bender with all my love

to the memory of my beloved grandparents: Giuseppe Valletutti, Filomena Cerino, Angelo Valente, and Rosina Di Stefano as well as to all their children

TEACHING
FUNCTIONAL ACADEMICS

chapter 1
INTRODUCTION AND OVERVIEW

CONCEPTUAL FRAMEWORK

This book presents a curriculum framework for developing functional learning activities and experiences appropriate to adolescents and adults who are experiencing learning problems. Functional learning activities and experiences are conceptualized to include the traditional basic-skill subjects of reading, writing, and mathematics. Learning problems are defined in the broadest sense to include all those factors that may interfere with the learning process, such as deviations in cognitive, physical, social, and emotional development. The curriculum framework is also meant to facilitate instruction for individuals who have been characterized as being mildly and moderately mentally retarded, learning disabled, emotionally handicapped, orthopedically impaired, or as having other developmental disabilities. Similarly, the term "adults" is meant to be viewed in its broadest sense to include *all* of the adult years in recognition of the need for life-long learning especially for those with learning problems.

In utilizing this framework to design relevant learning experiences, professionals, parents, surrogate parents, and other advocates must be judicious. Not only must they select activities, materials, and equipment, but they must provide experiences that are applicable to adolescents *and* adults. This emphasis becomes increasingly difficult as the age of the individual being instructed advances beyond the traditional years of schooling.

In establishing the curriculum framework and its component elements, a sociological perspective has been utilized. This perspective is based on the functional roles that an individual must assume to function fully in society. These roles are as follows:

1. The individual as a resident of a *home*.
2. The individual as a learner in traditional and non-traditional *school* settings.
3. The individual as a participant in the *community*.
4. The individual as a *consumer* of goods and services.
5. The individual as a *worker*.
6. The individual as a participant in *leisure experiences*.

FUNCTIONAL ESSENCE

In utilizing the curriculum framework in designing instructional objectives, experiences, and activities, the functional essence or reality must be kept constantly in mind. Many educators profess a commitment to the functional education of individuals with learning problems; however, their instructional plans are not congruent with their instructional purpose. Before creating instructional activities and experiences from specified objectives, instructors and others must diligently examine the functional reality that undergirds the stated objective. To do so requires a simple technique, namely the performance of the learning task in its actual context from the viewpoint of the learner and his role in that context. *Fail-*

ure to do so defeats the implied purpose of a functional curriculum. Failure to observe the functional essence renders the instructional act as impractical as more traditional approaches.

Examples of the functional essence for sample objectives in each of the six segments of the curriculum framework follow.

THE HOME
Functional Reading

The individual:

1. Turns on the desired burner after locating the appropriate dial or pushbutton that regulates that burner. The individual then, when applicable, selects the pushbutton that determines the desired temperature level for that burner.

Functional Essence

Instructional plans should have as their functional essence:

   a. the selection of a desired temperature level for the burner or heating element based upon recipe requirements and safety factors;
   b. the selection of foods that require cooking on top of the stove;
   c. the reheating of leftover foods;
   d. the matching of the type of pot or pan to the type of cooking desired (e.g., frying, boiling, or steaming);
   e. the matching of pot and pan size to burner size;
   f. the matching of pot and pan size to food quantity; and
   g. the selection of pots and pans according to their composition as specified by recipes (e.g., porcelain, stainless steel, or cast iron).

Throughout instructional activities, emphasis must be placed on safety.

THE SCHOOL
Functional Writing

The individual:

1. Writes down the requested information on school-related forms.

Functional Essence

Instructional plans should have as their functional essence the development of those integrated reading and writing skills involved in completing forms such as:

   a. class registration;
   b. library request;
   c. field trip permission;
   d. free breakfast or lunch requests; and
   e. musical instrument rental.

Key words should be culled from these forms and taught in relation to the individual's personal response, e.g., "Birthdate"—9/23/64. All forms used in the school program should be part of instructional activities.

THE COMMUNITY
Functional Mathematics

The individual:

14. Estimates the amount of time needed to meet bus, train, subway, and airline schedules.

Functional Essence

Instructional plans should have as their functional essence the estimating of time needed to meet transportation schedules. Experiences should include practice runs from the individual's home to selected bus stops, subway stations, train depots, airports, and bus terminals. After several trips to each site, assist the individual in arriving at a reasonable time estimate with an additional 10–15 minutes leeway added. Then assist the individual in subtracting this estimate, in each instance, from train, bus, airline, and subway departure or boarding times to determine his own times of departure. Actual trips should then be taken using the individual's estimates.

CONSUMER SKILLS
Functional
Reading

The individual:

2. Consults a shopping list and finds desired items in a supermarket by using a store directory.

Functional Essence

Instructional plans should have as their functional essence the development of the following skill sequences:

  a. preparation of a shopping list that reflects the individual's needs and budgetary constraints;
  b. identification of items by category, e.g., apples—*fruits*; carrots—*vegetables*; pepper—*spices*; etc.;
  c. location of categories on a store directory (bulletin board or hanging signs);
  d. identification of an aisle number when the directory is on a bulletin board;
  e. location of aisles by posted signs; and
  f. location of desired items on the shelves and in the bins or cabinets of that aisle.

Practice in each of these skills should be provided in simulated and actual shopping trips.

WORK
Functional Writing
(Office and Business
Occupations)

The individual:

10. Records customer's orders.

Functional Essence

Instructional plans should have as their functional essence the taking of customers' orders:

  a. over the phone;
  b. in person when an item must be ordered; and
  c. in person when the order form has to be routed to someone else for filling.

Instructional experiences should include all of the above situations. It may be necessary to develop a functional reading-writing list appropriate to the individual's business or business area of interest. Sample order forms should be collected and the individual given orders to record on these forms.

LEISURE
EXPERIENCES
Functional
Mathematics

The individual:

21. Determines the cost of automobile trips.

Functional Essence

Instructional plans should have as their functional essence the calculation of the cost of automobile trips including short as well as long trips. Instructional activities should include the determination of the total costs, including:

  a. tune-up;
  b. gas;
  c. oil;
  d. tolls;
  e. insurance; and
  f. depreciation.

Hypothetical trips should be planned originating from the individual's home or apartment. These trips should be scheduled to places of interest to the individual, and then the relative costs should be computed. Later, actual trips should be planned and the costs computed. Include, when applicable, the cost of accommodations, taxes, tips, and meals in the total cost.

DEVELOPING INSTRUCTIONAL PLANS

Once the sequence and scope of general or unit objectives and their supporting specific objectives are charted, the structure for educational evaluation and programming is present. These objectives serve as the framework for systematically observing and assessing the individual's performance in terms of processes and products. Evaluation occurs as the individual functions on a daily basis and when he responds to structured and simulated activities by parents, instructors, instructional aides, and other human-service professionals. These observations aid in determining those general and specific objectives to be selected for instructional planning. (*See* Sample Instructional Plan at the end of this chapter).

1. Instructional planning thus begins with the identification of a *General Objective* representing a major curriculum segment and the subsequent articulation of a relevant *Specific Objective* stated in behavioral terms. The specific objective is one that is deemed as contributing to the major curriculum goal implicit in the general objective.

2. After specifying a specific objective that serves as the focus of the instructional plan, a pertinent *Instructional Objective* is then composed. The instructional objective, as the specific objective, is student oriented and has the dual purpose of structuring the instructional sequence and suggesting the assessment strategy and assigned performance criterion level. Toward these ends, an instructional objective has three elements:
   a. The definition of the stimulus situation or conditions, e.g., "When given . . ." or "After being shown . . . ."
   b. The specification of the desired response, e.g., "The individual will . . . ."
   c. The establishment of a mastery level, e.g., "The individual will do so in four out of five trials." or "He will do so correctly within 5 minutes."

3. Next, *Materials and Equipment* are listed. The placement of this instructional plan segment is optional but is placed early in the plan for ease in reading as one skims the written plan before its implementation. In actuality, this section is filled in after the motivation and instructional procedures are identified. It is not expected that the instructional plan will be read in the teaching/learning context. Rather, its value lies in developing the plan before it is used. The design of the instructional plan aids the instructor in logically creating the educational program in a deliberate and reasoned professional manner.

4. Following the listing of materials and equipment, the *Motivating Activity* is stated. For many this is a challenging task, for it is difficult to specify a motivating activity that will capture the attention, imagination, and interest of those individuals for whom the instruction is designed. Many instructors who find it easy to motivate young children experience difficulty in formulating stimulating introductory activities, instructional procedures, and materials and equipment appropriate to individuals with mature interests and perspectives. The use of materials that appeal to young children are invariably counterproductive when used with adolescents and adults.

5. Next, *Instructional Procedures* are precisely and logically sequenced as suggested by the previously stated instructional objective. Instructional objectives are instructor oriented and are sequenced in logical steps from initial motivation to assessment.

6. *Individualized Reinforcement and Reinforcement Schedules* are then identified in recognition of the different reward preferences and needs of individuals and their varying response rates.

7. At this point a proposed *Follow-Up Activity/Objective* is written to ensure that the sequence of instruction is respected. A follow-up objective is specified when the instructor believes that the specific objective has been mastered and the individual is ready to proceed to the next specific objective. A follow-up activity is suggested when the specific objective requires additional experiences and activities for its complete attainment.

8. The *Assessment Strategy* to be employed is then specified. This strategy reflects the desired response and the mastery criterion or criteria stated in the instructional objective. It is instructor oriented and includes any record-keeping requirements.

9. *Instructional Resources* are articulated next. These suggested readings and resources are meant to support the instructional design and provide relevant information to readers and implementers of the instructional plan.

10. Finally, a concluding section is appended for the purpose of recording *Observations and Comments* for later reference and for use in completing checklists, for writing progress reports, and in designing individualized educational programs (IEPs). The instructor should schedule a time for recording observations and comments that provide special insights into the individual's characteristics and interests for educational and treatment purposes.

EVALUATING INDIVIDUAL PERFORMANCE AND PROGRESS

Instructors who fully appreciate the essential role of educational evaluation in designing instructional programs are aware that learners continually provide diagnostic information as they interact or fail to interact with people and objects in their environment. Strategies for observing and recording performance and progress are necessary to a systematic evaluation process. In addition, a framework must be provided that will structure and formalize observations. The scope and sequence of curriculum objectives provide that needed framework because learners are evaluated in terms of the tasks required of them. Therefore, a suggested companion to any curriculum framework is a complementary checklist that mirrors the objectives stated there.

A *Sample Completed Checklist* is provided here to clarify its composition and its use. The heading labeled "legend" in this checklist is supplied to elucidate the nature of possible responses and, when applicable, the types of assistance employed to obtain the desired responses.

Sample Completed Checklist

Individual's Name _____

Special Physical
Restrictions/Conditions _____
(if any)

General Objective:
The individual will function in leisure experiences as independently and skillfully as possible by performing diverse written tasks.

Evaluator(s) _____
_____
_____

Specific objectives	Response[a]	Number of observations	Dates	Observations and comments
The individual: 1. Writes down the scores obtained in various games.	PP	2	6/6/80 6/8/80	Did not complete. Refused to perform.
2. Writes and constructs words in knowledge and Word Games.	CAR (G)	3	7/6/80 7/8/80 7/12/80	Needed gestural help. Constantly moved in his seat.
3. Uses order forms to order sports and other recreational materials and equipment.	DFS (T)	1	5/5/80	No problems evidenced.
4. Writes or prints labels and headings for section dividers and other category/type designations in collections and albums.	IF	1	6/16/80	No problems evidenced.
5. Prints or writes words and sayings on arts and crafts products.	NA	—	—	There was insufficient time to do arts and crafts projects.
6. Writes greeting card verses, song lyrics, and poetry.	CAR (V)	4	7/8/81 7/10/81 7/21/81 7/23/81	Needed much assistance, and verbal clues were extremely helpful. Did not leave enough space between words and rhymed inappropriately.
7. Writes scenes and plays.	NA	—	—	There was insufficient time for activity.
8. Writes vignettes and simple prose selections.	CAR (V)	2	9/10/81 9/11/81	Had difficulty writing short sentences; wrote mostly in sentence fragments. Needs continual help and constant praise.

[a]Response legend: NA—not applicable; NR—no response; PP—partial performance; CAR—completed/assistance required; P—physical guidance; G—gestural prompts; V—verbal cues; IF—independent functioning; DFS—demonstrated in functional situation. Reported by: T—teacher; P/SP—parent/surrogate parent; I—individual; A—advocate; O—other team member.

SAMPLE INSTRUCTIONAL PLAN

Topic Area __WORK-FUNCTIONAL READING__   Date ___4/13/80___

Teacher___Mrs. Simms___

Time Allotted ___30-40 minutes___

Individual(s) or Group Members Involved:
A. Shallali, P. Cohen,
T. Nitti, J. McGerk

Special Notes or Precautions __J. McGerk has a significant visual problem and needs__ __a special magnifier for close visual work.__

General Objective

The individual will function as a worker as independently and skillfully as possible by identifying words and other symbols.

Specific Objective (Looking and Applying for Work - 2)

The individual locates the help wanted section of newspapers and identifies job offerings appropriate to his interests, needs, and skills.

Instructional Objective

When given a job category, the individual, using a local newspaper, will locate at least three different available jobs in that category.

Materials and Equipment

Copies of local newspapers

Motivating Activity

Discuss with the group those jobs of interest and those jobs for which they are qualified. Write down the job categories identified, adding those that are pertinent but not identified by the individuals.

Instructional Procedures

1. Pass out the help wanted section of the same newspaper to each member of the group.
2. Assist each individual in finding the job categories discussed in the motivating activity.
3. Ask the members of the group to identify job categories not mentioned previously.
4. Pass out complete editions of different local newspapers and ask each individual to locate at least three different jobs listed according to a specified category.

Individualized Reinforcement and
Reinforcement Schedules

For each correct response visually praise the individual by making a notation on a chalkboard that the response was correct. For J. McGerk provide verbal praise. Allow those individuals who complete activity independently and correctly to write in an IF (independent function) on their activity checklists.

Assessment Strategy

Check the individual's responses to make certain that he has correctly identified job listings by the assigned category. Reward the individual's response on the "Work: Functional Reading Checklist."

Follow-Up Activity/Objective

If the individual achieves the instructional objective, proceed to an instructional experience in which the individual is expected to identify other sources of information on job openings.

Instructional Resources

Bulletin boards in stores advertising job openings
Job bank flyers

Observations and Comments:

chapter 2
THE HOME

As adolescents and adults with learning problems deal with the functional reality of living in the greater community, they still must fulfill their role as residents in a home. To function as effectively, efficiently, and safely as possible, adolescents and adults must engage in a variety of practical reading, writing, and mathematical activities. A typical household is replete with tasks requiring the application of these fundamental processes. In each room, people find it necessary to perform these basics whether reading the varied directions on opening packages in the kitchen, writing telephone numbers and addresses in a personal directory in the bedroom, or balancing a checkbook in a living room or den.

To appreciate the scope of functional academic demands in the home, one must analyze the myriad tasks performed while participating in the activities of daily living. The automatic nature of these tasks, to those who are skillful at them, masks their subtle presence, thus interfering with the process of defining their scope and sequence. To be an effective instructor, therefore, it is necessary to view cognitive requirements from the different perspective of one with restricted ability. Once this new viewpoint is achieved, then it is less complicated to identify educational objectives and prepare for their facilitation in those individuals who need to be taught to be functioning members of a household.

Readers may wish to consult "Readings and Resources" at the end of this book for relevant information on programming for adolescents and adults as they function as residents of a home.

GENERAL OBJECTIVES

READING The individual will function in the home as independently and skillfully as possible by identifying words and other symbols found there.

WRITING The individual will function in the home as independently and skillfully as possible by performing diverse written tasks.

MATHEMATICS The individual will function in the home as independently and skillfully as possible by performing necessary mathematical operations.

FUNCTIONAL READING / INSTRUCTIONAL OBJECTIVES

GENERAL OBJECTIVE: The individual will function in the home as independently and skillfully as possible by identifying words and other symbols found there.

**THE KITCHEN
The Equipment and
Appliances**

Refrigerator

The individual:
1. Sets the temperature dial in a refrigerator at a medium setting for normal use.

Functional Essence

Instructional plans should have as their functional essence the setting of a refrigerator dial when:
   a. moving into a new apartment or home or
   b. obtaining a new or replacement refrigerator.

2. Sets the temperature dial in a refrigerator at the warmest (lowest) setting for defrosting purposes or sets the temperature dial in the freezer section of a refrigerator to the defrost position for defrosting purposes.

Functional Essence

Instructional plans should have as their functional essence the setting of a refrigerator dial at its lowest setting when the frost collected in the freezer is interfering with the easy storage of food and/or the closing of the freezer door. The initial emphasis should be on the identification of whether the refrigerator or freezer is frostfree.

3. Stores food in a refrigerator by responding appropriately to labels found on special compartments, drawers, and bins.

Functional Essence

Instructional plans should have as their functional essence:
   a. the storage of food needing refrigeration after a shopping trip and
   b. the return of unused food after food preparation or cooking.
Emphasis should be placed on food according to category types.

Sink

The individual:
1. Locates the cold (C) water faucet on a sink to draw a glass or container of water.

Functional Essence

Instructional plans should have as their functional essence the drawing of water:
   a. as part of one's daily water requirements;
   b. for taking vitamins, minerals, and medications;

    c.   for quenching thirst especially after physical activities and in hot weather;

    d.   as part of a diet regimen;

    e.   to fill containers of water for later use during times when water is shut off for plumbing repairs;

    f.   to fill water bottles to refrigerate for ice water;

    g.   to fill ice-cube trays;

    h.   to fill thermos bottles and canteens;

    i.   to collect water to be used to:

        (1)   water plants (to be used later at room temperature) or

        (2)   add or refill an aquarium;

    j.   to fill a pet's water bowl; and

    k.   to fill a vase used for fresh flowers.

2.   Locates the cold (C) water faucet to draw water for food preparation and cooking purposes.

Functional Essence   Instructional plans should have as their functional essence:

    a.   the filling of pots, pans, and kettles for cooking purposes;

    b.   the rinsing of poultry, fish, and meat when necessary;

    c.   the rinsing of fresh fruit and vegetables as necessary;

    d.   the measuring of water in cups and spoons for recipes;

    e.   the adding of water to powders and concentrates for the preparation of beverages, soups, salad dressings, etc.; and

    f.   the adding of water to foods as they are cooking.

3.   Locates the cold (C) water faucet and then the hot (H) water faucet to temper the water for rinsing and washing dishes and for general household cleaning purposes.

Functional Essence   Instructional plans should have as their functional essence:

    a.   the drawing of water for washing and rinsing dishes, glasses, pots, pans, and utensils and

    b.   the drawing of water in basins, pails, and buckets for general household cleaning.

Instructional activities should concentrate on safety in tempering water.

Stove

The individual:

1.   Turns on the desired burner after locating the appropriate dial or pushbutton that regulates that burner. The individual then, when applicable, selects the pushbutton that determines the desired temperature level for that burner.

Functional Essence   Instructional plans should have as their functional essence:

    a.   the selection of a desired temperature level for the burner or heating element based upon recipe requirements and safety factors;

    b.   the selection of foods that require cooking on top of the stove;

    c.   the reheating of leftover foods;

    d.   the matching of the type of pot or pan to the type of cooking desired (e.g., frying, boiling, or steaming);

    e.   the matching of pot and pan size to burner size;

    f.   the matching of pot and pan size to food quantity; and

    g.   the selection of pots and pans according to their composition as specified by recipes (e.g., porcelain, stainless steel, or cast iron).

Throughout instructional activities, emphasis must be placed on safety.

2. Sets the oven dial to a desired setting for broiling, roasting, and baking purposes.

Functional Essence Instructional plans should have as their functional essence:
  a. the preparation of snacks and meals by following recipes that require broiling, roasting, or baking;
  b. the preparation of snacks and meals by following heating, warming, and baking instructions found on frozen foods; and
  c. the heating and reheating of leftovers.

3. Sets the timer on a stove to a desired setting for cooking and baking purposes.

Functional Essence Instructional plans should have as their functional essence the setting of a timer when:
  a. following recipes that designate cooking times;
  b. adding ingredients according to time designations;
  c. determining when foods need to be stirred, turned over, spread out, or separated; and
  d. coordinating various foods being prepared in time for serving.

4. Locates the switch that activates the hood fan and sets it at a desired setting to remove cooking odors.

Functional Essence Instructional plans should have as their functional essence the setting of a hood fan when:
  a. cooking odors become offensive;
  b. burners smoke because of dropped foods; and
  c. on hot days when additional ventilation is needed.

5. Verifies the accuracy of the oven dial by comparing the reading on an oven gauge to that of the dial's setting.

Functional Essence Instructional plans should have as their functional essence the verification of the accuracy of an oven dial to ensure proper cooking.

6. Prepares nutritious snacks, parts of meals, and complete meals following the directions found in recipes.

Functional Essence Instructional plans should have as their functional essence the preparation of snacks, parts of meals, and complete meals that are nutritious. Instructional activities should emphasize the following of recipes for meal preparation and for snack preparation at times of hunger.

7. Prepares nutritious snacks, parts of meals, and complete meals using measuring spoons and measuring cups.

Functional Essence Instructional plans should have as their functional essence the accurate preparation of food and beverages as specified by recipes as well as the alteration of recipes to meet:
  a. different portion sizes;
  b. individual tastes; and
  c. creative experiments.
Instructional activities should provide sufficient experience in following and in modifying recipes with the various sizes of spoons and the various units appearing on measuring cups.

Kitchen Appliances and Items

The individual:

1. Activates a dishwasher by turning the dial to the beginning position of the washing cycle.

Functional Essence   Instructional plans should have as their functional essence the use of a dishwasher:
   a. when there are very few or no more clean dishes or utensils;
   b. when the dishwasher is fully loaded;
   c. when preparing for a party or other social gathering;
   d. after a party or other social gathering; and
   e. for shining dishes and utensils for display purposes.

2. Sets a kitchen timer to the numeral or slash marks required to prepare foods.

Functional Essence   Instructional plans should have as their functional essence the setting of a kitchen timer in order to:
   a. follow recipes that designate cooking times;
   b. add ingredients according to time designations;
   c. determine when foods need to be stirred, turned over, spread out, or separated; and
   d. coordinate various foods that are being prepared in time for serving.
Instructional activities should focus on the numeral and slash mark designations and their meanings.

3. Selects a desired setting on a toaster.

Functional Essence   Instructional plans should have as their functional essence the setting of a toaster when preparing a breakfast or other meal that includes toast, muffins, or other foods requiring toasting. Provide the individual with experience in toasting such items as Pop-tarts, waffles, and English muffins.

4. Weighs small quantities of food on a kitchen scale.

Functional Essence   Instructional plans should have as their functional essence the use of a food scale to weigh:
   a. small quantities of food as required by recipes *or*
   b. small quantities of food as required to conform to special diets.
Experiences should be provided in weighing the various quantities of food that the scale is capable of measuring. Review diets such as *Weight Watchers* and recipes requiring the measurement of solid food by weight.

5. Selects the appropriate dial setting on an electric fry pan to prepare simple snacks and meals.

Functional Essence   Instructional plans should have as their functional essence the setting of an electric frypan to:
   a. prepare foods that require stir or pan frying;
   b. prepare foods without using a stove; and
   c. heat and reheat leftovers.

6. Selects the desired setting on an electric percolator for desired coffee strength.

Functional Essence   Instructional plans should have as their functional essence the setting of an electric percolator to:
   a. prepare coffee for a large group at social gatherings and parties;

  b. prepare coffee beforehand when it is possible to activate the percolator by a timing mechanism; and

  c. prepare coffee without using the stove.

 7. Sets the dial or pushbutton on a food blender to a desired speed for food and drink preparation.

Functional Essence Instructional plans should have as their functional essence the use of a food blender to:

  a. follow recipe directions;

  b. prepare special diet foods;

  c. prepare beverages from powders or concentrates; and

  d. accelerate the process of preparing foods.

Instructional activities should involve experiences in the use of the blender for its various purposes (e.g., blending, whipping, chopping, pureeing) and at its several settings.

 8. Selects the dial or pushbutton position on an electric mixer to prepare a food item.

Functional Essence Instructional plans should have as their functional essence the selection of a desired setting on an electric mixer to:

  a. follow recipes and

  b. change consistency of foods such as puddings, cream, potatoes, and gravies.

Instructional activities should focus on the setting of the mixer to its various possible settings as dictated by recipe and package directions and should include the preparation of different foods.

 9. Dials or presses the pushbutton to obtain desired phone numbers on a telephone.

Functional Essence Instructional plans should have as their functional essence the dialing or pressing of pushbuttons on a telephone to:

  a. make personal phone calls;

  b. call for weather information and time reports;

  c. call the telephone company for billing and other business matters;

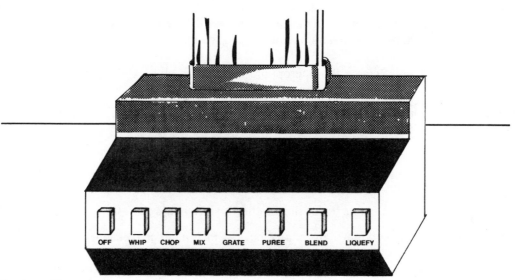

Figure 1. Blender settings.

     d.   call Information for numbers not listed in the local directory; and

     e.   make emergency phone calls in times of crisis.

Instructional activities should provide the individual with abundant opportunities to role play all of the above. Actual experiences should be furnished in using the telephone for relevant business and other purposes.

10.   Locates desired telephone numbers in a personal directory.

Functional Essence   Instructional plans should have as their functional essence the location of desired telephone numbers in a personal directory to make:

     a.   personal,

     b.   business, and

     c.   emergency calls.

11.   Locates desired telephone numbers in the general telephone directory ("White Pages").

Functional Essence   Instructional plans should have as their functional essence the location of desired telephone numbers in the telephone directory to make:

     a.   personal,

     b.   business,

     c.   emergency, and

     d.   information calls.

Instructional activities should stress that the telephone directory is used when desired numbers are not in the individual's personal directory. Provide sufficient practice in locating numbers found in all parts of the directory including municipal, state, and federal governmental agencies.

12.   Locates desired telephone numbers in the classified telephone directory (*Yellow Pages*).

Functional Essence   Instructional plans should have as their functional essence the location of business numbers in the *Yellow Pages*. Experiences should be provided in the use of the table of contents, guide words, and categories of business firms. Sufficient practice should be given in finding the categories of businesses that the individual is likely to need as he functions in the community.

The Kitchen Pantry

The individual:

1.   Stores food items in the appropriately labeled cannisters.

Functional Essence   Instructional plans should have as their functional essence the storing of food in cannisters:

     a.   after a shopping trip;

     b.   for display purposes;

     c.   for ease in obtaining frequently used food and food substances; and

     d.   for protection against spoilage and to keep foods as fresh as possible.

Activities should focus on the labels commonly found on food cannisters, e.g., flour, tea, coffee, and sugar.

2.   Selects the desired food item from its name on the package label.

Functional Essence   Instructional plans should have as their functional essence:

     a.   the selection of food packages from a pantry shelf to fulfill recipe requirements;

b. the selection of food packages for snacks and parts of meals; and

c. the inventorying of food on hand in compiling a shopping list.

Instructional activities should expose the individual to a large variety of packaged foods especially those that nourish and appeal to the individual's taste. Label cues such as pictures should be pointed out as should the names of commonly occurring foods. Ethnic and regional foods should be reviewed as well as food brands.

3. Stores unopened food packages in an appropriate place.

Functional Essence

Instructional plans should have as their functional essence the storing of unopened food according to:

a. the place it was stored in the supermarket, grocery, or food store *or*

b. "before-use" storage directions or cautions appearing on the label.

Experiences should be provided in the storage of food after returning from a shopping trip. Instructional activities should feature the most commonly used foods and the taste preferences of the individual.

4. Stores opened food packages according to the "after-opening" storage directions on the label.

Functional Essence

Instructional plans should have as their functional essence the storage of food according to the directions and cautions appearing on package labels. Instructional activities should focus on those foods that require different storage after a package is opened. Emphasis should be placed on health and safety factors, preventing spoilage (conservation), and saving money.

5. Selects the package size and the number of packages needed to meet the recipe requirements for preparing snacks and meals by checking weight designations on labels.

Functional Essence

Instructional plans should have as their functional essence the selection of quantity and size of package needed to meet recipe requirements to prevent waste and to maintain a reasonable food budget. Activities should focus on preparing snacks and meals involving different size portions and for serving different numbers of people. Throughout the emphasis must be on relating the net weight of the contents to portions desired.

6. Opens a food package by following the directions printed on its label.

Functional Essence

Instructional plans should have as their functional essence the opening of food packages according to directions found on the package label to:

a. facilitate the use of the contents;

b. prevent damage to the contents;

c. allow for closing for re-use;

d. minimize spillage and spoilage; and

e. maximize ease of transfer of contents to new containers.

Abundant experience should be provided in opening and reclosing packages in the diverse ways in which food packaging is made.

7. Prepares snacks and meals by following preparation directions printed on the labels of food packages.

Functional Essence

Instructional plans should have as their functional essence the preparation of snacks and meals according to directions appearing on package labels. Instructional activities should concentrate on foods that are preferred and on representative directions. A collection of label directions should be used to provide the individual with experience in preparing these foods as regular meals or snacks.

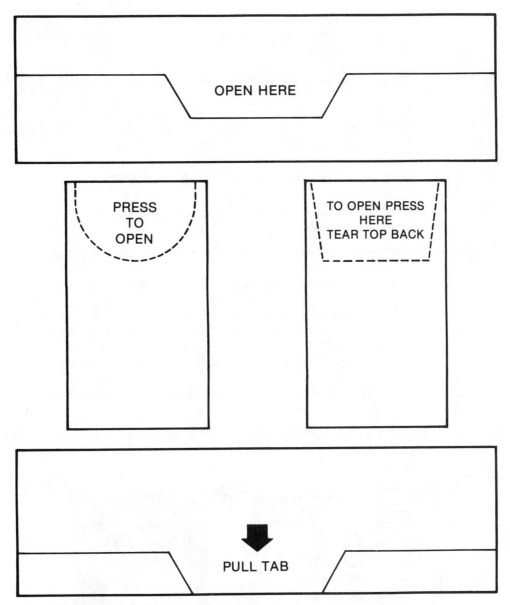

Figure 2. Directions for opening and closing food packages.

8. Buys packages of food only after checking sale expiration dates and then uses foods according to these dates.

Functional Essence Instructional plans should have as their functional essence the identification of expiration dates to avoid buying spoiled food or food that is likely to spoil soon or food that has lost its nutritional value. Furthermore, instructional activities should concentrate on using food before their expiration date for health and economic reasons.

9. Selects a food item for purchase or for use in meals after reviewing nutritional information appearing on its label.

Functional Essence Instructional plans should have as their functional essence the review of nutritional information on package labels to conform to a health or diet plan. Throughout the instructional activities, emphasis should be placed on nutritional contents and their relationship to nutritional needs of the individual. Attention must be paid to nutritional categories, vitamin and mineral specifications, and caloric values. Meal planning must be an integral part of instructional activities. Special attention should be given to food dyes, preservatives, and other chemical ingredients. The checking of ingredients for individual allergens should also be encouraged.

10. Prepares a snack or part of a meal from recipes appearing on a package label.

Functional Essence Instructional plans should have as their functional essence the use of special recipes appearing on package labels. Collect recipes found on labels of preferred foods and prepare them. The individual should be encouraged to save recipes of dishes liked and/or dishes that are easy to prepare and economical. Assist the individual in compiling and organizing a personal recipe box.

11. Appropriately uses kitchen paper products by reading the printed information found on packages.

Functional Essence Instructional plans should have as their functional essence the appropriate use of kitchen paper products to:
    a. clean up or absorb water after rinsing or washing food;
    b. clean the kitchen table, counter tops, and other surfaces; and
    c. protect clothing from being soiled.
Throughout instructional activities, emphasis should be placed on the proper utilization of paper products with particular attention to avoiding waste and to using the appropriate product for the specific job. Typical directions should be reviewed.

12. Obeys warning and caution words found on kitchen cleaning and other household products and stores them in a safe place.

Functional Essence Instructional plans should have as their functional essence the safe use of kitchen cleaning and other household products. Instructional activities should focus on find-

Homemade Barbecue Sauce

2 cups catsup
¼ cup brown sugar
1 teaspoon Durkee Chili Powder
¼ teaspoon Durkee Garlic Powder
⅓ cup water
¼ cup vinegar
3 tablespoons Worcestershire sauce
¼ cup **Durkee/Frank's RedHot Sauce**

Combine all ingredients thoroughly. Brush on beef, poultry, or pork while broiling or grilling.
  MAKES 3 cups sauce

Zing Wings

2½ pounds chicken wings
6 tablespoons **Durkee/Frank's RedHot Sauce**
¼ cup butter or margarine, melted

Split chicken wings at each joint and discard tips; pat dry. Deep fry at 400° (high) for 12 minutes or until crispy. Remove and drain well. (Can also be baked on a rack in a 400° oven for 25 minutes.) Combine hot sauce and butter. Dip chicken wings in sauce.
  MAKES 6 to 8 appetizer servings.

Figure 3. Recipes appearing on package labels.

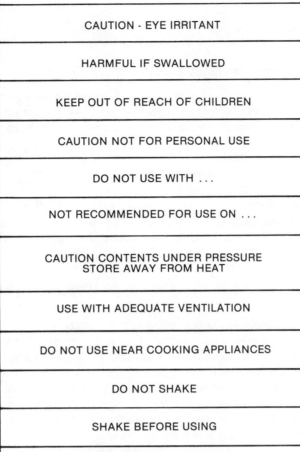

```
┌─────────────────────────────────────────┐
│         CAUTION - EYE IRRITANT          │
├─────────────────────────────────────────┤
│         HARMFUL IF SWALLOWED            │
├─────────────────────────────────────────┤
│      KEEP OUT OF REACH OF CHILDREN      │
├─────────────────────────────────────────┤
│      CAUTION NOT FOR PERSONAL USE       │
├─────────────────────────────────────────┤
│           DO NOT USE WITH . . .         │
├─────────────────────────────────────────┤
│      NOT RECOMMENDED FOR USE ON . . .   │
├─────────────────────────────────────────┤
│    CAUTION CONTENTS UNDER PRESSURE      │
│          STORE AWAY FROM HEAT           │
├─────────────────────────────────────────┤
│      USE WITH ADEQUATE VENTILATION      │
├─────────────────────────────────────────┤
│    DO NOT USE NEAR COOKING APPLIANCES   │
├─────────────────────────────────────────┤
│              DO NOT SHAKE               │
├─────────────────────────────────────────┤
│            SHAKE BEFORE USING           │
├─────────────────────────────────────────┤
│    WARNING - Keep this product out      │
│          of children's reach            │
├─────────────────────────────────────────┤
│          FLAMMABLE SUBSTANCE            │
├─────────────────────────────────────────┤
│               POISONOUS                 │
└─────────────────────────────────────────┘
```

Figure 4.   Warning words on household products.

ing storage places separate from food storage areas and out of the reach of children. Typical warning and caution words and phrases should be reviewed and their meanings exemplified in discussions on the possible consequences of ignoring these warnings. Assist the individual in finding an appropriate storage area in the home whenever practical. Further experiences should be provided that assist the individual in selecting the right product for a specific job and for avoiding misuse and waste. Attention should be paid to opening and operating these products especially when they are in special containers such as spray cans.

13.   Follows directions for assembling kitchen cleaning products and appliances.

Functional Essence   Instructional plans should have as their functional essence the following of written and diagrammatic directions for assembling kitchen cleaning products, e.g., placing the pump top on a window cleaner and the mop on a mop handle. Experiences should be provided in putting together and then using various products and appliances. A full range of experiences should be provided so that the individual will have had sufficient opportunities to explore materials and equipment he is most likely to encounter.

**Miscellaneous
Kitchen Items**

The individual:
1. Identifies the day and date on a wall calendar.

Functional Essence   Instructional plans should have as their functional essence the identification of the months, days of the week, and dates and on extracting this information based on the calendar's format. Instructional programs should concentrate on identifying the day and date to:
   a. write the date on checks and forms;
   b. carry out planned activities; and
   c. pay bills on time.

Special emphasis should be placed on encouraging the individual to note appointments, regularly scheduled activities, and upcoming special events on the wall calendar. Include in instructional plans alternate ways of identifying the day of the week and date, e.g., the radio and the newspaper.

2. Plans future activities using the wall calendar as a guide to future days and their dates.

Functional Essence   Instructional plans should have as their functional essence the use of the wall calendar as a means of identifying the day of the week of future activities in which he might wish to participate. Instructional activities should concentrate on various advertisements that announce future events and on assisting the individual in identifying the day of the week that the event will take place. Experiences should be designed to aid the individual in keeping a record of future appointments and possible activities and using the wall calendar as a means of planning and keeping track of these approaching activities.

3. Replaces light bulbs according to desired wattage.

Functional Essence   Instructional plans should have as their functional essence the selection of replacement light bulbs by the wattage information printed on these bulbs. Instructional activities should be provided in which the individual is expected to identify the appropriate wattage from the light bulb itself or the light bulb packaging. Experiences should emphasize the *safe* replacement of bulbs. Demonstrate the proper way to replace a light bulb and assist the individual in doing so. Assist him until he is able to replace a bulb safely and independently.

**ROOMS IN
THE HOME
The Living Room**

The individual:
1. Identifies and reviews mail addressed to him. (These instructional objectives are listed under the living room, although they can occur in other rooms in the home, e.g., kitchen and dining room.)

Functional Essence   Instructional plans should have as their functional essence the identification of the individual's name on cards and letters. Instructional activities should focus on sorting through mail addressed to various individuals and locating personal mail. Simulated mail should be used as part of instructional plans.

2. Follows directions and instructions in simple notes and written messages. (These instructional objectives are listed under the living room, although they can occur in other rooms in the home, e.g., kitchen and dining room.) (*See* Sample Instructional Plan.)

Functional Essence Instructional plans should have as their functional essence the identification of key information and directions found in simple notes and messages. Instructional experiences should be provided in which the individual is given:

    a. telephone messages;
    b. messages to carry out a household task or tasks;
    c. messages to carry out an errand; and
    d. messages informing him where the writer of the note may be reached.

Ample experience should be given in responding to each of these types of communication.

3. Sets the dial of a vacuum cleaner to the appropriate setting for cleaning the floor or floor covering.

Functional Essence Instructional plans should have as their functional essence the setting of a vacuum cleaner as part of a housecleaning schedule. Instructional activities should be designed to encourage the individual to develop a housecleaning schedule. Review instructional booklets for directions on vacuum cleaner settings as they relate to type of floor and floor covering. Show the individual samples of various floor coverings and point out the appropriate vacuum setting. Experiences should then be provided wherein the individual vacuums floors covered by various types of floor coverings.

4. Sets a thermostat for different times and different weather conditions.

Functional Essence Instructional plans should have as their functional essence the setting of a thermostat to conserve energy and to meet budgeted amounts for heat or air conditioning. Instructional activities should focus on setting the thermostat for different times, situations, and weather conditions. Included in these settings are:

    a. daytime operation;
    b. nighttime operation;
    c. seasonal operation (air conditioning or heating);
    d. operation when no one is at home; and
    e. operation for special health reasons.

Attention should be paid to numerical readings and to abbreviations and words that designate heating and air conditioning as well as on and off switches.

5. Operates a television set for leisure-time enjoyment.

Functional Essence Instructional plans should have as their functional essence the operation of a television set for leisure-time enjoyment. Numeral and word recognition skills should be developed to assist the individual in:

    a. turning a television set on and off when desired;
    b. adjusting the volume dial or knob to a desired listening level;
    c. selecting a channel;
    d. making simple adjustments for improved viewing using the focus, contrast, brightness, hold, color, and when appropriate tint dials.

Attention should be given to locating desired programs in program listings in newspapers and magazines. Throughout, an actual television set should be used for demonstration and practice purposes. Experiences should be provided in operating different brands and models.

6. Operates a stereo system for leisure-time enjoyment.

Functional Essence   Instructional plans should have as their functional essence the operation of a stereo system for leisure-time enjoyment. Numerical and word recognition skills should be developed to assist the individual in:
  a. turning the various sub-units of a stereo system on and off as desired;
  b. adjusting the volume dial or knob to a desired listening level;
  c. selecting desired sound adjustment by turning bass, treble, and volume dials or knobs;
  d. operating the record changer by moving dials or switches or pressing or sliding buttons for manual/automatic, record size, and play/reject options;
  e. selecting desired phonograph records to play on the stereo system;
  f. selecting and playing 8-track or cassette tapes on the stereo system; and
  g. recording musical and other selections on 8-track or cassette tapes.
Throughout instructional activities, an actual stereo system should be used for demonstration and practice purposes. Experiences should be provided in operating different brands and models.

7. Reviews radio and television schedules and selects desired program.

Functional Essence   Instructional plans should have as their functional essence the development of skills in reviewing radio and television program listings for the purpose of selecting desired programs. Instructional activities should center on identifying:
  a. station call letters, dial settings, and channel numbers;
  b. the names of programs; and
  c. the times that programs are scheduled.
Daily schedules should be obtained and reviewed with the individual, and plans should be made for listening or watching programs of interest.

8. Sets an electric timer to turn lights or lamps on or off for times when he will be away from home.

Functional Essence   Instructional plans should have as their functional essence the setting of an electric timer to turn lights or lamps on and off at preselected times when the individual will be away from home. Instructional activities should emphasize the steps the individual can take to prevent burglaries. Information should be obtained from local police departments on methods of crime prevention and then reviewed in discussions. Assist the individual in setting a timer to various time settings, e.g., so lights will be on when he comes home at night and go off when he is about to retire for the evening.

The Bedroom

The individual:
1. Turns on and then sets the speed of an electric fan to a desired cooling level and turns it off when cooling is no longer needed.

Functional Essence   Instructional plans should have as their functional essence the identification of numeral, letter, and word setting designations that appear on frequently used electrical fans. Practice should be provided in operating various brands and models. Throughout the experiences, major emphasis should be placed on safety.

2. Turns on and then sets an air conditioner to a desired cooling level and turns it off when cooling is no longer desired.

Functional Essence   Instructional plans should have as their functional essence the identification of numeral, letter, and word setting designations that appear on frequently used air

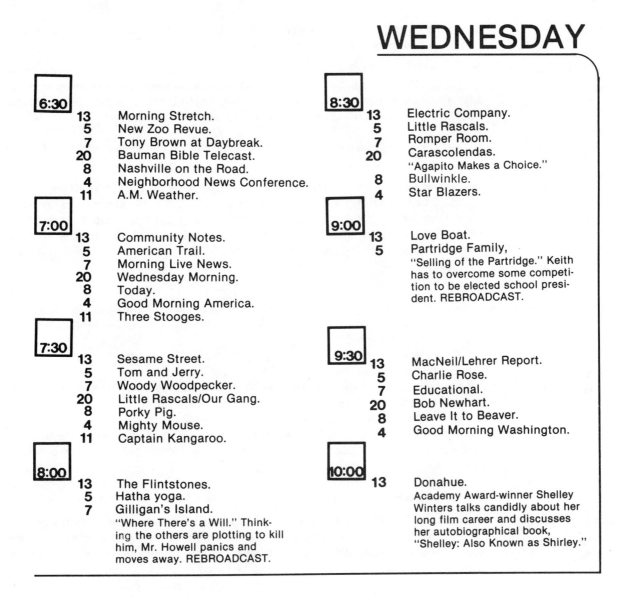

WEDNESDAY

6:30
13 Morning Stretch.
5 New Zoo Revue.
7 Tony Brown at Daybreak.
20 Bauman Bible Telecast.
8 Nashville on the Road.
4 Neighborhood News Conference.
11 A.M. Weather.

7:00
13 Community Notes.
5 American Trail.
7 Morning Live News.
20 Wednesday Morning.
8 Today.
4 Good Morning America.
11 Three Stooges.

7:30
13 Sesame Street.
5 Tom and Jerry.
7 Woody Woodpecker.
20 Little Rascals/Our Gang.
8 Porky Pig.
4 Mighty Mouse.
11 Captain Kangaroo.

8:00
13 The Flintstones.
5 Hatha yoga.
7 Gilligan's Island.
"Where There's a Will." Thinking the others are plotting to kill him, Mr. Howell panics and moves away. REBROADCAST.

8:30
13 Electric Company.
5 Little Rascals.
7 Romper Room.
20 Carascolendas.
"Agapito Makes a Choice."
8 Bullwinkle.
4 Star Blazers.

9:00
13 Love Boat.
5 Partridge Family,
"Selling of the Partridge." Keith has to overcome some competition to be elected school president. REBROADCAST.

9:30
13 MacNeil/Lehrer Report.
5 Charlie Rose.
7 Educational.
20 Bob Newhart.
8 Leave It to Beaver.
4 Good Morning Washington.

10:00
13 Donahue.
Academy Award-winner Shelley Winters talks candidly about her long film career and discusses her autobiographical book,
"Shelley: Also Known as Shirley."

Figure 5. Television program listings.

conditioners. Practice should be provided in operating various brands and models. Throughout the experiences, major emphasis should be placed on safety.

3. Turns on and then sets an electric heater to a desired heating level and turns it off when heat is no longer desired.

Functional Essence Instructional plans should have as their functional essence the identification of numeral, letter, and word setting designations that appear on frequently used electric heaters. Practice should be provided in operating various brands and models. Throughout the experiences, major emphasis should be placed on safety.

4. Turns on and then sets a heating pad to a desired heating level and turns it off when heat is no longer needed.

Functional Essence Instructional plans should have as their functional essence the identification of numeral, letter, and word setting designations that appear on frequently used heating pads. Practice should be provided in operating various brands and models. Throughout the experiences, major emphasis should be placed on safety.

5. Turns on and then sets an electric blanket to a desired heat level and turns it off when heat is no longer needed.

Functional Essence Instructional plans should have as their functional essence the identification of numeral, letter, and word designations that appear on frequently used electric blankets. Practice should be provided in operating various brands and models. Throughout the experiences, major emphasis should be placed on safety.

6. Sets a wind-up alarm clock, an electronic digital clock, or a clock radio to a desired wake-up time.

Functional Essence Instructional plans should have as their functional essence the setting of any type of alarm clock to a setting that considers the appropriate wake-up time to allow sufficient time for the individual to get to work, to keep appointments, or to arrive at scheduled events on time. Practice should be provided in setting the alarm at different times on various types of alarm clocks.

7. Operates a radio for leisure-time enjoyment.

Functional Essence Instructional plans should have as their functional essence the operation of a radio for leisure-time enjoyment. Numerical- and word-recognition skills should be developed to assist the individual in:
    a. selecting a desired radio program from a schedule listing;
    b. turning a radio on and off as desired;
    c. adjusting the volume dial or knob to a desired listening level;
    d. selecting the desired radio band (AM or FM) and;
    e. selecting the station by adjusting the tuner.
Throughout instructional activities, an actual radio should be used for demonstration and practice purposes. Experiences should be provided in operating different brands and models.

8. Follows washing and dry cleaning instructions found on clothing labels.

Functional Essence Instructional plans should have as their functional essence the identification of washing and dry cleaning instructions found on clothing labels. Instructional experiences should concentrate on separating clothes into clean and dirty piles and then identifying key words on labels that indicate cleaning instructions. Next, practice should be given in designating cleaning procedures to be followed.

The Bathroom

The individual:
1. Compares his weight shown on a bathroom scale to a previous weight and to a goal or desired weight.

Functional Essence Instructional plans should have as their functional essence the identification of numerals and slash-mark intervals as they appear on the bathroom scale's gauge. Instructional activities should include comparison to previous readings *and* to desired or goal weight as a preliminary step to altering dietary regimens. Consideration should be given to safeguarding the privacy of individuals who are self-conscious about their weight.

2. Turns on and then sets the dial control on an *electric* or *battery-operated shaver* to adjust for beard growth and skin sensitivity and turns if off when through.

```
WASH SEPARATELY

DRY CLEAN ONLY

DRIP DRY

WASH, WARM

TUMBLE DRY

MACHINE WASH, WARM

LINE OR TUMBLE DRY

DO NOT USE CHLORINE BLEACH

DO NOT BLEACH

HAND WASH IN COLD WATER WITH WOOLITE

LAY FLAT TO DRY

DO NOT IRON

DO NOT DRY CLEAN

HANGER DRY

DO NOT DRY IN DIRECT SUNLIGHT

FLAME RETARDANT, WASH BEFORE WEARING

DO NOT USE SOAP

MACHINE WASH AND DRY

WASH COLORS SEPARATELY

DRY CLEAN, FURRIER METHOD RECOMMENDED

HAND WASH, COLD WATER, MILD SOAP

SPONGE SPOTS WITH DAMP CLOTH
```

Figure 6.   Label instructions.

Functional Essence   Instructional plans should have as their functional essence the operation of an electric rechargeable or battery-operated shaver by attending to various dial settings. Instructional activities should focus on identifying a dial setting that is most comfortable and effective for the individual's hair growth. Once a suitable dial setting is decided upon, experiences should be designed to assist the individual in recalling this setting and then locating it on the shaver at times of use.

3. Turns on and then selects the appropriate setting on a hand dryer or blower to dry hair and then turns it off when hair is dry.

Functional Essence   Instructional plans should have as their functional essence the identification of the on and off switch and the selection of an appropriate setting on a hand dryer or blower. Instructional activities should focus on identifying a dial setting that is most comfortable and effective to the individual. Once a suitable dial setting is decided

THE CLOSENESS/COMFORT SELECTOR

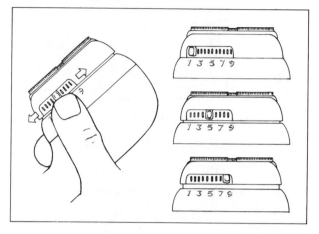

With the 9 shaving closeness/comfort settings, you can select a position which gives optimum shaving closeness and comfort for your individual skin and beard and the least possible skin irritation.

Position 1: Affords maximum closeness for tough (not so sensitive) skin.

Position 5: For normal skin. We recommend that you start at this position when shaving for the first time.

Position 9: Provides maximum protection for very soft (or sensitive) skin. For a "custom" shave, you may want to use one setting for cheeks and chin, and another "comfort" setting to shave your neck. If you are using an electric razor for the first time, please note that you must give your skin and beard several weeks to adapt to this new method. You will soon be rewarded with smooth, close shaves.

Figure 7. Electric shaver dial settings.

upon, experiences should be designed to assist the individual in recalling this setting and then locating it at times of use.

4. Takes and uses over-the-counter medicines and medications in dosages and at times recommended for adults.

Functional Essence   Instructional plans should have as their functional essence the identification of dosages, time of dosages, possible repeat dosages (amounts and times), maximum safe daily dosages, and specific warnings appearing on over-the-counter medicines and medications. Instructional activities should be provided that expose the individual to the most frequently used medications and the directions appearing on package and container labels.

5 . Takes and uses prescribed medicines and medications according to dosages, conditions, and at times identified on labels.

Functional Essence   Instructional plans should have as their functional essence the identification of personal medicines and medications as well as dosages and times of taking as they appear on prescription labels. Whenever possible, actual prescription drugs should be used if the individual's privacy is respected. Discussions should center on the possible consequences of modifying the directions and of taking drugs that are prescribed for others.

6. Takes vitamins and minerals in dosages recommended by a personal physician or in dosages listed on the label.

Functional Essence   Instructional plans should have as their functional essence the identification of vitamin and mineral contents, the recommended daily requirements, and the suggested dosage regimen as they appear on labels. Discussions should address the reasons for taking vitamins and minerals and the possible consequences of taking too high a dosage and the possible waste of money when dietary supplements are not needed.

7. Takes own temperature and informs significant others if a fever is present.

Functional Essence   Instructional plans should have as their functional essence the identification of numerals appearing on a thermometer. Instructional activities should focus on alerting the individual to:
   a. times when he should consider taking his temperature, e.g., if feeling ill, unusually hot, weak, or fatigued;
   b. the normal reading (occasionally someone's normal is slightly different so program for that when it occurs); and
   c. abnormal readings including slight variations and variations of concern.
Begin by taking his temperature and showing him the reading. Discuss the meaning of the reading. Demonstrate how to shake down the thermometer. Then ask him to take his temperature. Ask him to tell you his temperature and then discuss its meaning. Throughout emphasize the need to sterilize the thermometer before and after each use and to report variations of concern (temperature too high or too low) to a physician.

8. Takes the temperature of a member of his household and tells that person the reading.

Functional Essence   Instructional plans should have as their functional essence the identification of the numerals appearing on an oral thermometer. Instructional activities should concentrate on the following:
   a. making sure the thermometer is sterile;
   b. shaking the thermometer down;
   c. inserting it under the tongue;
   d. timing the procedure;
   e. identifying the reading;
   f. telling the individual the reading; and
   g. returning the thermometer to its container.
Experiences should also include discussions on giving the household members advice when abnormal readings are obtained.

9. Locates the cold (C) water faucet and then the hot (H) water faucet to temper the water in the bathroom sink.

Functional Essence   Instructional plans should have as their functional essence the location of cold and then the hot water faucet on a sink and their safe tempering, i.e., turning on the cold first and gradually turning on the hot while monitoring the warmth of the water with one's fingers. Instructional activities should include sufficient practice to ensure that the individual will follow these procedures to avoid burns. Experiences should involve tempering the water to:
   a. brush teeth;
   b. wash face and hands;
   c. shave with a razor; and
   d. take a sponge bath.

Practice each of the above activities. The individual's privacy must be respected in taking a sponge bath, so diagrams, adult mannequins, and/or verbal instructions may have to suffice instead of the more effective use of actual demonstration. Time should also be spent on turning off the water, hot water faucet first.

10. Locates the cold (C) water faucet and then the hot (H) water faucet to temper the water in the bathtub.

Functional Essence   Instructional plans should have as their functional essence the location of the cold and then the hot water faucet in a bathtub and their safe tempering, i.e., turning on the cold water first and gradually turning on the hot water while monitoring the warmth of the water collecting in the bathtub with one's fingers. Sufficient time should be spent on the tempering process as a precaution against burns. The individual's privacy must be protected in bathing activities, so diagrams, adult mannequins, and/or verbal instructions may have to suffice instead of the more effective use of actual demonstrations. Time should also be spent on turning off the faucets when the tub is sufficiently filled. In the turning off process, encourage the individual to turn off the hot water first.

11. Locates the cold (C) water faucet and then the hot (H) water faucet to temper the water in the shower.

Functional Essence   Instructional plans should have as their functional essence the location of the cold and then the hot water faucet in a shower and then safe tempering, i.e., turning on the cold water first and gradually adding hot water while monitoring the flow of water in the shower with one's fingers until a comfortable or desired level of warmth is obtained. Sufficient time should be spent on the tempering process as a precaution against burns. The individual's privacy must be protected so diagrams, adult mannequins, and/or verbal directions may have to suffice instead of the more effective use of demonstration. Time should also be spent practicing turning off the hot and cold faucets simultaneously or turning off the hot faucet first.

12. Uses grooming items according to directions printed on their labels.

Functional Essence   Instructional plans should have as their functional essence the identification of key words and phrases appearing on the labels of grooming items. These directions should be discussed and their meanings clarified through simulated and actual demonstrations. The preferred grooming aids of the individual should be ascertained, and they should be the key instructional materials.

13. Uses bathroom cleansers according to directions printed on their labels.

Functional Essence   Instructional plans should have as their functional essence the identification of key words and phrases appearing on the labels of bathroom cleansers. These directions should be discussed and their meanings clarified through simulated and actual demonstrations. The most commonly used cleansers should be obtained, and they should be the key instructional materials.

14. Uses an air freshener according to directions printed on its label.

Functional Essence   Instructional plans should have as their functional essence the identification of key words and phrases appearing on the labels of air fresheners. These directions should be discussed and their meanings clarified through actual demonstrations. The most commonly used air fresheners should be obtained, and they should serve as the key instructional materials.

**The Basement/
Laundry Area**

The individual:

1. Turns on and then sets an electric iron to the appropriate setting to iron various fabrics and then turns it off when ironing is complete.

Functional Essence

Instructional plans should have as their functional essence the identification of the words found on an electric iron. Instructional activities should concentrate on reviewing these words for fabric type and recommended settings from both a recognition and comprehension viewpoint. Sample clothing and other household items such as sheets, tablecloths, and pillow cases needing ironing should be gathered and fabric type identified through labels and/or touch. Once fabric type is identified, assist the individual in finding and selecting the appropriate setting. Proceed to ironing the clothing and other cloth items. Throughout, emphasis should be placed on the safe use of an iron, particularly because of the double danger of electric shock and burns.

2. Pre-sets the temperature dial of a washing machine to an appropriate setting for the type of laundry.

Functional Essence

Instructional plans should have as their functional essence the setting of a temperature dial on a washing machine in relation to laundry type. Instructional activities should feature a review of instruction booklets and directions found on the machine itself in isolating numerical and letter settings and in associating them with specific laundry load type. Instructional experiences should emphasize sorting of clothes to

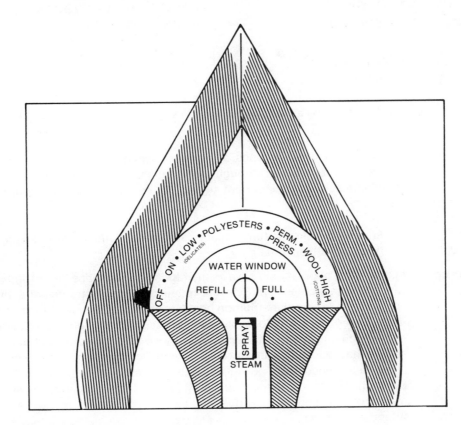

Figure 8.   Common words found on an electric iron.

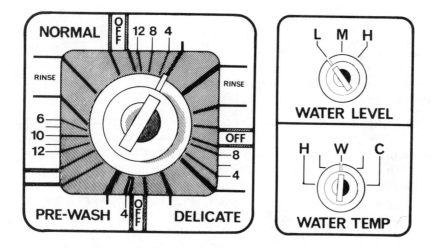

Here's how you wash a load of laundry

1   Carefully measure correct
amount of detergent. Put it
and your laundry into the tub.
Close the lid.

2   Turn the WATER LEVEL
Control to setting you want.

3   Turn the WATER TEMP
Control to setting you want.

4   Pull out and turn the Wash Time
Control clockwise to the cycle
and setting you want. Push the
control in, and your washing
is started.

TO STOP washer at any time, PULL Wash Time Control out.

Figure 9.   Temperature dials and directions on a washing machine.

be washed into different types, e.g., colored, white, synthetic, cotton, and wool. Once
sorting is accomplished through sight, touch, and review of labels, assist the individual in selecting the correct setting. Do so until he can carry out the task independently.

3.   Pre-sets the temperature dial of an automatic clothes dryer to an appropriate setting for the type of laundry.

Functional Essence   Instructional plans should have as their functional essence the setting of a temperature dial on a clothes dryer relevant to laundry type. Instructional activities should
focus on the review of instruction booklets and the directions found on the machine
itself. Experiences should involve isolating each of the letter or numerical settings
and associating them with specific laundry load type. Emphasis should be placed on
setting the dryer to the same level as selected for the washing machine temperature.
If necessary, encourage the individual to review laundry type by checking labels and
by touch. Work with the individual until he is able to independently and safely operate a dryer. Remind the individual that as a safety precaution always clean the filter
after using a dryer.

4.   Sets the timer on an automatic clothes dryer.

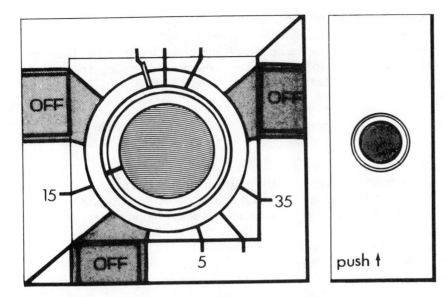

Here's how you dry a load of laundry

1 Put your laundry into the dryer. See your *Laundry Guide* for loading suggestions.

2 Shut the dryer door.

3 Turn the Dryness Control pointer to the cycle and setting you want.

4 Push the PUSH TO START control to start your dryer.

To STOP your dryer at any time, open the door, or, turn the Dryness Control to OFF.

Figure 10. Temperature dials and directions on a clothes dryer.

Functional Essence   Instructional plans should have as their functional essence the setting of a timer on an automatic clothes dryer to a time sufficient to dry a load of laundry. Instructional activities should develop:
    a.   the act of setting the timer and
    b.   the estimation of time needed for the clothes to be dried.
The first skill involves the identification of numeral and slash mark designations on the timer whereas the second skill involves time estimates based upon experience. To develop the latter skill, experiences should be provided in which the individual records the times needed to dry different size loads as well as different types of loads. From these exercises an average time should be computed and recorded for easy retrieval for future washing/drying sessions.

5.   Orders oil when the gauge on the oil burner indicates that oil is at a predetermined "alert" level.

Functional Essence   Instructional plans should have as their functional essence the identification of numeral and letter designations on an oil burner gauge as well as any marking on the gauge that signals a reorder alert. Instructional activities should revolve around the examination of:

a.   an actual gauge separate from an oil burner and

b.   an actual gauge connected to an oil burner.

Throughout, the emphasis should be on identifying various levels on the gauge *and* on the procedures to be followed for reordering. These processes should be germane to the individual's present situation yet general enough to be transferred to new situations.

6.   Checks the gauge on the water heater to determine that the water level is adequate.

Functional Essence   Instructional plans should have as their functional essence the identification of letter and numerical designations on a water heater gauge for the purpose of adding more water as needed. Instructional activities should deal with the use of an actual gauge and concentrate on adding water, when needed, to a predetermined level. Thus, the skills are as follows:

a.   reviewing the level of water;

b.   adding water as necessary; and

c.   stopping at a predetermined water level deemed adequate or as prescribed on the water heater's directions booklet.

7.   Checks electric, gas, and/or water meter readings to confirm official meter readings on utility bills.

Functional Essence   Instructional plans should have as their functional essence the comparison of electric, gas, and/or water meter readings to those readings as they appear on utility bills. This matching should be carried out to:

a .   verify the accuracy of the bills and

b.   arrive at a realistic and reasonable budget estimate for utility costs in formulating weekly and monthly budgets.

Instructional activities, therefore, should concentrate on both these aspects. Actual readings should be taken by the individual on reading dates, then recorded and retrieved when the bills arrive. Assist in this process until the individual is able to function independently.

8.   Replaces fuses or resets circuit breakers during power outages caused by factors occurring within the home.

Functional Essence   Instructional plans should have as their functional essence the identification of:

a.   fuse size markings on the fuse itself or on the package of fuses and

b.   circuit breakers that have shut down by the word "Off" appearing next to switches as opposed to the usual "On" that signals satisfactory operation.

Throughout instructional experiences, emphasis should be placed on the safe replacement of fuses. Be sure to point out that fuses must be always kept on hand in preparation for an emergency situation and that the individual must *never* use anything other than a fuse as a fuse replacement. Explain that total power outages *may* mean that the problem is outside the home and that replacing fuses or resetting circuit breakers will not help.

9.   Shuts off individual valves for the main water supply during emergency plumbing situations.

Functional Essence   Instructional plans should have as their functional essence the shutting off of water valves during a plumbing emergency. Instructional activities should be provided to assist the individual in locating the main emergency shut-off valve and in identifying the on and off direction. Experiences should also include tracing hot and cold water pipes to their main water supply. Discuss plumbing emergencies and the procedures to follow after the water supply has been shut off.

SPECIAL ITEMS FOR APARTMENT DWELLERS

The individual:

1. Locates mailbox and magazine slot.

Functional Essence Instructional plans should have as their functional essence the location of a personal mailbox and magazine slot for the purpose of obtaining mail for himself, for family, and other members of his household. Instructional experiences should deal with recognition of his name and/or his apartment number as they appear on mailboxes and magazine slots. Include the process to follow if someone else's mail is inadvertently put in his box or slot.

2. Locates laundry rooms.

Functional Essence Instructional plans should have as their functional essence the identification of laundry rooms from directional signs in hallways and from signs on or near doors. Instructional activities should emphasize that apartment dwellers frequently have laundry rooms or areas where they can launder and dry their wash. Ask him to locate the laundry rooms in his building and determine the cost of laundering and drying clothes. If possible, visit his building and assist him in:
   a. locating laundry rooms;
   b. operating them (including the use of coins); and
   c. selecting the right settings for type of laundry load.

3. Locates the garbage disposal/incinerator area or rooms.

Functional Essence Instructional plans should have as their functional essence the identification of garbage disposal/incinerator area or rooms from directional signs in hallways and from signs on or near doors. Instructional activities should emphasize that there may be restrictions on the use of these areas. Point out phrases and sentences that forbid the dumping of certain objects, e.g., a lighted cigarette, oily rags, paint and pressurized cans. Discuss why these restrictions are important, pointing out the dangerous consequences of ignoring these warnings.

4. Locates the family storage room or space.

Functional Essence Instructional plans should have as their functional essence the location of the family storage room or space for the purpose of storing or retrieving excess or unused clothing, furniture, appliances, furnishings, and equipment. Instructional activities should concentrate on maintaining security over this storage area because it is removed from his daily surveillance. Discuss what objects are realistically and reasonably stored in this area. Be sure to stress that highly valuable objects and papers must be kept in alternate places such as a safe deposit box or in the apartment itself.

5. Opens a combination lock found on a family storage room/space.

Functional Essence Instructional plans should have as their functional essence the use of a combination or other lock to secure the contents of a storage room or space. When a combination lock is used as opposed to a key-activated lock, experience should be provided in:
   a. carrying out the combination sequence;
   b. recording and safekeeping the combination;
   c. retrieving and using the combination to gain access to or to store unused or excess household material or equipment.

6. Locates all exits and entrances.

Functional Essence Instructional plans should have as their functional essence the location of exits and entrances from signs over doorways and from directional signs in hallways. Instructional activities should deal with the use of entrances and exits:
   a. during normal use and
   b. in emergency situations.

Whenever possible, visits should be taken to the apartment building to practice entering and exiting the building in casual use and rapidly and safely during emergency use. Remember, when there is an elevator or elevators, program the individual to avoid them during a fire emergency or fire drill.

7. Locates a fire alarm panel or box.

Functional Essence Instructional plans should have as their functional essence the location of a fire alarm panel or box for use in a fire emergency. Instructional activities must emphasize that he must only use these alarm systems when there is an actual fire and when the fire department is not already at the premises. Discuss thoroughly the legal consequences of sending a false alarm as well as the danger to apartment residents and responding fire personnel.

8. Locates areas where fire extinguishers are stored.

Functional Essence Instructional plans should have as their functional essence the location of areas where fire extinguishers are stored. Instructional activities should focus on the use of extinguishers only after the fire department has been alerted and only to contain a small fire that is interfering with the ability of people to move freely out of a dangerous area. Include in instructional experiences, a visit from a firefighter who can explain the directions on an extinguisher, demonstrate its safe and effective use, and discuss precautions to be observed.

9. Obtains an elevator by pressing the appropriate call button.

Functional Essence Instructional plans should have as their functional essence the location and pressing of the appropriate call button to facilitate his movement in and out of the building. Experiences may be provided with any self-service elevator. Concentrate on the words "Up" and "Down," pointing out their meaning in relationship to "What floor am I on now?" and "Where do I want to go?" Remember to warn the individual never to use an elevator in times of fire emergencies or drills.

10. Operates a self-service elevator.

Functional Essence Instructional experiences should focus on locating the buttons on a self-service elevator to operate it effectively and safely. Instructional activities should review all the numerical (floor number), letter (L-Lobby and P-Penthouse), and word ("Close Door" and "Open Door") designations found on most elevators. Explain their use in getting him in and out of the building and helping him to move within the building. Also, make it clear that "Open Door" is to be used to assist passengers in getting in and out of elevators. Practice on self-service elevators at any site because most have uniformity of button controls.

11. Obtains help while in a malfunctioning or nonfunctioning self-service elevator.

Functional Essence Instructional plans should have as their functional essence the location of emergency buttons and/or telephones while in a malfunctioning or nonfunctioning elevator. Instructional activities should concentrate on the use of the:
   a. automatic stop switch/button;

b. alarm button;

c. emergency power switch; and

d. telephone call box.

Discuss the dangers of panicking during a real emergency. Obtain permission to use an elevator to demonstrate the use of these emergency elements. Permission may be obtained in a public building after closing hours. Program the individual to check these buttons and devices on entering an elevator and only on using them during the malfunction or nonfunction of the elevator.

SAMPLE INSTRUCTIONAL PLAN

Topic Area ___THE HOME-FUNCTIONAL READING___   Date ___9/23/80___

Teacher ___Mr. Murchison___

Time Allotted ___50-60 minutes___

Individual(s) or Group Members Involved:
J. DeSheilds, W. Breman,
M. Micks, D. Stanley,
K. Jones, D. Smeltzer,
J. Swain

Special Notes or Precautions ___None___

General Objective

The individual will function in the home as independently and skillfully as possible by identifying words and other symbols found there.

Specific Objective (The Living Room - 2)

The individual follows directions and instructions in simple notes and written messages.

Instructional Objective

When given a simple note with shopping instructions, the individual will carry out the requested task and return with all of the desired items or a receipt as appropriate.

Materials and Equipment

1. Shoes needing repair
2. A suit to be dry cleaned
3. A phone bill and check
4. A shopping list and cash (for super market)
5. A shopping list and cash (for specialty food store)
6. A shopping list and cash (for a clothing store)
7. A deposit slip and a check to be deposited
8. Seven hand-written notes.

Motivating Activity

Tell the group members that you need their help on a shopping trip to a nearby shopping center. Inform them that you will give each a note that gives the assignment.

Instructional Procedures

1. Give each a handwritten note and, when applicable, items or papers to be brought to the shopping center. Each note should be individually prepared with a different assignment. Included are:
   a. shoes to be repaired ("Please take these shoes to the shoe repair shop and ask for new heels and soles. Remember to get a receipt.")

b. a suit to be dry cleaned ("Please take this suit to the dry cleaners. I need it by Wednesday afternoon. Remember to get a receipt.")

c. a deposit slip and an endorsed (For deposit only) check (Please take this to the Maryland Cosmopolitan Bank and make a deposit. Remember to get a deposit receipt.")

d. a shopping list ("Please go to the Apex Super Market and buy these items. Remember to count your change.")

e. a shipping list for a specialty food shop ("Please go to Samsone's Cheese Shoppe and buy a half pound of cheddar cheese and a half pound of blue cheese. Remember to count your change.")

f. a phone bill and a written check ("Please go to the telephone company office and pay my bill. Remember to bring back a paid receipt.")

g. a shipping list for a men's clothing store ("Please go to Wilson's Men's Shop and buy a pair of black knee-length socks, size 12. Remember to count your change.")

2. Proceed to the shopping center and show the group the Directory. Arrange for a meeting time and place.

Individualized Reinforcement and Reinforcement Schedules

Provide praise for correct responses and give the individual permission to shop independently.

Assessment Strategy

Check to see whether each individual has carried out the task correctly. Check receipts, items purchased, and change for accuracy. Record the individual's responses on "The Home: Functional Reading Checklist."

Follow-Up Activity/Objective

If the individual achieves the objective, proceed to an instructional experience in which the simple note has instructions for two different stores or stops at the shopping center.

Instructional Resources

Shopping center directory
Sample receipts

Observations and Comments:

> **GENERAL OBJECTIVE:** The individual will function in the home as independently and skillfully as possible by performing diverse written tasks.

The individual:

1. Writes down and files desired recipes for future use.

Functional Essence

Instructional plans should have as their functional essence the copying and filing of desired recipes. Instructional activities should include reviewing recipes found:
   a. on package labels;
   b. in cookbooks;
   c. in newspapers and magazines; and
   d. in the files of friends and family members.

These recipes should be reviewed for taste preferences, ease of preparation, and cost factors. Those selected as meeting the individual's needs should then be tried whenever possible and then copied if successful. Assist the individual in developing a filing system. Include experiences in obtaining recommended recipes from friends and family members with the goal of encouraging the individual to exchange recipes.

2. Writes simple notes and messages for family members and other members of the household.

Functional Essence

Instructional plans should have as their functional essence the development of the concept that notes and messages may have to be left for members of the household when the individual is not able to speak to them either in person or on the telephone. Instructional activities should include the following types of notes:
   a. a telephone message;
   b. a message telling where the individual has gone, where he may be contacted, and when he expects to return; and
   c. a note that outlines work that has to be done by the reader when that person awakens or returns home.

Practice should be provided, through various simulations, in composing each of the above types of notes.

3. Adds names, telephone numbers, and addresses to his personal telephone directory.

Functional Essence

Instructional plans should have as their functional essence the development of a personal telephone directory. Instructional experiences should involve obtaining the names, telephone numbers, and addresses of the individual's friends and family members for entry into a telephone directory. These entries should then be made from:
   a. dictation (i.e., as if the friend were telling the individual the information);
   b. notes and letters that contain this information (i.e., as if the friend were including the information in a letter);
   c. the telephone directory; and
   d. the telephone information operator.

Activities should include the inclusion of emergency numbers and business numbers often called, e.g., personal physician, dentist, work number, gas and electric company, member of the clergy, etc.

4. Prepares shopping lists.

Functional Essence

Instructional plans should have as their functional essence the preparation of a shopping list from:

a. an inventory of food, household products, household supplies, and clothing on hand;

b. planned meals and snacks;

c. planned cleaning, repair, and other household tasks and activities;

d. planned activities and events that require additional or special clothing; and

e. an examination of the individual's budgeted amounts for purchases.

Instructional activities should demonstrate the relationship between each of the above elements to the composition of a shopping list. Items on sale and discount coupons should be considered when preparing a shopping list. Care should be taken, however, that these factors do not unduly influence shopping behaviors because the individual might purchase items that are not needed just because they are "bargains."

5. Prepares weekly and monthly budgets.

Functional Essence   Instructional plans should have as their functional essence the preparation of a personal budget. Consideration should be given to:

a. anticipated or actual net income;

b. fixed expenditures;

c. expenditure averages in fluctuating items such as food and utility bills;

d. interest payments;

e. anticipated activities and events such as trips, visits from friends and relatives, etc.; and

f. savings.

Whenever possible, actual income and expected expenditures should be used in composing and calculating a budget. Experiences must include the development of a budget format with explanations and clarifications explored for each budget category.

6. Makes notations on a wall calendar, an appointment book, or desk diary.

Functional Essence   Instructional plans should have as their functional essence the writing down of appointments, scheduled events, and approaching activities and events on a wall calendar, an appointment book, or a desk diary. Experiences should include the review of newspapers, magazines, bulletin board notices, and other printed notices for information on activities and events of possible interest to the individual. Practice should be given in noting the dates of these events on a wall calendar or in an appointment book. Appointments with physicians, businesses and agencies, and friends and relatives should also be noted. Regularly scheduled events such as leisure-time pursuits, e.g., bowling league, aerobics classes, and club meetings should be posted. Sufficient experience in posting all these activities should be provided.

7. Writes down key dates in the lives of special friends and relatives in a personal calendar.

Functional Essence   Instructional plans should have as their functional essence the encouragement of the individual to note key dates such as birthdays and anniversaries of special friends and relatives for the purpose of sending greeting cards on these occasions.

8. Writes greeting cards, post cards, and letters to relatives and friends. (*See* Sample Instructional Plan.)

Functional Essence   Instructional plans should have as their functional essence the development of skills in corresponding with relatives and friends. Activities should be provided in using a personal calendar of key dates to send birthday and anniversary cards to special friends and relatives. Experiences should include: addressing the envelope, writing the return address, writing the greeting, and signing the card. In addition, activities should deal with addressing, writing a brief message, and signing post cards when on a vacation trip. Abundant experiences must also be provided in writing simple personal letters to friends and relatives, especially when reaching these people is not easy by telephone or would involve long-distance calls. The writing of special occasion cards should also be practiced (e.g., get well, sympathy, Mother's and Father's Day, baby congratulations, etc.).

SAMPLE INSTRUCTIONAL PLAN

Topic Area __THE HOME-FUNCTIONAL WRITING____   Date __11/13/82_____

Teacher____Mr. Russell_____

Time Allotted ___30-35 minutes_____

Individual(s) or Group Members Involved:
D. Frey, P. Moncur, G. Munzu,
R. Jones, R. Cassell, J. Jones,
M. Pierce

Special Notes or Precautions ____None_____

General Objective

The individual will function in the home as independently and skillfully as possible by performing diverse written tasks.

Specific Objective (8)

The individual writes greeting cards, post cards, and letters to realtives and friends.

Instructional Objective

When given a list of five names of relatives and friends, the individuals will address, write a brief message, and sign post cards. They will do so without errors.

Materials and Equipment

1. Individualized listing of names and addresses
2. Sample post cards.

Motivating Activity

Collect sample post cards that you received over the years. Show the picture and message side of each card by using an opaque projector, commenting on the vacation sites and the pleasure experienced upon receiving these cards.

Instructional Procedures

1. After showing the cards with the opaque projector, pass them around to the members of the group.
2. Ask each to tell:
    a. the vacation site;
    b. the message;and
    c. the name of the person sending the card.
3. Pass out the individualized list of names and addresses from each person's personal directory.
4. Say, "I will pass out to each of you a travel packet that contains:
    a. a travel brochure;
    b. five sample post cards;and
    c. a ballpoint pen.
    Use the information in the travel brochure to write a simple message."

5. Then say, "Now, write your post cards and bring them to me for mailing." Remind them to sign the post card and that this is a practice session to prepare them for a future vacation trip.

Individualized Reinforcement and
Reinforcement Schedules

Reinforce individuals periodically with verbal praise. Comment on how well the post cards are written. Tap shoulder of D. Frey for praise.

Assessment Strategy

Collect the post cards and check the mailing address, the message, and the signature. Record the individual's performance on "The Home: Functional Writing Checklist."

Follow-Up Activity/Objective

If the individual achieves the instructional objective, proceed to an instructional experience on writing special occasion greeting cards.

Instructional Resources

Travel posters
Travel brochures
Maps

Observations and Comments:

GENERAL OBJECTIVE: The individual will function in the home as independently and skillfully as possible by performing necessary mathematical operations.

THE KITCHEN
The Equipment and
Appliances

The individual:

1. Sets the timer and/or heating level (numerical) on a stove, microwave oven, or other appliance to a desired setting for cooking and baking purposes.

Functional Essence

Instructional plans should have as their functional essence the matching of the time designation on a timer, to that time specified in a recipe or in the package directions of a food item. Instructional activities should focus on providing the individual with experience in setting various (numerical) temperatures and different times. Throughout, the emphasis should be on the matching of numbers *and* the estimation of time left before an item is ready to be removed from the appliance and then served.

2. Verifies the accuracy of the oven dial and corrects for measured errors in setting when necessary.

Functional Essence

Instructional plans should have as their functional essence the verification of the accuracy of the oven dial by matching the numerical reading of an oven gauge to the number of the dial's setting. The key instructional activity must be the actual use of an oven gauge. Be sure to include paper and pencil and/or oral *arithmetic computations* in making adjustments in the oven dial setting to correct for measured errors. Also, include techniques for getting the oven setting corrected, e.g., calling the building superintendent when appropriate, or the gas and electric company.

3. Weighs small quantities of food using a kitchen scale.

Functional Essence

Instructional plans should have as their functional essence the use of a kitchen scale to:
   a. prepare snacks and meals;
   b. conform to a special diet; and
   c. conform to a daily health and nutrition regimen.
Instructional experiences should be provided that assist the individual in measuring solid foods according to recipes as well as nutritional guidelines. Activities should include adding quantities or subtracting quantities to reach desired weight levels.

4. Selects the dial or pushbutton on an electric mixer or blender and uses this setting for a predetermined amount of time to prepare a food item.

Functional Essence

Instructional plans should have as their functional essence the timing of the use of an electric mixer or blender in the preparation of beverages and food items. Emphasis should be placed on following time designations as specified in recipes and package directions as they correspond to specific dial or pushbutton settings. The use of a kitchen clock, kitchen timer, or watch should be featured. Experiences should be provided for different time periods.

Food Items

The individual:

1. Selects the package size and/or the number of packages needed to meet the recipe requirements for preparing snacks and meals by checking weight designations on labels.

Functional Essence   Instructional plans should have as their functional essence the computation of package size and/or the number of packages needed by net weight designations as they compare to weight designations specified in recipes. Instructional activities should focus on preparing recipes for different numbers of people so that the individual practices multiplying and dividing recipe quantities and then selects the food package and/or packages needed to meet these requirements.

2. Prepares a snack or part of a meal using measuring spoons and cups.

Functional Essence   Instructional plans should have as their functional essence the preparation of snacks or meals by using measuring spoons and cups to measure out the ingredients as called for in:
   a. recipes and
   b. directions printed on package labels.
Instructional activities should concentrate on using all the possible measurements of which these devices are capable. Experiences also should include multiplying and dividing recipe formulations to accommodate different numbers of people.

3. Buys packages or containers of food only after checking sale expiration dates and uses them before expiration dates.

Functional Essence   Instructional plans should have as their functional essence the identification of sale expiration dates and their comparison to the day's date to determine:
   a. whether the item has expired or
   b. the number of days left that the product can be used.
Instructional activities should feature the computation of days left of possible use before purchasing a food item. Throughout, the emphasis should be placed on relating days left to the planned use of the item. The planning of meals according to nutritional and other considerations including budgetary constraints must play an integral part in instructional plans.

4. Selects a food item for purchase and for use in meals after reviewing nutritional information on its label.

Functional Essence   Instructional plans should have as their functional essence the calculation of nutritional elements supplied by a food item as they fit into a daily health plan or special diet regimen. Attention must be paid to meeting food group requirements, vitamin and mineral elements, and caloric intake factors. Throughout, the emphasis should be on arithmetic computations to ensure that nutritional needs are satisfactorily met.

Kitchen-Related Items

The individual:

1. Obeys cleaning instructions found on kitchen cleaning products.

Functional Essence   Instructional plans should have as their functional essence the measuring out of quantities of cleaning products as specified on the package directions. Throughout the instructional activities, emphasis should be placed on the safe use of these products and on using exact amounts to avoid waste. Experiences should be provided in measuring the most commonly used products.

2. Anticipates future activities using the wall calendar as a guide to days left and their dates.

Functional Essence   Instructional plans should have as their functional essence the calculation of the days left until a planned activity or event. Instructional activities should center on recording appointments, regularly scheduled activities, and special events on a wall calendar and then on checking periodically to determine the days and dates of these approaching events.

ROOMS IN THE HOME
The Living Room

The individual:
1. Sets an electric timer to turn lights, lamps, and radios on and/or off.

Functional Essence   Instructional plans should have as their functional essence the setting of electric timers to specific times so that lights, lamps, radios, and other appliances may be turned on and off when the individual is away. Instructional activities should focus on the prevention of burglaries through this technique. Other techniques that should be followed when the person will be away from home for more than several days should also be included. Discussions should include alerting neighbors and stopping mail and newspaper deliveries. Information from local police departments on burglary prevention should be obtained and shared with the individual.

2. Sets a thermostat for different times and different weather conditions.

Functional Essence   Instructional plans should have as their functional essence the setting of a thermostat for:
   a. daytime operation;
   b. nighttime operation;
   c. seasonal operation (air conditioning versus heating); and
   d. times when no one is at home.
Activities should include the examination of appropriate numerical settings for these various situations and conditions. Throughout, emphasis must be placed on setting thermostats in such a way as to conserve energy from national and individual economic perspectives. Relate conservation of energy to the preparation of weekly and monthly budgets.

The Bedroom

The individual:
1. Sets an alarm clock, an electronic digital clock, or a clock radio to a desired wake-up time.

Functional Essence   Instructional plans should have as their functional essence the setting of an alarm to a desired wake-up time. Instructional activities should concentrate on the calculations involved in determining this time. Included should be:
   a. time required to be at work or other activity;
   b. time needed to carry out morning activities such as toileting, dressing, grooming, meal preparation, and eating; and
   c. time needed to travel to work.
Instructional plans should communicate the concept that once these various time factors are computed, the task of setting the alarm is carried out.

2. Selects the numerical settings for appliances used in the bedroom according to instruction booklets. (*See* Sample Instructional Plan.)

Functional Essence   Instructional plans should have as their functional essence the selection of settings on bedroom appliances such as fans, air conditioners, heaters, heating pads, and electric blankets to match numerical designations recommended in instructional booklets. Instructional activities should emphasize the relative performance levels of these pieces of equipment in terms of numerical value, i.e., a setting of 5 on an electric blanket is warmer than a setting of 4 or lower, but less warm than a setting of 6 or greater.

The Bathroom

The individual:

1. Compares his weight shown on a bathroom scale to a previous weight or to a goal or desired weight.

Functional Essence   Instructional plans should have as their functional essence the calculation of:
   a. weight gained or lost and
   b. weight to be lost or gained.

Instructional activities should focus on monitoring one's weight for the purpose of modifying eating habits and practices. The computation of weight loss or gain or the determination of weight to be lost or gained as part of a goal or desired weight plan should be the key mathematical skill developed in instructional plans.

2. Takes and uses over-the-counter medicines and medications in dosages and at times recommended for adults.

Functional Essence   Instructional plans should have as their functional essence the observation of dosage recommendations as they are suggested on product labels. Throughout, the emphasis should be on numerical designations for quantity of medication, for maximum daily dosages, and for suggested times of repeated dosages. Commonly used medicines and medications should be reviewed for their suggested uses.

3. Takes and uses medicines and medications according to prescribed dosages and at times identified on labels of prescribed medicines and medications.

Functional Essence   Instructional plans should have as their functional essence the observation of:
   a. prescribed dosages and
   b. times of dosage administration.

Instructional activities should feature the actual medicines taken by the individual whenever feasible. Care should be taken to ensure the individual's privacy is safeguarded. Sample labels of commonly prescribed medicines and medications should be reviewed with particular attention paid to counting and measuring out dosages.

4. Takes vitamins and minerals in dosages recommended by his physician or in dosages listed on the label.

Functional Essence   Instructional plans should have as their functional essence the observation of dosage recommendations as they are suggested on vitamin and mineral bottles or containers. Throughout, the emphasis should be on numerical designations for dosage, suggested minimum daily requirements, cautionary notes on maximum limits, and suggested times of taking. Commonly recommended vitamins and minerals should be reviewed. Whenever possible, however, individual programs should be used while safeguarding the individual's privacy.

The Basement

The individual:

1. Orders oil or other fuel when the gauge on the oil burner or other fuel gauge is at a predetermined alert level.

Functional Essence

Instructional plans should have as their functional essence the calculation of fuel left to order replacement fuel before there is none left. Instructional experiences should focus on reading various levels on fuel gauges and determining quantity of fuel left. Emphasis should always be placed on estimating the time to order based on:

    a.   seasonal consumption rates and

    b.   delivery times.

Activities should also stress the relationship between consumption and the formulation of a budget.

2. Checks electric, gas, and/or water meter readings to confirm official meter readings on utility bills.

Functional Essence

Instructional plans should have as their functional essence the matching of meter readings to the recorded readings on utility bills. Emphasis should be placed on verifying the accuracy of the bills and on using consumption rates in determining budget entries.

SAMPLE INSTRUCTIONAL PLAN

Topic Area __THE HOME-FUNCTIONAL MATHEMATICS__   Date __9/15/83__

Teacher __Ms. Stanhope__

Time Allotted __25-35 minutes__

Individual(s) or Group Members Involved:
C. Hopewell, G. Simmons,
B. Mihalski, H. Hernandez

Special Notes or Precautions __Because this instructional plan involves the operation of electrical appliances, emphasis throughout must be on safety.__

General Objective

The individual will function in the home as independently and skillfully as possible by performing necessary mathematical operations.

Specific Objective (Bedroom - 2)

The individual selects the numerical settings for appliances used in the bedroom according to instructional booklets.

Instructional Objective

When asked to decrease and increase the temperature settings of a variety of bedroom appliances (air conditioners, heaters, heating pads, and electric blankets), the individual will correctly change the setting by the designated amount, e.g., "Make the electric blanket warmer by two settings."

Materials and Equipment

1. An electric blanket
2. A heating pad
3. A heater
4. An air conditioner
5. Instructional booklets for these appliances

Motivating Activity

Talk about recent weather conditions, e.g., "It has been so hot this summer that there is a need to use the air conditioner to protect against the heat." Discuss degrees of heat and what being comfortable may mean. Discuss instructional booklets for typical appliances in the home that control temperature. Give each individual a different booklet and tell him he will get to examine the dial controls.

Instructional Procedures

1. Ask each individual to identify the appliance to which the booklet that he received applies.
2. When he identifies it, give him the appliance or its facsimile (in the case of an air conditioner) to examine.

3. Explain that if one wants an air conditioner that is set on high to make the room or area colder, one must set the numerical dial to higher number. Demonstrate. Give each person an opportunity to change the numerical setting by specified amounts.
4. Explain that if one wants an air conditioner that is set on high to make the room or area less cold, one can:
   a. change to the low setting, or
   b. lower the numerical dial to a lower number.
5. Explain that if one wants to operate a heating appliance at a higher temperature, one must change the numerical dial to a higher number. Demonstrate. Give each person an opportunity to change the numerical setting by specified amounts.
6. Explain that if one wants to operate a heating appliance at a lower temperature, one must change the numerical dial to a lower number. Demonstrate. Give each person an opportunity to change the numerical setting by specified amounts.
7. Give each person problems to solve, e.g., "You have the electric blanket, and it is set on '3' and you are getting cold. Make it two numbers warmer."

Individualized Reinforcement and Reinforcement Schedules

Praise the individuals for correctly setting the appliance. Fade out the praise for G. Simmons after initially providing it.

Assessment Strategy

Observe each individual as he solves the oral problem. Check to see of he resets the control dial/button to the requested setting. Record his response on "The Home: Functional Mathematics Checklist."

Follow-Up Activity/Objective

If the individual achieves the instructional objective, proceed to an instructional experience involving the review of various appliances and their accompanying instructional booklets with particular reference to numerical settings.

Instructional Resources

Instructional booklets

Observations and Comments:

chapter 3
THE SCHOOL

As society becomes increasingly responsive to the need for continuing education and actively supports life-long education, adolescents and adults with learning problems will spend substantially greater segments of their lives in school settings. To function successfully as students, adolescents and adults must acquire a variety of skills in reading, writing, and mathematics. Essential language, problem solving, and computational competencies range from those critical to functioning in teaching and learning contexts to those involved in moving and communicating within the school building and engaging in extra-curricular activities. As perceptions of educational and training needs evolve, adolescent and adult education will not be limited to traditional secondary and post-secondary offerings but will encompass all types of instructional programs, especially those that emphasize vocational and avocational development.

Preparation for the role of a student, therefore, must become an integral part of instructional experiences for all persons, especially for those individuals whose learning problems interfere with their facile, incidental learning from actual life experiences. For these persons, a functional and practical education must focus on activities that will make it possible for them to meet the functional demands of a school program.

Readers may wish to consult "Readings and Resources" at the end of this book for relevant information or programming for adolescents and adults as participants in school programs.

GENERAL OBJECTIVES

READING   The individual will function in the school as independently and skillfully as possible by identifying words and other symbols found there.

WRITING   The individual will function in the school as independently and skillfully as possible by performing diverse written tasks.

MATHEMATICS   The individual will function in the school as independently and skillfully as possible by performing necessary mathematical operations.

FUNCTIONAL READING / INSTRUCTIONAL OBJECTIVES

GENERAL OBJECTIVE: The individual will function in the school as independently and skillfully as possible by identifying words and other symbols found there.

The individual:

1. Obeys safety signs and directions on school buses.

Functional Essence   Instructional plans should have as their functional essence the development of an appreciation for and the strict observance of safety signs and directions on school buses, including:
   - a. "No Smoking";
   - b. "Watch Your Step";
   - c. "Emergency Exit";
   - d. "Stay in Your Seats";
   - e. "Keep hands inside windows"; and
   - f. "Do not cross white line while bus is in motion".

Tours of school buses should be scheduled before students are allowed to ride them.

2. Obeys signs outside the school building.

Functional Essence   Instructional plans should have as their functional essence the location and observance of entrance way signs and signs that direct pedestrians and vehicles. For those individuals who drive to school, special attention should be paid to signs that designate parking areas. Also, review signs found on outside playground and play areas such as tennis courts.

3. Locates classrooms, offices, and special facilities and areas such as the cafeteria, auditorium, shops, gymnasium, and fallout shelters, from names and numbers printed on doors, and on signs placed on or near doorways.

Functional Essence   Instructional plans should have as their functional essence the location of special sites in the school so that the student can:
   - a. follow a schedule of classes and activities;
   - b. take messages to teachers, administrators, and other staff;
   - c. schedule and keep appointments with key school personnel (principal, assistant principal, guidance counselors, department heads, therapists, nurse, etc.); and
   - d. take shelter during emergencies or emergency drills involving the non-evacuation of the building.

4. Follows a class and activity schedule as it appears on the personal schedule card.

Functional Essence   Instructional plans should have as their functional essence the identifying of class names and/or abbreviations, class periods, teacher names, and room assignments as they appear on official class schedules. Instructional activities should include reference to school floor plans and directional signs in hallways. Experiences should include practice schedules in which the student walks through identified schedule patterns.

5. Locates exits and entrances, stairways, and elevators from signs near these areas and from directional signs leading to these locations.

Functional Essence   Instructional plans should have as their functional essence the location of exits and entrances, stairways, and elevators so that the student can:
   a. enter the school building;
   b. move about the school during the school day;
   c. exit the building at the end of the school day; and
   d. exit the building during emergencies and during emergency drills.

6. Operates a self-service elevator to facilitate his movement within the school building.

Functional Essence   Instructional plans should have as their functional essence the operation of a self-service elevator as the individual moves about the school building. Activities should

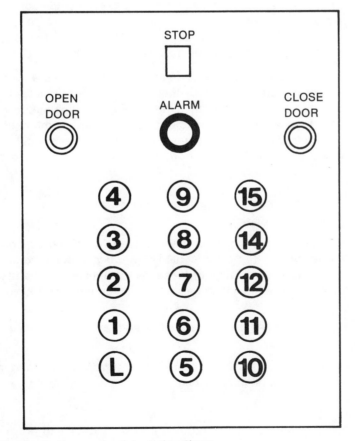

Figure 11.   Self-service elevator buttons and safety designations.

center on the meanings and use of the various buttons and safety elements including:

    a.   floor numbers or letters;

    b.   door-control buttons ("Close Door"—"Open Door");

    c.   emergency buttons and switches ("Alarm"—"Stop"); and

    d.   emergency telephone directions and numbers.

7.   Locates restrooms from names printed on doors and signs placed on or near doorways.

Functional Essence   Instructional plans should have as their functional essence the location of restrooms when needed according to:

    a.   sex designation ("Girls" and "Boys");

    b.   category designation ("Student" and "Faculty"); and

    c.   foreign language designations ("Señor" and "Señorita").

8.   Obeys warning signs appearing throughout the school environment.

Functional Essence   Instructional plans should have as their functional essence the location of and compliance with safety signs that appear throughout the school environment, including those found in gymnasiums, cafeterias, boiler rooms, science laboratories, shop areas, shelter areas, store rooms, maintenance areas, and areas where signs prohibit entry by students.

9.   Locates his personal locker and/or gym locker.

Functional Essence   Instructional plans should have as their functional essence the location of a personal locker and/or gym locker from the name, number, or personal rebus appearing on the locker.

10.   Unlocks a combination lock used on his school locker.

Functional Essence   Instructional plans should have as their functional essence the memorization of the number and turn sequences that unlock the individual's school locker. Emphasis should be placed on matching the memorized combination with the numbers on the lock. If the individual is unable to memorize the combination, it should be written down and kept in his wallet. Instructional activities should include experiences with the storage in and removal from the school locker of clothing and other appropriate personal items.

11.   Places notes in the correct mail slots or boxes in the teachers' and staff's mail room or area.

Functional Essence   Instructional plans should have as their functional essence the identification of teacher and staff members' names in order to place notes and messages in mail slots or boxes. A review of these names should include identification of subjects taught and room locations as an aid in locating their rooms and work areas.

12.   Reads aloud the letters and numerals appearing on a chart designed to evaluate visual acuity.

Functional Essence   Instructional plans should have as their functional essence the identification of the letters of the alphabet, the numerals 1–9, and zero in preparation for visual screening assessments.

13.   Compares weight and height measurements to previous measurements obtained in school check-ups.

Functional Essence   Instructional plans should have as their functional essence the identification of:

      a.   representative height designations including the abbreviations "ft." and "in." the symbols (') and ("), and the numerals 1 through 12 and

      b.   a realistic range of possible weights appropriate to the students in the group.

Experiences should also include the computation of differences in both weight and height measurements, preferably from the actual records of the student. Be careful not to embarrass any student who might be self-conscious about his weight or height.

14.   Orders desired breakfast and lunch items.

Functional Essence   Instructional plans should have as their functional essence the selection of desired foods from a:

      a.   menu checklist and

      b.   cafeteria directory.

Instructional experiences should focus on the names of food items that are found on the menus for the school year. Identify the most frequently occurring items. Early in the instructional program, use those item names along with the student's favorite foods.

15.   Locates items in a school store from the information found on a store directory.

Functional Essence   Instructional plans should have as their functional essence the identification of the names of school supplies and other typical school store items. Conduct an analysis of the items and use these in instructional plans. Visit the school store to locate the items found there and then locate the names on a directory. Prepare activities in which the student is expected to match names with their actual counterparts.

16.   Identifies athletic team members by the names and/or numbers appearing on team uniforms. (*See* Sample Instructional Plan.)

Functional Essence   Instructional plans should have as their functional essence the identification of school team members by their numbers and/or names as they appear on uniforms. Review the rosters of the team and arrange for their visit to the learning area. Obtain pictures of the individual team members in uniforms and team shots and use them in instructional plans.

17.   Locates the scores of the "Home" and "Visitors" teams during sporting events.

Functional Essence   Instructional plans should have as their functional essence the identification of the words and numbers on score boards including:

      a.   the words "Home" and "Visitors";

      b.   representative numbers appropriate to possible scores, inning, and period numbers, and other game statistics like runs, hits, and errors;

      c.   the words that label key situations including "runs," "hits," and "errors"; and

      d.   words that label general information (batting averages, home dates, and attendance).

18.   Uses an electronic calculator to perform simple computations.

Functional Essence   Instructional plans should have as their functional essence the identification of words, abbreviations, initials, and process signs as a preliminary step to carrying out various functional mathematical computations. (*See* "Functional Mathematics" for objectives involving computations.)

HEIGHT-WEIGHT CHART*

Height	Females	Males
4'7"	74–90	
4'8"	77–94	
4'9"	80–97	
4'10"	83–101	88–110
4'11"	87–104	92–110
5'0"	90–108	96–118
5'1"	94–111	100–123
5'2"	97–115	104–127
5'3"	100–118	108–131
5'4"	103–122	112–135
5'5"	106–125	116–139
5'6"	110–129	120–145
5'7"	113–132	124–151
5'8"	116–136	129–156
5'9"	120–141	133–160
5'10"	123–146	137–164
5'11"	127–151	140–168
6'0"	131–156	154–173
6'1"		148–178
6'2"		152–182
6'3"		155–185
6'4"		159–189

* Small Frame - use lighter end of weight chart

Large Frame - use heavier end of weight chart

Figure 12.   Height and weight chart.

CALCULATION EXAMPLE

- Set the decimal selector as specified in each problem.
- Enter all numbers exactly as you would write them (except when using the Add mode).
  EXAMPLE: To enter 123.45, you would press the following keys:

  [1] [2] [3] [·] [4] [5]

- All totals and sub-totals may be used for further calculations. RE-ENTER the number into the calculator by using a FUNCTION key and continue the problem.
  EXAMPLE: (123 + 456) x 2 = 1,158

Set Selector @2			
Enter	Press	Tape	Note
123	* [⬛] [±] [=]	123·00 +	* Depress the [⬛] key to clear the calculation registers before starting an addition or subtraction.
456	[±] [=]	456·00 +	
	[⬛]	579·00 ✳	
	[x]	579·00 x	
2	[±]	2· =	
		1158·00 ✳	Re-entry of total

Figure 13. Electronic calculator terminology.

19. Follows written directions found throughout the school environment.

Functional Essence   Instructional plans should have as their functional essence the development of those reading skills involved in comprehending and carrying out written directions appearing on or accompanying:
   a. seat work assignments;
   b. learning stations;
   c. tests and examinations;
   d. homework assignments;
   e. teaching machines; and
   f. vending machines.
Experiences should be provided to familiarize the individual with typical directions accompanying each category listed above. Sufficient practice should be given for each area.

20. Completes assignments as specified in workbooks, lab and shop manuals, mimeographs, and dittos.

Functional Essence   Instructional plans should have as their functional essence the following of written instructions as they appear in workbooks, lab and shop manuals, mimeographs, and dittos. Collect representative workbooks, manuals, mimeographs, and dittos that are part of the student's curriculum. Explore the scope and sequence of the curriculum to plan a pattern of exposing the student to typical directions as required by that curriculum.

21. Engages in calisthenics and other physical activities as outlined in posters and charts.

Functional Essence   Instructional plans should have as their functional essence the development of skills involved in following the diagrams that depict the movements required to carry out specified physical activities. These charts/posters should be used to demonstrate

Figure 14.   Physical fitness diagrams.

various activities. Once the individual develops some skill in interpreting diagrams, provide him with diagrams that he had never seen before.

22.   Participates in educational board games.

Functional Essence   Instructional plans should have as their functional essence the development of skills involved in following the written directions found on:
        a.   game boxes;
        b.   game boards;
        c.   cards; and
        d.   scoring sheets.
Review the various games found in the school to determine patterns of written rules. Read these rules aloud and carry them out in playing games or in executing individual steps that are part of games.

23.   Reviews his notes and notebooks for studying purposes.

Functional Essence   Instructional plans should have as their functional essence the development of skills in note-taking as a means of reinforcing learning and for later study purposes. Instructional activities should concentrate on techniques of note-taking and on methods of reviewing these notes in preparation for quizzes and examinations. Outlining procedures must especially be developed.

24.   Locates books, records, tapes, and magazines in the school library.

Functional Essence   Instructional plans should have as their functional essence the development of skills involved in using a card catalog, a book-locator index, or *Books in Print* to locate desired print and other media materials. Instructional activities should include the retrieval of materials from shelves and files and through the process of completing order forms to be submitted to the librarian.

MOVES

1. A player may move two stones (one for each count) or one stone the sum of both counts. Example: with a roll of 6-3, a player may move one stone 6 points and another by 3 points, or he could move one stone by 9 points.

2. Stones may be moved to any point except a point which is occupied by two or more opposing stones. Such a point is called "made." There is no limit to the number of stones on any point.

3. If a stone is being moved more than one count, each count must be taken separately (in any order) and no single count may end on a point "made" by the opposing player.

continued

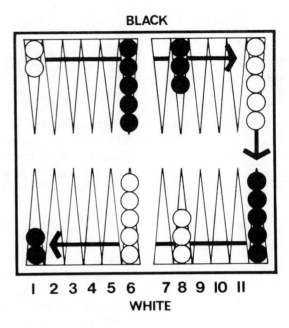

Figure 15.   Written game rules.

25.   Locates special school activities and events listed on the student calendar and attends those of interest.

Functional Essence   Instructional plans should have as their functional essence the development of reading skills involved in interpreting the information found on student calendars. Instructional experiences should focus on identifying days, dates, and typical student activities. The actual student calendar should be used in functional instructional activities. Special emphasis should be placed on identifying events of special interest to the student.

26.   Locates key words on school-related forms and provides the requested information.

Functional Essence   Instructional plans should have as their functional essence the completion of school-related forms. Instructional activities should include experiences in filling out the following forms as appropriate:
   a.   class registration;
   b.   library request;
   c.   field trip permission;
   d.   free breakfast or lunch;
   e.   musical instrument rental; and
   f.   special event requests.

Key words should be extracted from these forms and taught as specialized vocabulary words. All forms used in the school should be reviewed in instructional activities. The relationship between personal information and key words must always be emphasized.

27.   Locates important information on written announcements and memos and responds appropriately to the information and special requests.

Functional Essence   Instructional plans should have as their functional essence the development of those reading skills involved in interpreting the information found in memos and written announcements. Instructional activities should include providing the individual with experiences in which he is expected to respond to special request for information from school authorities. Collect representative forms and past announcements as instructional materials. Whenever new announcements or forms are distributed, review these with the student.

28. Locates information and articles of interest in the school newspaper.

Functional Essence   Instructional plans should have as their functional essence the development of those reading skills involved in finding and comprehending information and articles of interest in the school newspaper. Issues of the school newspaper should serve as the core of instructional experiences in which the student reviews the newspaper for information of general and individual interest.

29. Obeys the rules of behavior specified in the *Student Handbook.*

Functional Essence   Instructional plans should have as their functional essence the development of reading skills involved in the comprehension of written rules found in the *Student Handbook.* Each rule should be reviewed in terms of its rationale and the consequences of noncompliance. The more relevant rules should be culled from the text and used for individual instructional experiences. These rules may be placed on wall charts or bulletin boards for easily accessible reference.

30. Locates key information found on personal records and reports.

Functional Essence   Instructional plans should have as their functional essence the development of those reading skills involved in comprehending the information found in pertinent records and reports including:
  a. progress reports;
  b. report cards;
  c. grade reports;
  d. progress charts; and
  e. individualized educational plans.
In each case, efforts should be taken to ensure that the student understands the implications and participates both in record keeping and in identifying educational objectives and instructional procedures as appropriate.

SAMPLE INSTRUCTIONAL PLAN

Topic Area __THE SCHOOL-FUNCTIONAL READING__   Date __5/3/82__

Teacher __Ms. Pesik__

Time Allotted __25 minutes__

Individual(s) or Group Members Involved:
M. Bryznowski, L. Currier,
O. Cooke, C. Wright, M. Cohen,
D. Crown, F. Laina, C. Ives,
S. Joyner, M. Kaplan

Special Notes or Precautions __None__

General Objective

The individual will function in the school as independently and skillfully as possible by identifying words and other symbols.

Specific Objective (16)

The individual identifies athletic team members by the names and/or numbers appearing on team uniforms.

Instructional Objective

When shown the jerseys of the school or local baseball team, the individual will name the players with 100% accuracy.

Materials and Equipment

1. Photographs of the team members
2. Jerseys of the team members
3. Paper and pencils
4. List of anticipated team line-up

Motivating Activity

Announce to the group that it will be going to an upcoming school or local baseball game. Tell the group members that they will be able to meet each of the players of their team after the game is over.

Instructional Procedures

1. Tell the group members that, if they are going to meet the players in person, it would be nice to say their names and numbers.
2. Show the group photographs of the team members. When showing each photograph, immediately afterwards show the athlete's uniform shirt. Point out the names and numbers on each jersey, associating each with the picture of the player.
3. Hang each jersey over a chair.
4. Ask the group members to make up their own score sheets by listing the names and numbers of the team members in the order of pictures shown. (Check the anticipated line-up for the game. Make sure the jerseys are in clear view.)
5. Then show the pictures of each player and ask the individuals to name each player.
6. Point to each jersey and ask the individual to name its owner.

Individualized Reinforcement and
Reinforcement Schedules

Provide praise for correct responses. Take individual(s) to a
professional baseball game.

Assessment Strategy

Check to see if the members of the group have written down the names
and numbers in the order of the pictures shown. Listen to see
if the individuals name the baseball players when shown the jerseys
of the players. Record the individual's response on "The School:
Functional Reading Checklist."

Follow-Up Activity/Objective

If the individuals achieve the instructional objective, proceed to
an instructional experience in which the individuals fill in their score
sheets while listening to a tape of a previous game.

Instructional Resources

Team rosters
Team pictures
School year book
Professional team souvenir booklet

Observations and Comments:

FUNCTIONAL WRITING / INSTRUCTIONAL OBJECTIVES

GENERAL OBJECTIVE: The individual will function in the school as independently and skillfully as possible by performing diverse written tasks.

The individual:

1. Writes down the requested information on school-related forms. (*See* Sample Instructional Plan.)

Functional Essence

Instructional plans should have as their functional essence the development of those integrated reading and writing skills involved in completing forms such as:
   a. class registration;
   b. library request;
   c. field trip permission;
   d. free breakfast or lunch request; and
   e. musical instrument rental.

Key words should be culled from these forms and taught in relation to the individual's personal response, e.g., "Birthdate — 9/23/64." All forms used in the school program should be part of instructional activities.

2. Completes written assignments as specified in workbooks, lab and shop manuals, mimeographs, and dittos.

Functional Essence

Instructional plans should have as their functional essence the following of written instructions as they appear in workbooks, lab and shop manuals, mimeographs, and dittos. Collect representative workbooks, manuals, mimeographs, and dittos that are part of the student's curriculum. Explore the scope and sequence of the curriculum to plan a pattern of exposing the student to typical directions. In all cases, emphasize the relationships existing between the instructions and the nature of the written response. Provide sufficient practice so that the student will have enough experience and confidence to perform independently. Review periodically to make certain that the student is not practicing incorrect responses.

3. Writes down words, phrases, and sentences and fills out score sheets as required in educational board games.

Functional Essence

Instructional plans should have as their functional essence the development of skills involved in responding in writing as required by educational board games. Review the various games found in the school to determine the specific writing requirements. Practice each of these tasks individually and then incorporate them into the total experience of playing them. Stress accuracy of response and legibility.

4. Completes written class and home assignments.

Functional Essence

Instructional plans should have as their functional essence the development of skill in carrying out oral and written directions by translating them into action. Particular emphasis should be placed on those assignments requiring written responses. Instructional experiences should involve assignments given by instructors and instructional aides. Assignments should run the gamut of the entire scope of the student's curriculum. Special attention should be directed to sequencing these assignments to program for increasing difficulty and for emerging skills.

5. Writes relevant notes in notebooks during class sessions.

Functional Essence

Instructional plans should have as their functional essence the development of skills in note-taking as a means of reinforcing learning and for later study purposes. Instructional activities should concentrate on techniques of note-taking and on methods of reviewing these notes in preparation for quizzes and examinations. Outlining procedures must especially be developed.

6. Supplies answers on written quizzes and examinations.

Functional Essence

Instructional plans should have as their functional essence the development of those skills involved in test-taking. Experiences should be provided in taking the following types of tests:

    a. matching;
    b. true-false;
    c. completion;
    d. multiple choice;
    e. listings; and
    f. essay.

Techniques for responding to each type of test should be reviewed. Quizzes and examinations in each appropriate subject area should be used in practice sessions and should reflect the scope and sequence of the individual's curriculum.

SAMPLE INSTRUCTIONAL PLAN

Topic Area ___THE SCHOOL-FUNCTIONAL WRITING___   Date ___12/14/80___

Teacher ___Mr. Ferris___

Time Allotted ___35 minutes___

Individual(s) or Group Members Involved:
L. Banks, M. Krishnan, R. Kim,
R. DeStefano, W. Carter,
E. Partridge, M. Kasabian,
E. Lane, G. Parks, M. Marten

Special Notes or Precautions ___None___

General Objective

The individual will function in the school as independently and skillfully as possible by performing diverse written tasks.

Specific Objective (1)

The individual writes down the requested information on school related forms.

Instructional Objective

When given invitation forms to a school exhibit or performance, the individual will fill in the correct time and date of the event on the invitation and will address the envelopes without any errors.

Materials and Equipment

1. Invitation forms
2. Envelopes for the invitations
3. Pens
4. Individual address books

Motivating Activity

As part of an exhibit or performance activity sequence, give out invitation forms to the group members. Tell them they may have up to five invitations for each of two separate recitals or scheduled exhibits.

Instructional Procedures

1. Pass out invitation forms.
2. Ask the group members to look in their address books and decide whom they would like to invite. Remind them they can only invite five people to each show.
3. Tell them to separate the invitation forms into two piles.
4. Announce the time and date of the first performance.
5. Ask them to fill in that information on the first pile of invitations.
6. Announce the time and date of the second performance.
7. Ask them to fill in that information on the second pile of invitations.
8. Tell them to address the envelopes and put the invitations in them.

Individualized Reinforcement and
Reinforcement Schedules

Praise all individuals for satisfactory performance.

Asessment Strategy

Check each envelope against the entries in the individual's address book. Then check to see whether the individual has written the right time and date in the appropriate place on the invitations for each of the two performances. Record the individual's performance on "The School: Functional Writing Checklist."

Follow-Up Activity/Objective

If the individual achieves the objective, proceed to an instructional experience involving the preparation of the official program for the performance or exhibit.

Instructional Resources

Sample invitation forms

Observations and Comments:

FUNCTIONAL MATHEMATICS / INSTRUCTIONAL OBJECTIVES

GENERAL OBJECTIVE: The individual will function in the school as independently and skillfully as possible by performing necessary mathematical operations.

The individual:

1. Unlocks a combination lock used on his school locker.

Functional Essence   Instructional plans should have as their functional essence the memorization of the number and turn sequences that unlock the individual's school locker. Emphasis should be placed on matching the memorized combination with the numbers on the lock. If the individual is unable to memorize the combination, it should be written down and kept in his wallet. Instructional activities should include experiences with the storage in and removal from the school locker of clothing and other appropriate personal items.

2. Completes assignments involving computation as specified in math and other workbooks, lab and shop manuals, and dittos.

Functional Essence   Instructional plans should have as their functional essence the development of computational skills as required in workbooks, manuals, and dittos. Collect representative workbooks, manuals, and dittos that are part of the student's curriculum. Isolate those pages and sections that feature computational activities. Assist the student in translating written examples and problems found there into his own paper and pencil representations and their solution. Encourage him to check answers through estimation, standard mathematical operations, and electronic pocket calculators.

3. Moves on a game board a specified number of places, records and tallies scores, and carries out other required mathematical computations in educational board games.

Functional Essence   Instructional plans should have as their functional essence the development of mathematical skills necessary to the student's participation in educational board games. Score-keeping, movements of tokens or pawns, paying out money replicas, and other mathematical operations required by the educational games available in the school should be isolated and practiced and then incorporated into the total game experience.

4. Keeps appointments at scheduled times with school personnel.

Functional Essence   Instructional plans should have as their functional essence the following skills:
   a. the recording of the scheduled time in a personal diary;
   b. the identification of time on watches and clocks;
   c. the estimation of time left before the scheduled appointment; and
   d. the estimation of time needed to arrive at the appointed place on time.
Activities should include moving from the learning area to various locations, e.g., the offices of administrators, guidance counselors, department heads, therapists, and the school nurse to arrive at realistic estimates of travel time.

5. Compares weight and height measurements obtained in school check-ups to previous measurements.

Functional Essence   Instructional plans should have as their functional essence the computation of differences in both weight and height measurements, preferably from the actual records of the student. Be careful not to embarrass any student who might be self-conscious about his weight or height. Mathematical problems should focus on before and after measurements of individuals who have gained or lost weight and who have grown taller. In each problem, the student is expected to calculate the change.

6. Locates the scores of "Home" and "Visitor" teams during sporting events and determines who is leading and by what amount. (*See* Sample Instructional Plan.)

Functional Essence Instructional plans should have as their functional essence the identification of the words and numbers on score boards for the purpose of monitoring the score, the leader, and the spread of the score. Use previous game scores during practice instructional activities. Supplement these scores with scores from community, semi-professional, and professional teams as added motivation and practice whenever appropriate.

7. Checks the prices of desired food and beverage items from a menu checklist or from a cafeteria food directory before ordering.

Functional Essence Instructional plans should have as their functional essence the selection of desired foods from a:
    a. menu checklist and
    b. cafeteria directory.
Instructional activities should focus on the cost of the items in terms of the student's budget *and* money on hand. Encourage the student to use a pocket calculator and/or to estimate the cost of desired items before ordering. Actual menu checklists and charts of cafeteria price lists should be used during instructional sessions.

8. Pays for breakfast or lunch.

Functional Essence Instructional plans should have as their functional essence the use of currency and/or coins to purchase desired food items. The skills involved include:
    a. identification of prices on a menu checklist and cafeteria directory;
    b. determination of money on hand and budgetary constraints;
    c. selection of coins and currency as payment; and
    d. verification of change when applicable.
Actual menu checklists and charts of cafeteria directories used in the school should be used in practice sessions. Daily menus should be previewed before trips to the cafeteria until the student is able to function independently.

9. Purchases needed or desired items in a school store.

Functional Essence Instructional plans should have as their functional essence the use of currency and/or coins to purchase needed or desired items in a school store. Instructional activities should emphasize:
    a. reference to the individual's budget;
    b. reference to money on hand;
    c. paying the exact amount or paying more than exact amount and anticipating change; and
    d. verifying correctness of change received.
Visit the school store to locate items of interest and need to determine future purchases. Practice role plays of these purchases before actual shopping.

10. Pays for school trips and other special events.

Functional Essence
Instructional plans should have as their functional essence the use of currency and/or coins to pay for school trips and other special events. Reference should be made to amounts designated on field trip permission forms and in memos and bulletins announcing special events. Practice sessions should include the presentation of cost figures from previous school trips and special events announcements to the student who then must identify the money he should use to pay the bill.

11. Puts exact amount of change in a vending machine or puts in more than exact change and verifies correctness of change received.

Functional Essence
Instructional plans should have as their functional essence the selection of coins needed to operate a vending machine. Emphasis throughout should be placed on purchasing nutritious snacks and not on the substitution of snack items for breakfast or lunch. Be sure to include verification of change when more than exact change is used.

12. Pays fines for overdue library books.

Functional Essence
Instructional plans should have as their functional essence the use of currency and coins to pay for overdue library books. Emphasis should be placed on developing the awareness that he should not return books late. Instructional activities should involve the study of fine schedules and the tabulation through multiplication of the rates for different number of days.

13. Uses an electronic pocket calculator to perform simple computations.

Functional Essence
Instructional plans should have as their functional essence the development of skills in the effective and efficient use of the calculator as an aid in carrying out

Figure 16. Calculation example.

mathematical computations. Oral problems, written examples, and written problems should be used to provide abundant experience in the calculator's use. Instructional programs should include activities that practice each of the operations and combination of operations of which the calculator is capable. Stress the importance of checking the accuracy of answers through estimation and second or multiple runs.

14. Uses measuring devices in science, industrial arts, vocational education, and home economics classes.

Functional Essence Instructional plans should have as their functional essence the development of skill in using various measuring devices including:
  a. measuring cups;
  b. measuring spoons;
  c. rulers;
  d. beakers;
  e. flasks;
  f. scales;
  g. tapes; and
  h. instruments such as micrometers, callipers, and depth gauges.

Provide the individual with sufficient practice with each of the above as appropriate. Use these devices to carry out various experiments and work projects.

SAMPLE INSTRUCTIONAL PLAN

Topic Area THE SCHOOL-FUNCTIONAL MATHEMETICS   Date 1/12/83

Teacher Ms. MacIntosh

Time Allotted 25-30 minutes

Individual(s) or Group Members Involved:
C. Lynwood, M. O'Connor,
S. Liotta, M. Evans,
N. Austin, K. Mueller

Special Notes or Precautions None

General Objective

The individual will function in the school as independently and skillfully as possible by performing necessary mathematical operations.

Specific Objective (6)

The individual locates the scores of "Home" and Visitors" teams during sporting events and determines who is leading and by what amount.

Instructional Objective

When given three sample box scores, the individual will identify the winner correctly and indicate the winning amount exactly.

Materials and Equipment

1. Sample box scores
2. Photographs of the scoreboard taken during and after recent school sporting events

Motivating Activity

Using an opaque or slide projector show the individuals photographs or slides of the scoreboard taken during and after recent school sporting events. Ask them to identify the score of the home team and by how much they are winning or losing.

Instructional Procedures

1. Review the key words found on the scoreboard, i.e., Home and Visitors.
2. Provide the individuals with practice in identifying numerals that are likely to appear in the specific sporting event being discussed. Use flash cards to encourage rapid recognition of these numerals.
3. Practice computing the winning margin on sample box scores.
4. Give each individual three sample box scores, and ask him to identify the winner and the winning amount.

Individualized Reinforcement and
Reinforcement Schedules

Praise all individuals after they complete the activity correctly. If feasible, provide tickets to a ball game.

Listen to each person as he identifies the winner and winning amount on each box score. Record the individual's response on "The School: Functional Mathematics Checklist."

Follow-Up Activity/Objective

If the individual achieves the instructional objective, proceed to an instructional experience in which the individual is expected to carry out diverse mathematical operations in interpreting the box scores of community, semiprofessional, and professional teams.

Instructional Resources

Sports Illustrated Magazine
Sporting News
Sports sections of newspapers
Books on sports
Sport record books

Observations and Comments:

chapter 4
THE COMMUNITY

As individuals participate in the general community, they must be able to interpret and use signs, symbols, and rebus systems. Despite the critical nature of these functional receptive and expressive skills, they have only recently been assigned an important place in educational programming. For many enlightened educators, "basic skill" instruction has come to include preparation for living and participating in the community.

Skill in reading, writing, and mathematics is fundamental if one is to cope successfully with the demands of participating in society. Paying for one's food, transportation, and personal items and interpreting time tables, signs, maps, schedules, and store directories are examples of functional challenges in the community. Taking notes, recording appointments, completing forms, using public telephones, and operating self-service elevators are representative tasks that adolescents and adults

with learning problems must master as they move about the community.

Individuals with learning problems must become proficient at obtaining information from written media such as newspapers, posters, flyers, brochures, and other forms of advertising. They must learn how to set aside extraneous information while utilizing relevant facts and other data.

It is an overwhelming task to review all the information, signs, and symbols present in the community. However, if people are to participate functionally as pedestrians, drivers, purchasers of goods and services, and as workers, attention must be given to educational programming in community skills.

Readers may wish to consult "Readings and Resources" at the end of this book for relevant information on preparing adolescents and adults for functioning in the community.

GENERAL OBJECTIVES

READING   The individual will function in the community as independently and skill-fully as possible by identifying words and other symbols.

WRITING   The individual will function in the community as independently and skill-fully as possible by performing various written tasks.

MATHEMATICS The individual will function in the community as independently and skill-fully as possible by performing necessary mathematical operations.

FUNCTIONAL READING / INSTRUCTIONAL OBJECTIVES

GENERAL OBJECTIVE: The individual will function in the community as independently and skillfully as possible by identifying words and other symbols.

The individual:

1. Locates public restrooms.

Functional Essence Instructional plans should have as their functional essence the locating of public restrooms when the individual has to:
   a. go to the bathroom;
   b. wash face and/or hands;
   c. remove spots from clothing;
   d. comb hair;
   e. apply make-up;
   f. change clothes; or
   g. put on or change a sanitary napkin.

2. Finds telephone booths and other locations of public telephones.

Functional Essence Instructional plans should have as their functional essence the locating of telephone booths and other locations of public telephones to:
   a. make a telephone call and
   b. look up an address in the telephone book.

3. Uses a pay telephone.

Functional Essence Instructional plans should have as their functional essence the placing of coins into their appropriate slots and the dialing of numbers from memory, a personal directory, and from the telephone directory.

4. Identifies and uses the correct value of stamps to mail letters, greeting cards, and post cards.

Functional Essence Instructional plans should have as their functional essence the selection of the correct amount of postage for mailing personal correspondence.

5. Mails letters observing mailbox pickup schedules.

Functional Essence Instructional plans should have as their functional essence the location of mailboxes in the individual's home and work communities and the actual mailing of personal correspondence according to mailbox pickup schedules.

MAIL COLLECTION TIMES					
MONDAY THRU FRIDAY EXCEPT HOLIDAY		SATURDAY		SUNDAY	
A.M.	P.M.	A.M.	P.M.	A.M.	P.M.
8:05	1:09	8:15	5:05		4:50
	5:02			HOLIDAY	
Monument and Wolf St.				A.M.	P.M.
					4:56

BOX LOCATION FOR LATER COLLECTION
DAILY EXCEPT SATURDAYS, SUNDAYS AND HOLIDAYS
2116 E. Monument St.   #504

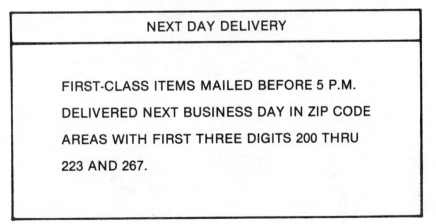

NEXT DAY DELIVERY
FIRST-CLASS ITEMS MAILED BEFORE 5 P.M. DELIVERED NEXT BUSINESS DAY IN ZIP CODE AREAS WITH FIRST THREE DIGITS 200 THRU 223 AND 267.

Figure 17.   Mailbox pickup schedules.

6. Operates vending machines to obtain desired items.

Functional Essence   Instructional plans should have as their functional essence the operating of vending machines for snacks, beverages, and for small items of personal need such as combs and other grooming and health aids.

7. Orders meals from a restaurant menu.

Functional Essence   Instructional plans should have as their functional essence the ordering of actual meals at a variety of restaurants. Simulated ordering of meals may precede actual visits to restaurants but only as preliminary instructional experiences and activities.

8. Orders a meal from a cafeteria or fast-food restaurant bulletin board or directory.

Functional Essence   Instructional plans should have as their functional essence the ordering of actual snacks and meals at cafeterias and fast food restaurants. Simulated ordering of snacks and meals may precede actual visits but only as preliminary experiences.

MENU

May We Suggest Our

SEAFOOD COMBINATION DINNER FOR 2
Jumbo Shrimp Lobster Sauce
Barbecued Pork Fried Rice
2 Egg Rolls or
Egg Drop Soup or Cookie
975

Genuine Native Cuisine

Butterfly Shrimp with Tomato Sauce and Cracked Almonds	5.50
Breaded Jumbo Shrimp Sweet and Pungent	5.00
Fried Pork Sweet and Pungent	4.50
Beef with Boktoy (Chinese Vegetables)	4.60
Diced Chicken with Vegetables and Almonds	5.00
Moo Goo Gai Pan (Chicken, Mushrooms, Bamboo Shoots, Water Chestnuts, Snow Peas and Vegetables)	5.00
Beef or Shrimp with Bean Sprouts	4.60
Char Sue Ding (Diced Barbecue Pork with Assorted Vegetables)	5.00
Beef with Snow Pea Pod	6.00
Chow Char Sue Pan (Moo Goo Gai Pan Style with Barbecued Pork)	5.00
Chow Gow Yok Pan (Moo Goo Gai Pan Style with Beef)	5.00
Chow Har Kew (Jumbo Shrimp Dipped Egg Batter with Mushrooms, Snow Peas, Bamboo Shoots and Vegetables)	5.10

Figure 18.   Sample menu for ordering meals.

9. Finds a desired location in the community by street signs.

Functional Essence Instructional plans should have as their functional essence the location and identification of street names on posts and poles. Preliminary to actual excursions into the community, the individual should be exposed to street maps of the community. Instructional experiences should be of a problem-solving nature, e.g., "You are at Warwick Avenue and North Avenue and want to go to Gwynns Falls and the corner of Braddish Avenue. Show me which way you would walk and what street name signs you would encounter." After these problem-solving sessions, instructional activities should be devoted to locating street locations on errands in the community. Various errands could include the use of automobiles, public transportation, taxis, and walking, as appropriate to the task, budgetary constraints, and weather and health conditions.

10. Finds a desired location in the community by building or house numbers.

Functional Essence Instructional plans should have as their functional essence the location of building and house numbers on doorways, windows, building facades, and signs. Before locating a specific building or house, the individual should have experienced identifying the street name from street signs (*see* 9 above). Experiences should also be provided in identifying odd and even numbers as an aid in locating a specific site. Although simulated experiences may be used in the beginning, later instructional plans should feature locating:
   a. the residences of relatives and friends;
   b. frequently needed resource agencies in the community; and
   c. business offices and buildings of places personally used by the individual.

11. Locates the apartment number from names and numbers on or near doorbells or mailboxes.

Functional Essence Instructional plans should have as their functional essence the identification of apartment numbers of friends and relatives from names and numbers on or near doorbells or mailboxes. Before actually locating an apartment number, the instructor should obtain pictures of the mailboxes or doorbells of friends and relatives of the individual who lives in a multiple dwelling. Pictures must be clear enough to see name and apartment number designations. This instructional activity should be followed by actual trips to the locations.

12. Locates a specific room, apartment, or office from directional signs and numbers and/or letters on doors.

Functional Essence Instructional plans should have as their functional essence the location of specific rooms, apartments, and offices from directional signs in hallways and from numbers and/or letters on doors. Preliminary experiences should be provided in which floor plans of apartment and other buildings are studied and in which trips are made to various buildings including apartment houses, schools, hospitals, and office buildings. Attention should be directed toward numerical clues that indicate floor location and hallway side (odd-even). Attention must also be paid to alphabetical and numerical progressions. Finally, instructional activities should include experiences in locating rooms, apartments, and offices where the individual is likely to go if he is to be actively involved in community activities.

13. Using key words on signs and marquees locates a desired store or business.

Functional Essence Instructional plans should have as their functional essence locating signs on business establishments that signal the type of goods and/or services provided. The names of supermarket, department store, fast-food, and other chain or company stores found in the individual's community should be emphasized. Instructional plans should feature a problem-solving approach, e.g., "You need to have your shoes repaired; find the store in this shopping mall where shoes are repaired."

14. Locates a business or store in an office building from the building directory.

Functional Essence   Instructional plans should have as their functional essence the use of a building directory to locate a business office or store in an office building. Attention should be devoted to identifying actual offices and stores in buildings in the community with special emphasis on those places that the individual is most likely to visit or need to visit as he meets the requirements of daily existence.

15. Using signs on doors and windows, identifies and observes store and office hours posted.

Functional Essence   Instructional plans should have as their functional essence the scheduling of visits to public places according to posted hours. A problem-solving approach is most beneficial, i.e., one in which the individual is to plan a daily itinerary where visits to a store, library, museum, bank, etc. must be accomplished by considering hours of operation. After preliminary hypothetical problem-solving activities are engaged in, the scheduling of required or desired visits should be pursued.

16. As he moves about the community, obeys warning signs and avoids places designated as dangerous. (*See* Sample Instructional Plan.)

Functional Essence   Instructional plans should have as their functional essence the development of safe behavior as the individual moves about the community. A necessary first step is the identification of common warning signs found in the community. The identification of signs should then be followed by exploring the meaning behind the warnings and the simulation of obeying those signs. Finally, trips within the community are necessary to field test the individual as he moves about the community to determine whether he truly behaves safely and is not merely reading the signs.

17. Enters and exits buildings through appropriate doorways, attending to "In" – "Out" and "Enter" – "Exit" designations on doors.

Functional Essence   Instructional plans should have as their functional essence actual trips into the community in which the individual is expected to enter and exit a variety of buildings through a variety of doorways including: automatic doors, sliding doors, revolving doors, ones that open by pushing a hinged steel bar, ones that must be pushed, and ones that must be pulled. In all cases, attention must be directed toward word clues printed on and over doors and on directional signs.

18. Exits from buildings by locating fire and other exits during fire emergencies and fire drills.

Functional Essence   Instructional plans should have as their functional essence the development of safe behavior when facing an emergency situation or an emergency drill requiring rapid exit from a building. Abundant experience should be provided in participating in fire drills both in the instructional area and while in public buildings. Particular attention must be paid to the visual exit signs and to emergency exit signs. Attention must also be directed toward warning signals including bells, buzzers, sirens, speakers, and other alarms. Rapid, orderly walking and exiting to remove oneself as far from the building as feasible must always be emphasized.

In the Country	No Hunting
	No Campfires
	Remember To Put Fires Out
	No Trespassing
	Private Road
	Private Property
	Do Not Drink The Water
	No Picnicking

For the Pedestrian	Beware of Dogs
	Pedestrians Prohibited
	No Trespassing
	Keep Out
	No Loitering
	Quiet Zone
	Curb Your Dog
	No Hitchhiking
	PEDXING
	DANGER - Men At Work
	Private
	Railroad Crossing
	DANGER - High Voltage

In Parks and Zoos	Do Not Pick The Flowers
	Do Not Feed The Animals
	No Bicycling
	Bicycling Prohibited
	Stay Behind Guard Rail
	Keep Off The Grass
	Keep Out
	Closing Times
	No Littering
	No Standing Up On Rides

For the Passenger	Fasten Seat Belts
	Watch Your Step
	No Smoking
	Emergency Door
	No Spitting
	No Littering

In Buildings	Hold On To Moving Hand Rail
	Watch Your Step
	Emergency Exit
	Elevator Out of Order
	Closing Times
	Warning Elevators Should Not Be Used During Fires

At Beaches, Lakes, Quarries, and Other Bodies of Water	No Swimming
	No Wading
	No Fishing
	No Diving
	Keep Off The Rocks
	Polluted

At a Library	No Talking
	No Smoking
	No Eating

Figure 19. Common warning signs in the community.

19. Locates shelter areas in buildings during emergencies and emergency drills.

Functional Essence   Instructional plans should have as their functional essence the development of safe behavior when facing an emergency situation or an emergency drill requiring movement to a shelter or sheltered area. Experiences should be provided in the instructional area and in public buildings. Attention must be directed to signs that signal shelters and shelter areas. Attention should also be paid to alarms and to the rapid but orderly walking to shelters. Finally, experience should be provided designed to facilitate safe and proper behavior while in the shelter area.

20. Avoids entering doorways and corridors in buildings and other places designated as "No Entry" or open to "Authorized Personnel Only."

Functional Essence   Instructional plans should have as their functional essence the development of safe and acceptable behavior as one moves within public buildings. Actual written designations found in buildings in the community should be reviewed and explanations given for the reasons behind each of the directions. Final experiences should involve moving through the buildings in the community and checking to see whether the individual avoids entering doorways and corridors where entry is forbidden for safety and privacy reasons.

21. As a pedestrian, obeys detour and rerouting signs near construction and repair sites.

Functional Essence   Instructional plans should have as their functional essence the development of safe behavior as the individual walks near construction and repair sites. Actual trips in the community where work sites are located are essential if the objective is to be realized.

22. As a pedestrian, uses a map to find his way about the community.

Functional Essence   Instructional plans should have as their functional essence the use of a community street map to find desired locations in the community. Early instructional experiences should center on hypothetical situations, e.g., "You are at the corner of Lake Avenue and York Road and want to get to the doctor's office on York and Overbrook Roads. Show me the way you would walk to get there." After sufficient experience with hypothetical situations, involve the individual in using a street map in unfamiliar areas of the community.

23. As a commuter, locates the bus stop for a desired bus.

Functional Essence   Instructional plans should have as their functional essence the exploration of bus stops in the community, walking trips in the community to identify sidewalk and curb markings as well as signs on poles and stanchions. Particular attention should be paid to numerals on signs indicating the route or routes at the bus stop as well as hours of operation when applicable. Bus trips throughout the community should be taken so that the individual will have the opportunity to find bus stops in unfamiliar places.

24. As a commuter, signals buses to stop from numeral and destination names appearing on the bus.

Functional Essence   Instructional plans should have as their functional essence the identification of buses as they approach from numeral and destination names appearing in the front window. Actual trips should be planned and taken.

25. As a commuter, uses maps to travel on a bus, subway, and other mass transit vehicles and systems.

Instructional plans should have as their functional essence the use of maps found in subway stations, on subways and buses, and in depots. Copies of the maps found in the community should be used to plan trips from the individual's home, place of employment, and/or instructional site to various places in the community including residences of friends and relatives, locations of leisure activities of interest, and offices and agencies that are important resources contributing to a more satisfying existence. Once the individual develops skill in getting from his home, work, and instructional site to key locations in the community, attention should be directed to using the map from any location in the community. Particular attention should be devoted to the numerals and destination names on buses, bus stop stanchions, subway trains, subway stops, depot bulletin boards, subway passage ways, etc.

26. As a traveler, schedules and plans trips according to bus, train, and airline schedules.

Functional Essence Instructional plans should have as their functional essence the use of printed and posted travel schedules to plan trips. At first, hypothetical trips should be planned using all the possible means of transportation available in the community. Various types of trips should be planned including visits to out-of-town relatives and friends and to vacation spots. Schedules should be referred to throughout the planning. Whenever possible, trips should be taken that employ consideration of time, money, packing, and other pertinent factors.

27. As a driver, obeys rebus symbols on dashboard and within car.

Functional Essence Instructional plans should have as their functional essence using rebus designations found in the car to operate:
    a. seat belts;
    b. lights;
    c. defogger;
    d. directional signals;
    e. windshield wipers; and
    f. radio.

28. Obeys traffic signs.

Functional Essence Instructional plans should have as their functional essence the development of safe behavior through the identification and obeying of the variety of traffic signs. Instructional experiences should be varied to include several different orientations including the individual as:
    a. a pedestrian;
    b. a bicyclist;
    c. a runner/jogger; and
    d. a driver.

29. As a driver or a passenger in a car, uses road maps to arrive at desired locations.

Functional Essence Instructional plans should have as their functional essence the use of a road map as an aid in arriving at a desired location. Maps of the community itself should be the instructional starting point. This activity is then followed by using maps of the state and region in hypothetical trips to locales of regional and individual interest. Specific destinations and specific travel routes should be charted. Trips should be taken for

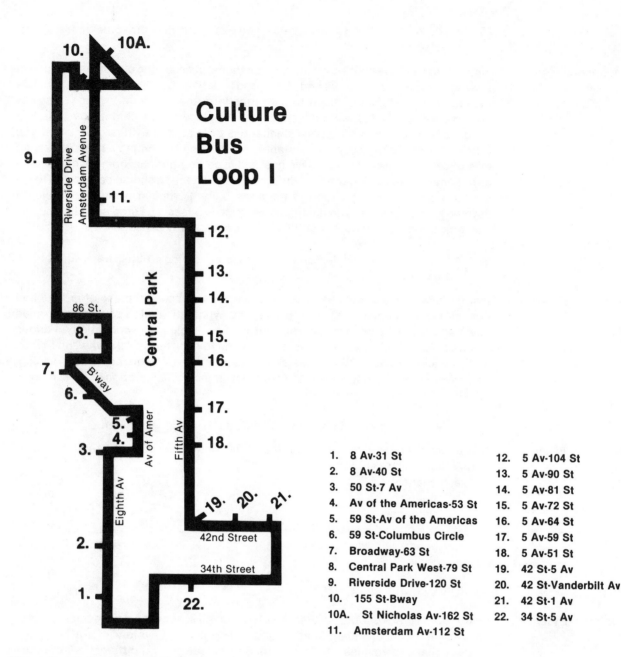

Culture Bus Loop I

1. 8 Av-31 St
2. 8 Av-40 St
3. 50 St-7 Av
4. Av of the Americas-53 St
5. 59 St-Av of the Americas
6. 59 St-Columbus Circle
7. Broadway-63 St
8. Central Park West-79 St
9. Riverside Drive-120 St
10. 155 St-Bway
10A. St Nicholas Av-162 St
11. Amsterdam Av-112 St

12. 5 Av-104 St
13. 5 Av-90 St
14. 5 Av-81 St
15. 5 Av-72 St
16. 5 Av-64 St
17. 5 Av-59 St
18. 5 Av-51 St
19. 42 St-5 Av
20. 42 St-Vanderbilt Av
21. 42 St-1 Av
22. 34 St-5 Av

Figure 20.   Public transportation map.

the purpose of matching highway signs, such as route numbers, exit numbers, and exit names, to map designations. Take simulated trips in which the individual acts as a passenger giving directions to a driver based on map readings.

30.   As a driver, obeys parking signs.

Functional Essence   Instructional plans should have as their functional essence the interpretation of parking signs to avoid breaking the law and risking getting a fine or having the car towed away. Instructional plans must include telling the time, reading the sign to determine whether parking is legal on that day and at that time, and then returning to move the car if there are time restrictions on parking or if there is an approaching time period when parking is no longer allowed.

BM-1 BERGEN BEACH—MANHATTAN (See notes for all routes on reverse side)

Departures from 56th Drive

A.M.	P.M.
6:00T	12:10T
6:10M	12:30T
6:20PR	12:50T
6:30T	1:10T
6:35M	1:30T
6:40T	1:50T
6:50M	2:10T
7:00T	2:30T
7:10PR	2:50T
7:10M	3:10T
7:20T	3:30T
7:25T	3:50T
7:30PR	4:10T
7:30M	6:50T
7:35T	
7:40T	
7:45T	
7:55T	
8:05T	
8:15T	
8:30T	
8:45T	
8:55T	
9:10T	
9:25T	
9:50T	
10:10T	
10:30T	
10:50T	
11:10T	
11:30T	
11:50T	

Brooklyn Boarding/Drop-off Locations

56 Drive	& Strickland Ave.
	& East 63rd St.
	& East 66th St.
East 66th St.	& Dakota Place
	& Bassett Ave.
	& Mayfair Dr. N.
	& Ohio Walk
	& Strickland Ave.
	& Avenue U
Avenue U	& Bergen Ave.
	& East 71st St.
	& East 69th St.
	& East 66th St.
Mill Avenue	& Avenue T
Ralph Avenue	& Avenue N
	& Avenue N
	& Avenue L
Avenue K	& East 57th St.
	& East 52nd St.
	& Schenectady Ave.
	& East 43rd St.
	& East 38th St.
	& New York Ave.
	& East 29th St.
	& Bedford Ave.
Ocean Ave.	& Avenue K ##
	& Avenue I ##
	& Glenwood Rd. ##
	& Ditmas Avenue ##
Cortelyou Rd.	& East 19th St. ★ ★
	& Stratford Rd. ★ ★
Coney Island Ave.	& Beverly Rd. ★ ★
Church Avenue	& East 7th St. ★ ★

Departures from Manahttan ★

A.M.	P.M.
10:00T	12:00T
10:20T	12:20T
10:40T	12:40T
11:00T	1:00T
11:20T	1:20T
11:40T	1:40T
	2:00T
	2:20T
	2:40T
	3:00T
	3:20T
	3:45T
	4:10M
	4:25M
	4:35M
	4:35PR
	4:45T
	4:45PR
	4:55T
	5:00PR
	5:00M
	5:10M
	5:15PR
	5:20M
	5:25T
	5:35PR
	5:45T
	6:20T
	7:10T
	8:00T

Figure 21.   Sample travel schedule.

31.   As a driver, puts coins into a parking meter as needed.

Functional Essence   Instructional plans should have as their functional essence the identification of times that the meter is in effect, the telling of time, and the use of specified coins in specified numbers to obtain desired parking time. The computation of money needed relevant to time segment required must be an essential part of instructional activities and procedures.

32.   Operates self-service elevators in various places in the community.

Functional Essence   Instructional plans should have as their functional essence the identification and appropriate and safe use of the call button and the various operating buttons on a self-service elevator as the individual encounters them in:
  a.   department stores;
  b.   office buildings;
  c.   hospitals, schools, and museums;
  d.   apartment houses; and
  e.   other public or private buildings.
Wherever possible in the community, demonstrate the operation of an elevator and encourage the individual to model your behavior.

33.   Pays the correct fare as shown on a taxi meter and gives a tip as appropriate.

Functional Essence   Instructional plans should have as their functional essence the computation of the fare and a tip based upon the reading on the taxi meter. Instructional plans should deal with the situations in which a taxi is appropriate for travel and include a consideration of budgeting constraints.

SAMPLE DASHBOARD SYMBOLS

(1) HIGH-BEAM INDICATOR;
(2) HEADLAMP SWITCH;
(3) DIRECTIONAL SIGNAL;
(4) HAZARD WARNING FLASHER;
(5) SEAT BELT;
(6) FUEL;
(7) FRONT HOOD;
(8) REAR HOOD;
(9) RADIO SELECTOR:
(10) WINDSHIELD DEFOGGER:
(11) REAR DEFOGGER;
(12) VENTILATING FAN;
(13) HORN;
(14) CIGARETTE LIGHTER;
(15) RADIO VOLUME;

Figure 22.   Dashboard rebus symbols.

34.   Obtains information of interest from local newspapers.

Functional Essence   Instructional plans should have as their functional essence the use of a newspaper as a source of:

    a.   current news;
    b.   weather information;
    c.   sports events and scores;
    d.   leisure time events and schedules (television, movies, and radio schedules);
    e.   sales and prices including special coupons;
    f.   help wanted ads;
    g.   business and financial information;
    h.   real estate information;
    i.   death notices and obituaries;
    j.   schooling and specialized training information; and
    k.   editorial comments and opinions.

Instructional activities and experiences should include all these areas, especially those of interest to the individual, his peers, and his family.

35. Obtains information of interest from posters and notices displayed in public places in the community.

Functional Essence   Instructional plans should have as their functional essence encouraging the individual to review actual posters and notices appearing in the community for events of interest.

36. Obtains information of interest and need from brochures and flyers prepared by public and private agencies and businesses.

Functional Essence   Instructional plans should have as their functional essence the reviewing of flyers and brochures for sales and other events of interest and need.

37. Determines time by observing clocks and electronic time signs placed on buildings in the community.

Functional Essence   Instructional plans should have as their functional essence locating clocks and electronic time signs in order to keep appointments and to meet schedules. Also, clocks and electronic time signs may be used to check the accuracy of the individual's watch or to set a watch that has stopped.

38. Determines the temperature by observing electronic temperature signs placed on buildings in the community.

Functional Essence   Instructional plans should have as their functional essence locating electronic temperature signs and determining the temperature. Instructional activities should be geared to modifying apparel, eating and drinking plans, and general activities when unexpected temperatures are noted.

39. Locates various personal cards when needed from his wallet or billfold.

Functional Essence   Instructional plans should have as their functional essence the location of cards carried in the individual's wallet when needed in real situations, e.g., a medical insurance card at a hospital or doctor's office, an AAA card for auto service, a library card to borrow books, etc. Both simulated and actual situations should be experienced.

SAMPLE INSTRUCTIONAL PLAN

Topic Area ___THE COMMUNITY-FUNCTIONAL READING___   Date _____2/14/81_____

Teacher_____Ms. Schauben_____

Time Allotted ____35-40 minutes_____

Individual(s) or Group Members Involved:
J. Carla, M. Lego,
B. Hartgrove, C. Capute,
C. Leonard

Special Notes or Precautions ___None_____

General Objective

    The individual will function in the community as independently and skillfully as possible by identifying words and other symbols.

Specific Objective (16)

    The individual, as he moves about the community, obeys warning signs and avoids places designated as dangerous.

Instructional Objective

    When shown five flashcards upon which "Warning Signs" that might be found at a zoo have been printed, the individuals will read aloud each card and will explain what they must refrain from doing. They will respond correctly to four out of five signs on the first review trial.

Materials and Equipment

    1. Postcards of zoo animals
    2. Direction signs
    3. Entrance and exit signs
    4. Warning signs
    5. Tape and chalk

Motivating Activity

    Tape postcards of zoo animals on a chalkboard. As the pictures are being taped, ask the members of the group to identify each animal. Fill the chalkboard with easily recognized zoo animals to create a "Zoo Mural." Place an "Entrance" and "Exit" sign in appropriate places.

Instructional Procedures

    1. Ask the group member to identify where they might find these wild animals all in one place. After a discussion, write an appropriate geographic title such as "The Baltimore Zoo" on the board.
    2. Give each group member a direction sign (review of previous lesson) on which has been written an animal's name and an arrow. Ask each individual to place his sign on the board. Praise each one for his contribution to the mural.
    3. Tell the group that there are more signs needed to complete the mural, that is, "Warning Signs." Ask the group to explain what "warning" means.

4. Encourage the members of the group to suggest "Warning Signs" they might see at a zoo. If a sign is named, use a magic marker to prepare the sign. Give the individual the sign to place on the mural. Review the sign's meaning.
5. Make "Warning Signs" for the mural not mentioned by the group. Include the following: "Do Not Feed The Animals," "Stay Behind The Guard Rail," "Do Not Pick The Flowers," "Keep Off The Grass," and "Keep Out."
6. Place each sign on the mural. For each sign discuss its meaning.

Individualized Reinforcement and Reinforcement Schedules

Provide praise for correct responses. Give each individual a map of the local zoo. Stay close to C. Leonard and increase amount of praise as he provides correct responses.

Assessment Strategy

Listen to each individual's oral responses during a review of the "Warning Signs" on an individual basis. Record any difficulties evidenced during the first review trial on "The Community: Functional Reading Checklist."

Follow-Up Activity/Objective

If the individual achieves the instructional objective, proceed to an instructional experience on "Warning Signs" found at beaches, lakes, quarries, and other bodies of water.

Instructional Resources

Map of a zoo
National Geographic or animal magazines

Observations and Comments:

GENERAL OBJECTIVE: The individual will function in the community as independently and skillfully as possible by performing various written tasks.

The individual:

1. Adds telephone numbers to a personal notebook or telephone directory. (*See* Sample Instructional Plan.)

Functional Essence

Instructional plans should have as their functional essence the provision of experiences in which the individual writes down telephone numbers obtained as he moves about the community. Sources of new telephone numbers include:
   a. meetings with friends or relatives;
   b. signs, posters, and bulletin boards;
   c. meetings with representatives from business;
   d. meetings with persons providing service to the individual; and
   e. flyers and brochures.

2. Writes down items of interest in a personal notebook.

Functional Essence

Instructional plans should have as their functional essence the provision of experiences in which the individual takes notes based on items of interest found:
   a. on signs;
   b. on posters;
   c. on store fronts and windows;
   d. on bulletin boards;
   e. in flyers; and
   f. in brochures.
A key factor is the identification of information that is of interest and is, consequently, worthy of note-taking.

3. Writes down appointments in a personal appointment or schedule book.

Functional Essence

Instructional plans should have as their functional essence the simulation of experiences in which appointments are made as the individual moves about the community. Sample appointments should include:
   a. appointments with physicians, dentists, counselors, therapists, and other human service professionals and
   b. appointments, dates, and meetings with family members and friends.
The relationships existing between a wall calendar and the calendar in a personal appointment or schedule book should be highlighted. Entries should also be made from appointment cards obtained from office secretaries and receptionists.

4. Signs petitions and fills out surveys as desired as he moves about the community.

Functional Essence

Instructional plans should have as their functional essence the simulation of experiences in which the individual is asked to fill out surveys and to sign petitions. Survey forms and sample petitions should be included in instructional experiences. Emphasis should be placed on exposing the individual to typical directions and to usual formats.

What those meat stamps tell you— and what they don't

Consumers are often confused by the stamps, tags and package imprints
which indicate the meat has been examined by government inspectors.
But if you want to be sure of getting what you pay for, it will help
if you understand the government meat symbols.

RED MEAT   **POULTRY**

The U.S. Department of Agriculture
inspection stamp in the form of a *circle*
is your assurance of *wholesomeness*. This
circle appears as a stamp on the meat
itself, on metal tags or printed on cans
and containers. The USDA inspection
stamp is required by law for all meat

sold in interstate commerce. This marking is the government statement that a
federal inspector personally inspected the
carcass and determined that it came from
a healthy animal and, further, that it was
processed in sanitary surroundings.

RED MEAT   **POULTRY**

The Department of Agriculture *grade*
stamp is always in the form of a *shield*
and is your assurance of *quality*. This
mark also is affixed to various meats or
containers in the most convenient way.
Unlike the USDA inspection stamp, a
federal grade stamp is not required by
law. Its use is strictly at the option of
the processor. In order to get meat products graded by federal inspectors, the
processor must pay for the service. While
much meat is not federally graded, the
lack of a stamp does not mean the product is inferior. THOSE BRAND NAMES
YOU KNOW AND TRUST SHOULD
OFFER EQUAL ASSURANCE OF
SATISFACTION.

Figure 23.   Information found in brochures and flyers.

5.   Fills out and signs order, request, and application forms when in the community.

Functional Essence   Instructional plans should have as their functional essence the completion of application, order, and request forms. Included should be:
   a.   job applications;
   b.   order forms in catalog stores;
   c.   order forms in department stores;
   d.   credit card application forms;
   e.   library reserve forms; and
   f.   deposit and withdrawal slips.

Initial experiences should involve the mechanics of completing these forms in the instructional area to be rapidly followed by visits into the community to fill out and sign
these forms as needed.

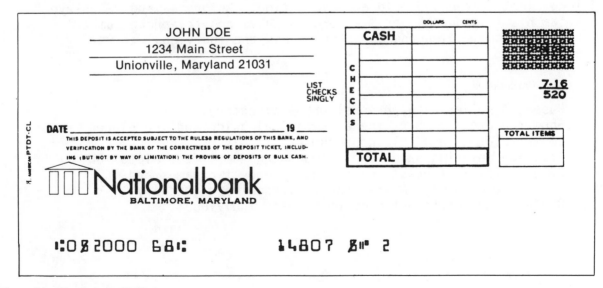

Figure 24.   Bank deposit slip.

SAMPLE INSTRUCTIONAL PLAN

Topic Area __THE COMMUNITY-FUNCTIONAL WRITING__   Date ___12/13/81___

Teacher ___Ms. Lightfoot___

Time Allotted ___30-40 minutes___

Individual(s) or Group Members Involved:
M. Slavic, M. Martins,
P. Savidge, T. Porter,
A. Pepitone

Special Notes or Precautions ___M. Slavic, because of a physical handicap, needs___ additional time to complete assigment.

General Objective

The individual will function in the community as independently and skillfully as possible by performing various written tasks.

Specific Objective (1)

The individual adds telephone numbers to a personal notebook or telephone directory.

Instructional Objective

When four different phone numbers are dictated to the individual, he will write down the person's name and telephone number in a personal directory. He will do so in the appropriate alphabetical section and will record the name and telephone number accurately.

Materials and Equipment

Personal telephone directories

Motivating Activity

Role play a scene in which you play the person moving through the community. As you meet each one of the group members, pretend he is a long, lost friend and hold a conversation. Before saying "Good-bye," ask for his telphone number. Record the name and telephone number in your personal telephone directory. Ask the individual to verify the accuracy.

Instructional Procedures

1. Pass out copies of a personal phone directory.
2. Show the group members the alphabetical guide and the places to write names and telephone numbers.
3. Practice entering names and telephone numbers from dictation.
4. After sufficient practice, dictate one or two names and telephone numbers. Assist the individual as necessary.
5. Dictate four different numbers to each individual.

Individualized Reinforcement and
Reinforcement Schedules

Praise the individuals for correct written responses. Make sure each entry is checked before providing this praise. Allow individuals to keep personal phone directories.

Assessment Strategy

Collect the individual's personal directory and check to see whether he has placed the name in its appropriate alphabetical section and has written the name and telephone number accurately.

Follow-Up Activity/Objective

If the individual achieves the instructional objective, proceed to an instructional experience in which the individual is expected to record in his personal directory telephone numbers of interest from signs, posters, bulletin boards, flyers, and brochures.

Instructional Resources

Telephone Company Directories

Observations and Comments:

GENERAL OBJECTIVE: The individual will function in the community as independently and skillfully as possible by performing necessary mathematical operations.

The individual:

1. Uses a pay telephone.

Functional Essence

Instructional plans should have as their functional essence the selection of coins needed to make local and long-distance phone calls.

2. Mails letters observing mailbox pickup schedules.

Functional Essence

Instructional plans should have as their functional essence the comparison of postal time with present time and the estimation of time needed to get to a mailbox with the actual time left.

3. Puts exact amount of change in a vending machine or puts in more than exact change and verifies correctness of change received.

Functional Essence

Instructional plans should have as their functional essence the selection of coins needed to purchase a desired item. Experiences should include the use of more than exact amount and the computation and verification of change received. Various coin combinations should be experienced. Special attention should be directed toward the observation of "Exact Change Only" signs. After sufficient practice, actual vending machines should be used.

4. Pays for meals at restaurants and cafeterias.

Functional Essence

Instructional plans should have as their functional essence the following mathematical operations:
   a. estimation of the cost of the meal;
   b. comparison of money on hand and/or money budgeted with estimated cost of meal;
   c. verification of check subtotal;
   d. verification of sales tax;
   e. verification of check total; and
   f. computation of a tip.

5. Using signs on doors and windows, identifies store and office hours, and plans to arrive or leave these destinations according to this information.

Functional Essence

Instructional plans should have as their functional essence the comparison of present time to times of operation of stores and offices to estimate time of departure (to get to place at or after time of opening) and time left (to complete shopping or business before closing). Actual trips should be taken with the calculation of time differences as the central point of the experiences.

6. As a driver, obeys parking signs.

Functional Essence

Instructional plans should have as their functional essence the comparison of present time to parking times and the calculation of time remaining when there exists either a time limit ("Two Hour Parking"), or the lapsing of time permitted ("Parking from 9 A.M. to 4 P.M. only").

7. As a driver, places coins into a parking meter as needed and returns before the time expires.

Functional Essence Instructional plans should have as their functional essence the selection of coins needed for a parking meter in terms of estimated time needed as well as the calculation of time left on the meter.

8. Pays the correct fare as shown on a taxi meter, leaving a tip as appropriate.

Functional Essence Instructional plans should have as their functional essence the calculation of currency and coins needed to pay the fare and the computation of an appropriate tip.

9. Puts the correct amount of postage on letters, post cards, greeting cards, and packages.

Functional Essence Instructional plans should have as their functional essence the selection of stamps for mailing letters, post cards, greeting cards, and packages. This selection involves knowledge of the typical rate and the various possible combinations of stamps that make up that rate. Knowledge of special rates such as those for air mail and first class should also be utilized when appropriate. Activities should involve mailing cards on special occasions and the writing of business and personal letters.

AMOUNT OF BILL	TIP
$ 1.00	15¢
2.00	30¢
4.00	60¢
5.00	75¢
6.00	90¢
7.00	$1.05
8.00	1.20
9.00	1.35
10.00	1.50
12.50	1.90
15.00	2.25
17.50	2.60
20.00	3.00

Figure 25. Tip chart.

10. Locates the side of the street where residences and businesses are located from odd and even house numbers.

Functional Essence　　Instructional plans should have as their functional essence the identification of odd and even sides of streets for the purpose of locating residences and businesses by their odd or even number designation. Experiences should include locating the side of streets of actual places of interest and need in the individual's life.

11. Finds residences and businesses by number sequences appearing on surrounding houses. (*See* Sample Instructional Plan.)

Functional Essence　　Instructional plans should have as their functional essence the locating of residences and businesses from address sequences. Information and the use of street maps should be followed by visits to places of interest and need in the individual's life.

12. Finds a specific apartment number from numbers appearing on nearby apartment doors.

Functional Essence　　Instructional plans should have as their functional essence the locating of specific apartments from number sequences found on nearby apartment doors. Experiences should include the presenting of information with apartment house floor plans. This should be followed by visits to the apartment houses of friends and relatives.

13. Finds a business or store in an office building from the numbers appearing on the doors and windows of nearby offices.

Functional Essence　　Instructional plans should have as their functional essence the locating of businesses and stores from numbers appearing on doors and windows of nearby offices. Experiences should include the presentation of information and floor plans of office buildings. This should be followed by visits to offices of interest and need in the individual's life.

14. Estimates the amount of time needed to meet bus, train, subway, and airline schedules.

Functional Essence　　Instructional plans should have as their functional essence the estimating of time needed to meet transportation schedules. Experiences should include practice runs from the individual's home to selected bus stops, subway stations, train depots, airports, and bus terminals. After several trips to each site, assist the individual in arriving at a reasonable time estimate with an additional 10–15 minutes leeway added. Then assist the individual in subtracting this estimate, in each instance, from train, bus, airline, and subway departure or boarding times to determine his own times of departure. Actual trips should then be taken using the individual's estimates.

15. Estimates the amount of time needed to arrive at a bank, business, or store after opening time.

Functional Essence　　Instructional plans should have as their functional essence the estimating of time needed to arrive at banks, businesses, and stores. Experiences should include practice runs from the individual's home to selected banks, businesses, and stores important in the individual's life. After several trips to each site, assist the individual in arriving at a reasonable time estimate for the average trip. Then assist the individual in subtracting this estimate from the scheduled opening time of the bank, business, or store. Repeat the estimation process for each bank, business, and store on a list of important places. Make a list of time estimates for the individual to keep for future reference. Actual trips should be taken using the individual's estimates. Be sure to provide the individual with activities that involve considering time of day, type of weather, and seasonal variations in using and modifying time estimates.

16. Estimates the amount of time needed to arrive at a bank, business, restaurant, or store before closing time.

Functional Essence   Instructional plans should have as their functional essence the estimating of time needed to arrive at a bank, business, restaurant, or store before closing. Experience should include practice runs from the individual's home to selected banks, businesses, restaurants, and stores of interest and need in the individual's life. After several trips to each site, assist the individual in arriving at a reasonable time estimate for the average trip. Then assist the individual in subtracting this estimate from the scheduled closing time plus an additional amount of time to conduct the business matters. Repeat the estimation process for each bank, business, restaurant, and store on a list of important places. Make a list of time estimates for the individual to keep for future reference. Actual trips should be taken using the individual's estimates. Be sure to provide the individual with activities that involve considering time of day, type of weather, and seasonal variations in using and modifying time estimates.

17. As a driver, obeys traffic signs designating specified time intervals that change patterns and flow of traffic.

Functional Essence   Instructional plans should have as their functional essence the identification of time variations found on traffic signs that designate changes in turning, traffic flow, and other vehicular movement patterns. Simulated trips should be made with adjustments made in driving behavior to correspond to posted times. When feasible, take the individual on automobile trips into the community, pointing out how you change driving patterns because of signs. Show the individual how to check his watch and outside clocks for the time of day and to then refer to time in guiding driving behavior. When applicable, accompany the individual as he drives in the community.

18. As a driver, uses a map scale to estimate the number of miles to be traveled from one point on a map to another on an automobile trip.

Functional Essence   Instructional plans should have as their functional essence the estimation of distance from one point on a map to others. Trips to various points of interest should be planned and mileage estimates obtained and recorded. After sufficient map study involving hypothetical trips, schedule actual trips estimating the mileage from maps and then estimating travel time and gasoline needed.

19. As a driver, uses a map scale and an odometer to estimate the time needed to travel from one point to another on an automobile trip.

Functional Essence   Instructional plans should have as their functional essence the use of an odometer and the scale on a map to estimate the time needed to complete an automobile trip. Activities must involve the taking of actual trips in which car speed, mileage readings, and estimated mileage are computed to arrive at an understanding of the time needed for trips of various distances. Activities should include dealing with variations in weather, time, and road conditions and their impact on time needed for trips. Caution should also be taken to ensure the map is a recent one indicating any new routes or detours.

THE COMMUNITY-
Topic Area FUNCTIONAL MATHEMATICS   Date _____ 3/20/82

Teacher_____ Mr. Mitchel

Individual(s) or Group Members Involved:
J. Lovelock, Y. DeSouza,
Time Allotted ___ 30-35 minutes   M. Gomez, M. Goldberg

Special Notes or Precautions _As you move around the community make sure all safety_
precautions are observed. Pay special attention to J. Lovelock, who walks
with a cane.

General Objective

The individual will function in the community as independently
and skillfully as possible by performing necessary mathematical
operations.

Specific Objective (11)

The individual finds residences and businesses by number
sequences appearing on surrounding houses.

Instructional Objective

When given the numbers of adjacent houses, the individual will
identify correctly the house number of an unmarked house. When
given the number of a house, the individual will identify correctly
the house numbers of nearby houses.

Materials and Equipment

1. Worksheets with visual problems in which there are marked and
   unmarked houses, e.g.
2. Diagram of a community street

Motivating Activity

Take the group members for a walk in the community. Walk down
the street and point out the progression of numbers. Point out
that one side of the street has even progressions while the other
has odd.

Instructional Procedures

1. Give the individuals oral problems in which they are expected
   to find houses from numbers you tell them.
2. Return to the learning area and review the experience by providing
   each person with a diagram of the street just visited. Ask the
   group members to fill in missing numbers on the diagram.
3. Pass out a worksheet of a hypothetical street, ask the individual
   to fill in all the missing house numbers.

Occasionally reinforce with praise for correct responses. Praise M. Gomez more often than other group members and use some of his correct responses as models for the other individuals.

Assessment Strategy

Collect the individual worksheets and check to determine whether the individual has written the missing house numbers correctly. Record the individual's response on "The Community: Functional Mathematics Checklist."

Follow-Up Activity/Objective

If the individual achieves the instructional objective, proceed to Specific Objective #12, "The individual finds a specific apartment number from numbers appearing on nearby apartment doors."

Instructional Resources

Polaroid pictures of neighborhood houses with some house numbers clearly marked and others missing.

Observations and Comments:

chapter 5
CONSUMER SKILLS

All individuals are consumers of goods and services. Some people, however, are skillful in selecting quality merchandise and in purchasing services for reasonable prices and fees and others are not. Unskilled consumers often purchase unneeded merchandise, sign unclear service contracts, or buy poorly made products.

Enlightened consumerism is difficult because of false and misleading advertisements, the relentless bombardment of the mass media, and the sophisticated urgings by skilled and, often unscrupulous salespersons.

Individuals with learning problems, as all individuals, must learn to be selective in purchasing goods and services and must resist impulse buying. High inflation rates, increased personal and sales taxes, and reduced personal income and purchasing power demand that individuals consume wisely.

Good consumer judgment includes: buying food and household products selecting among generic, store, or brand name products, and purchasing items on the basis of need and budgetary considerations. Individuals need to be aware of energy-saving procedures that result in lower utility bills and strategies for purchasing quality products that are not widely advertised or openly displayed in a store. Using coupons, understanding serving and food portion information on labels, and interpreting whether sale items should be purchased are additional examples of consumer skills.

Learning how to budget one's finances including interpreting bank statements, interest notes, and participating in savings programs are other major instructional areas requiring consumer proficiency and sophistication. Information on writing and depositing checks, making periodic bank withdrawals from savings accounts, and computing one's taxes are also important to a successful consumer education program.

Finally, the importance of becoming a consumer advocate and of understanding one's rights as a consumer must also be a part of educational experience for adolescents and adults.

Readers may wish to consult "Readings and Resources" at the end of this book for relevant information on programming for adolescents and adults as they fulfill their role as wise consumers of goods and services.

GENERAL OBJECTIVES

READING
The individual will function as a consumer of goods and services as independently and skillfully as possible by identifying words and other symbols.

WRITING
The individual will function as a consumer of goods and services as independently and skillfully as possible by performing diverse written tasks.

MATHEMATICS
The individual will function as a consumer of goods and services as independently and skillfully as possible by performing necessary mathematical operations.

FUNCTIONAL READING / INSTRUCTIONAL OBJECTIVES

GENERAL OBJECTIVE: The individual will function as a consumer of goods and services as independently and skillfully as possible by identifying words and other symbols.

FOOD AND HOUSEHOLD PRODUCTS

The individual:

1. Prepares a shopping list and then purchases the food on that list.

Functional Essence

Instructional plans should have as their functional essence the development of a meaningful and reasonable shopping list. Toward that end, the following skills should be developed:
   a. review of food on hand;
   b. review of planned meals and snacks for the week or a selected period of time;
   c. review of food budget for the week or a selected period of time;
   d. review of discount coupons; and
   e. review of store advertisements.

After each of these tasks are practiced, experiences should be provided in purchasing the items on the list in the store or stores where they cost less. Travel time and travel expenses must always be considered in determining the relative amount of money saved.

2. Consults his shopping list and finds desired items in a supermarket by using a store directory. (*See* Sample Instructional Plan.)

Functional Essence

Instructional plans should have as their functional essence the development of the following skill sequences:
   a. preparation of a shopping list that reflects the individual's needs and budgetary constraints;
   b. identification of items by category, e.g., apples—*fruits*; carrots—*vegetables*; pepper—*spices*, etc.;
   c. location of categories on a store directory (bulletin board or hanging signs);
   d. identification of an aisle number when the directory is on a bulletin board;
   e. location of aisles by posted signs; and
   f. location of desired items on the shelves and in the bins or cabinets of that aisle.

Practice in each of these skills should be provided in simulated and actual shopping trips.

3. Reviews the cost of desired food items at different stores and buys those items where they are most economical.

Functional Essence   Instructional plans should have as their functional essence the review of newspaper advertisements and flyers from several stores in the individual's community to determine differences in cost. Attention must be paid first to the reasonableness of shopping in the stores under study in terms of travel time and cost. Once, however, the number of stores is delimited, assist the individual in developing a comparative shopping list, i.e., one in which the store that is selling an item the cheapest can be checked and/or the prices entered for each store. Once a preliminary list is prepared, provide the individual with opportunities to visit various markets to check differences in price. Add relevant information to the "comparison shopping list." During these trips be sure to point out the unit price signs. Frequently help the individual in preparing "comparison shopping lists" from advertisements and trips to stores. Impress him with the fact that frequent changes in prices make lists out-of-date fast.

SHOPPING LIST

PRODUCE
lettuce	☐	onions	☐
celery	☐	potatoes	☐
cucumbers	☐	peppers	☐
tomatoes	☐		

MEATS
steak	☐	roast beef	☐
lamb	☐	pork	☐
fowl	☐	sausage	☐
liver	☐	ham	☐
fish	☐	hamburger	☐
hot dogs	☐	bacon	☐

CANNED VEGETABLES
asparagus	☐	carrots	☐
corn	☐	green beans	☐
potatoes	☐	peas	☐
beets	☐	baked beans	☐

DAIRY PRODUCTS
butter(marg.)	☐	milk	☐
eggs	☐	cream	☐
cheese	☐	ice cream	☐

FROZEN FOODS
vegetables	☐	pizza	☐
juices	☐	dinners	☐

DINNERS & SAUCES
tomato	☐	tom. paste	☐
spaghetti	☐	chili	☐
soups	☐	tuna	☐

PACKAGED FOODS
inst. potatoes	☐	rice	☐
spaghetti	☐	noodles	☐

BREAKFAST FOODS
syrup	☐	pancake mix	☐
waffles	☐	cereals	☐

BAKED GOODS
bread	☐	cake	☐
rolls	☐	cookies	☐

SPICES & CONDIMENTS
salt	☐	pepper	☐
ketchup	☐	mustard	☐
mayonnaise	☐	pickles	☐
oil	☐	vinegar	☐
garlic	☐	relish	☐

BAKING NEEDS
sugar	☐	flour	☐
cake mix	☐	baking powder	☐
pie filling	☐	pie crust mix	☐

BEVERAGES
coffee	☐	tea	☐
soft drinks	☐	mixer	☐

SOAP & LAUNDRY
bleach	☐	detergent	☐
softener	☐	starch	☐
bar soap	☐	dish liquid	☐

Figure 26.   Suggested shopping list.

4. Compares the cost of generically labeled food with brandname and store brands and selects the food item that best meets his budget and taste preferences.

Functional Essence   Instructional plans should have as their functional essence the development of skills involved in purchasing food according to quality and cost factors. Begin by selecting a favorite food of the individual and purchase that same size package in several name brands, the store brand, and a generically labeled item. Cover the label so that the individual is unable to see the label. Open the package and together examine the contents. Note any difference in color, odor, texture, size, amount of food in relation to liquid contents, etc. Record any differences in quality evaluation, listing items in rank order. Then prepare the items in the same way and ask the individual to taste each item, again without knowing the brand. Record any differences in taste evaluation, listing items in rank order. After taste and quality evaluations are conducted, review them in terms of the individual brands and their difference in cost. When the individual prefers a brand that is higher in cost help him to examine the question, "Is it worth spending more money to buy a name brand than a store or generic brand?" Repeat this type of activity with different foods.

5. Compares the unit prices of food items (price per ounce or pound) and selects the food item that is most economical and best meets personal food quality and quantity requirements.

Functional Essence   Instructional plans should have as their functional essence the purchasing of food packages by size and brand according to quality and quantity requirements, utilizing unit price information in making the selection. Take a trip to supermarkets and other stores that display unit prices. First examine the difference in unit price by brand, i.e., look at the various sizes of tuna and then at the unit price of each size. Then refer to package size and assist the individual in deciding which size will meet his food preparation needs. Once the individual experiences success with handling unit pricing as it relates to the item in a specific brand, combine the experiences suggested in #3 above to assist the individual in determining the most economical purchase across brands and sizes. On your trips to stores, record typical item prices and unit prices by size and brand to use later in instructional activities that will be more realistic because they are based on actual products and prices.

6. Clips discount coupons from daily newspapers, magazines, and store handouts and uses them to purchase desired food products.

Functional Essence   Instructional plans should have as their functional essence the encouragement of the individual to use discount coupons in purchasing needed items. Emphasis must be placed on only using those coupons for needed items while discouraging their use "just because they are there." Also, instructional experiences should include reference to activities in 2, 3, and 4 above because some products, even with discounts, are still not good buys. Instructional activities should include reviewing various sources of coupons, their clipping, their filing, their expiration dates, and their use especially when there are double-coupon savings. As part of the instructional program, bring in newspapers, magazines, and store handouts so that the individual can clip discount coupons. Use an index file to store coupons. Plan meals and parties and use the discount coupons to reduce costs.

7. Uses food stamps to purchase needed food.

Functional Essence   Instructional plans should have as their functional essence the use of food stamps in purchasing food. Throughout the various instructional activities, emphasize the relationship between food stamp denominations and their currency counterparts. In-

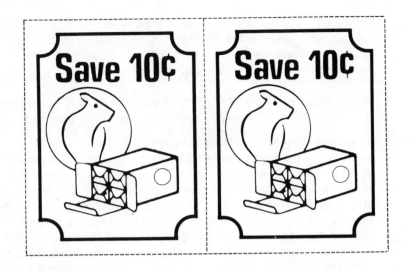

Figure 27. Sample coupon sheet.

structional activities involving purchasing food with cash can be easily modified to practice with food stamps. Time should be spent on acquainting the individual with each denomination and with the limitations on use of food stamps, i.e., restricted to food purchases only. Throughout, reference to a budget plan remains important.

8. Locates serving and portion information on food packages and buys the size and number of packages needed for planned meals and snacks.

Functional Essence   Instructional plans should have as their functional essence the purchase of food based on planned meals and snacks. Emphasis should be placed on planning for the weekly food needs, within budgetary constraints, before shopping. Once the quantity of food is determined, demonstrate how printed information on food packages relevant to portion and serving factors helps to determine the size and number of packages to buy. Include in instructional activities cost factors as they interrelate with item storage possibilities and longevity factors. At this point, the *expiration dates* on packages should be located and discussed. Instructional activities should also involve the individual in translating recipe recommendations into item purchases. Show the individual how to conduct an inventory of food on hand as a critical element in composing a shopping list.

9. When dining out, reviews the menu and orders a meal.

Functional Essence   Instructional plans should have as their functional essence the development of those reading skills involved in interpreting a menu. Instructional experiences should first emphasize the exploration of the menu to ascertain what foods are available as well as the different ordering options, i.e., daily special, full-course dinners, fixed price dinners, and à la carte. Throughout this endeavor, attention should be paid to money on hand, budgetary constraints, dietary requirements, other foods to be eaten that day, and to the relative costs of each ordering option. Explain that daily specials are usually less expensive and sometimes fresher than other menu items and that it may be wiser to order a second choice on the menu for economy purposes. When restaurant discount coupons are available, encourage the individual to use them at restaurants where he enjoys eating.

TO MAKE	DRINK MIX	ADD COLD WATER TO MAKE
1 SERVING	1½ TABLESPOON OR FILL SCOOP TO INSIDE LINE	6 FL. OZ.
1 PINT	1 SCOOP	16 FL. OZ.
1 QUART	2 SCOOPS	32 FL. OZ.
½ GALLON	4 SCOOPS	64 FL. OZ. (2 QUARTS)
1 GALLON	8 SCOOPS	128 FL. OZ. (4 QUARTS)

Figure 28.   Serving and portion information on food packages.

10. Reviews the information and directions found on vending machines and selects an item according to the directions.

Functional Essence   Instructional plans should have as their functional essence the purchase of nutritional snacks as the individual moves about the community. Although there is general uniformity of prices, vending machine prices tend to be higher in public areas such as bus and train stations, movie houses, and airports. Take trips to vending machines in the area to compare prices and to discuss nutritious snacks. Review coin names and their numerical counterparts as well as the written directions that typically appear on these machines. Review the meaning and the process involved when the words "Exact Change Only" appear.

11. Compares the accuracy of store receipts with products purchased.

Functional Essence   Instructional plans should have as their functional essence the development of those skills involved in carrying out the following:
a. identifying of item names as they appear on receipts (computerized checkout systems list the names of items) and matching of price labels, *or*
b. identifying of product prices by reference to price labels on items and to initials that designate food department, e.g., Dy for Dairy, Pr for Produce, and Mt for Meat.

Actual shopping trips should be taken and receipts checked as each item is unpacked. Throughout instructional activities, the individual should be encouraged to estimate the cost of his purchases *and* to check each item as it is rung up on the register.

GR	.00
GR	1.99
MT	1.91
MT	7.81
MT	1.58
GR	.31
GR	.31
GR	.31
MT	1.81
MT	3.94
GR	.95
PR	.89
PR	.45
GR	1.19
GR	.63
GR	.69
GR	.75
GR	.59
	26.11TL
	.50C
A	26.00AT
	.39CD
	6/23
	4722

Figure 29.   Grocery receipt.

The individual:

1. Checks the prices of prescription drugs, over-the-counter drugs, and medications at different stores and buys needed items where they are most economical.

Functional Essence

Instructional plans should have as their functional essence the purchase of needed drugs and medications where they are the most economical. Instructional activities should include visits to pharmacies and to pharmacy departments of larger stores. The purpose of these visits is to record prices of over-the-counter drugs and medications so that the prices can be compared. Plan instructional experiences in which the individual checks directly with the pharmacist, calls up the pharmacist, or refers to a directory of prescription drug prices. Ask the individual to refer to his records in deciding upon where to buy the item. Be sure to include the factors of travel time and travel costs in the decision process. After sufficient study, opportunities should be provided in which the individual shops for needed items.

2. Compares name, store, and generic brands of over-the-counter drugs and medications and selects the one best suited to his budgetary needs and quality preferences.

Functional Essence

Instructional plans should have as their functional essence the selection of over-the-counter drugs and medications as suited to budgetary needs and quality preferences. Unlike food, quality preferences in drugs and medications are too subjective to program for. Instructional experiences, however, should be geared to exploring the cost differences among these three levels of products so that the individual who selects a higher-priced item is aware that he is paying more for the brand of his choice. Also, throughout the experiences make certain to remind the individual that budgetary considerations should play a part in his decision.

3. Compares the sizes and prices of various over-the-counter drugs and medications and purchases the one appropriate to his needs.

Functional Essence

Instructional plans should have as their functional essence the development of skill in comparing unit prices of over-the-counter drugs and medications to determine which size of a specific item is the most economical. Instructional experiences should include discussion of longevity factors and storage space needs of large-size packages with special attention paid to expiration dates on packages. Discussions should also include a review of the need for each item needed in an attempt to determine size.

4. Compares prices of generic and brand names of prescription drugs and selects the one best suited to his budget.

Functional Essence

Instructional plans should have as their functional essence the identification of prices for generic and brand names of prescription drugs. Make a chart of typically used prescriptions presenting the generic name and brand name for each drug. Along side each name present the cost-per-one-hundred or per-a-specific-number of units. Assist the individual in determining which type is more economical. Experiences should be provided in which the individual refers to posted price lists, checks in person with the pharmacist, and/or calls the pharmacist to determine comparative prices. Do not attempt to influence the individual in favor of either generic or brand name drugs because it is a highly subjective choice. The functional essence merely involves stimulating the awareness of the existence of generics and the potential savings.

5. Differentiates medications that are applied externally from medicine, vitamins, and minerals.

Functional Essence   Instructional plans should have as their functional essence the development of skill in differentiating medications that are to be applied externally from those that are ingested. Collect a variety of medications that are applied externally and review their names and directions on their labels. Cautionary words should be pointed out, e.g., "For external use only" and "Do not put near the mouth or eyes." For each precaution, review the reasons and the possible consequences of not heeding it. Point out directions that clearly imply that the item should not be swallowed, e.g., "Apply to your face with cotton," "Squeeze a little on your finger," and "Rub gently into the skin over the affected area."

CLOTHING

The individual:
1. Reviews the labels on clothing items and purchases clothing items that best meet his budgetary and other needs.

Functional Essence   Instructional plans should have as their functional essence the review of labels on items of clothing to determine:
   a. item size;
   b. brand name;
   c. washing and cleaning instructions;
   d. fabric contents; and
   e. prices.
Instructional experiences should include the collection of representative labels that are then reviewed with the individual in discussions of his size, preferred brand, preferred washing/cleaning needs, desired fabric contents, and price he is both able and willing to pay. Weekly and monthly budgets should be created and maintained as part of this instructional sequence.

2. Checks advertisements, posters, and store handouts for announcements of clothing sales and purchases needed at sale prices.

Functional Essence   Instructional plans should have as their functional essence the development of the awareness that it may be a savings to:
   a. postpone shopping trips for an anticipated sale or until there is a sale and
   b. purchase beforetime an item of anticipated need when there is a sale in progress.
In both cases, weekly and monthly budgets should be considered and revisions made that are realistic in terms of income and need for items in different budget categories. As part of instructional activities, collect a variety of advertisements, copies of posters, and store handouts that announce sales. In each case look for budgeted items that are on sale and determine money that would be saved. Whenever practical, arrange for a shopping trip in which the individual actually purchases sale items. During these trips, point out crossed-out old prices, sale signs on racks and shelves, and special tags that signal a sale item (red tag sale).

3 . Checks the prices of clothing at different stores and buys needed items where they are most economical.

Functional Essence   Instructional plans should have as their functional essence the development of comparative shopping skills. This objective involves trips to various stores in the community to determine where the price is the most economical. Care should be taken to make sure items compared are of similar quality or the same style number and manufacturer before decisions are made on the relative value of the purchase. Instructional experiences should also be provided in which cost of alterations modify the relative price resulting in a decision to purchase an item at a different store.

4. Locates clothing and other stores to purchase needed clothing.

Functional Essence   Instructional plans should have as their functional essence the identification of clothing stores from store names and from display windows. Trips should be scheduled to shopping districts, centers, plazas, and malls for the purpose of identifying store type and store contents by label clues, e.g., Jerry's Men's Store, Jill's Dry Cleaners, Jane's Shoe Repair, and Stoll's Pharmacy. During this trip, a review of display items should also be emphasized as a clue to the items being sold. Experiences should involve finding general clothing stores, department stores that are likely to sell clothing, and specialty shops.

5. Locates laundromats and dry cleaners to take clothing to be washed and cleaned.

Functional Essence   Instructional plans should have as their functional essence the identification of laundromats and dry cleaners to take clothing to be washed and cleaned. Trips should be scheduled to shopping districts, centers, and malls for the purpose of identifying laundromats and dry cleaners from store titles and from window displays and equipment on display. Sometime during the instructional program, discuss the relationship between clothing label instructions and garment cleaning requirements. Also, include comparative shopping at these facilities to determine their price list. Throughout, emphasize that a place with a higher price may provide better service and that the individual must decide on paying more for that service. Budget considerations must always be taken into account.

6. Locates tailor shops to have desired alterations and repairs made on clothing.

Functional Essence   Instructional plans should have as their functional essence the location of tailor shops. Trips should be taken to shopping areas, centers, and malls to locate tailor shops. Discuss the need to have clothing repaired and altered. Instructional experiences should emphasize that it may be necessary to repair or alter a garment rather than to purchase a new one. Throughout, the emphasis should be placed on budgeted items and budgetary constraints. Activities should be provided in which the individual is expected to differentiate between items beyond repair or alteration and items that are reasonable to alter or repair.

FURNITURE AND APPLIANCES

The individual:
1. Checks out prices of furniture and appliances at different stores and buys needed items where they are most economical.

Functional Essence   Instructional plans should have as their functional essence the development of comparative shopping skills. Advertisements of furniture and appliance stores and stores with these departments should be used for comparison purposes. Throughout, the individual must be instructed to be certain to compare the items to be sure they are made by the same manufacturer and are the same model. When there are different manufacturers, the items must be inspected for quality and special features before a cost judgment is made. Ample experiences should be provided in reviewing the products of different manufacturers in an effort to assist the individual in making judgments of relative value.

2. Reviews sale advertisements in newspapers, store handouts, and posters for furniture, appliances, and other items, compares their prices with non-sale item prices, and purchases desired items.

Functional Essence   Instructional plans should have as their functional essence the review of printed materials for sale items. Comparisons should be made between pre-sale and post-sale prices and the sale price. In each case the expected savings should be computed and reference made to weekly and monthly budgets to determine whether an expected purchase can be postponed until the sale or moved up to benefit from the sale.

3. Reviews ads for heavy duty and non-heavy duty appliances and purchases those most suited to his needs.

Functional Essence   Instructional plans should have as their functional essence the review of heavy-duty and non-heavy-duty appliances in terms of their work specifications. The instruction booklets of these appliances should be reviewed to determine their work capacity. Specific jobs should be presented and decisions made whether it is necessary to pay the increased cost of a heavy duty appliance. Repeat for various heavy duty items such as:
   a. vacuum cleaners;
   b. power tools;
   c. dishwashers;
   d. washing machines and dryers; and
   e. freezers.

4. Identifies warning signs on appliances and observes their precautions.

Functional Essence   Instructional plans should have as their functional essence the identification of warning signs on appliances and in their instruction booklets. Collect the words, phrases, and sentences warning and review them with the individual. Include:
   a. "Shock";
   b. "220 Volts Only";
   c. "Do Not Use Near Water";
   d. "Use Grounded Outlets"; and
   e. "For Outside Use Only".
The rationale for each and the consequences of noncompliance should be discussed before demonstrating their use. After sufficient demonstration by the instructor, proceed to supervise use by the individual.

5. Reviews markings and notations on packages and cartons and observes their directions.

Functional Essence   Instructional plans should have as their functional essence the identification of markings and notations on packages and cartons. Collect the words, phrases, and sentences frequently found on appliance packages and review their meaning, rationale, and consequences of non-compliance when it is a precautionary message. Include:
   a. "This End Up";
   b. "Open Other End";
   c. "Store in Dry Place";
   d. "Fragile";
   e. "Invoice Enclosed"; and

f. "Keep from Freezing".

Prepare packages with each of these notations and ask the individual to treat each package appropriately and safely.

6. Locates the installation and assembly directions on booklets that accompany furniture, appliances, and other products and observes these directions.

Functional Essence   Instructional plans should have as their functional essence the development of those comprehension skills involved in following diagrams and written instructions that describe installation and assembly procedures. Instructional experiences should include a variety of appliances and recreational equipment to be assembled and/or installed. These items should include:
a. outdoor cooking grills and related equipment;
b. bicycles and other sports equipment;
c. electric switches and related devices; and
d. indoor and outdoor furniture.

SERVICES IN THE HOME AND COMMUNITY

The individual:
1. Reviews monthly bills and statements for accuracy and, after verification, pays bills by the due date.

Functional Essence   Instructional plans should have as their functional essence the review of bills and statements against services received under the conditions and costs specified at the time of contract. Simulated experiences should be provided that take the individual through the following sequential stages:
a. services are needed;
b. several suppliers of service are interviewed for cost factors and quality of service and nature of guarantees;
c. a contract is signed with conditions of service and conditions of payment specified;
d. services are rendered satisfactorily;
e. bills and statements are received;
f. bills and statements are verified as accurate; and
g. bills are paid by the due date.

2. Reviews energy-saving hints in pamphlets that accompany fuel bills and, when possible, follows their suggestions.

Functional Essence   Instructional plans should have as their functional essence the development of the awareness that energy saving is critical in times of rapidly accelerating prices and in terms of conservation. Obtain energy-saving hints from government publications and in pamphlets and brochures developed by utility companies. Review these suggestions and discuss their present cost, their cost spread over time, and anticipated energy savings. Throughout, reference must be made to present budget and anticipated budgets in future years. If it is possible, a survey of the individual's home should be made for an analysis of specific needs.

3. Reviews the *Yellow Pages* for places to purchase services.

Functional Essence   Instructional plans should have as their functional essence the use of the *Yellow Pages* as a reference resource in locating individuals and companies who provide

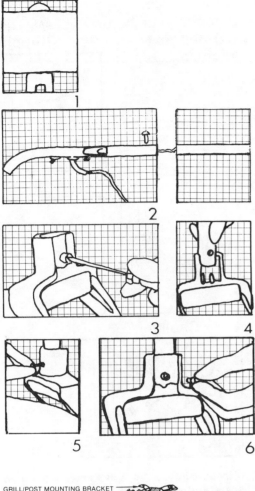

HOW TO ASSEMBLE

A. Put handle together

Be sure you have removed cardboard from the end of handle pieces. Slide the two handle pieces together. Check to see that cord storage hooks are on the same side of handle. Insert bolt through small holes and secure with nut. Tighten nut with screwdriver. Fig. 1.

If the nut and bolt are not assembled as shown in the illustration, the holes in the handle are not lined up correctly. Fig. 2.

B. Attach handle to the cleaner

Unscrew nut and remove bolt and plate from handle socket. Fig. 3.

Take assembled handle and place so that the socket holes in the bottom of the handle are directly in line with the electrical prongs. Position the handle so that the ON-OFF switch is to the rear of the cleaner. Fig. 4.

Push down until handle is securely in place. Insert bolt into small hole in front of handle. Fig. 5.

Place plate over end of bolt and hole. Fit curve of plate to curve of handle. Plate is properly in place when the tabs of the handle bail fit into the cutout areas of the plate.

Secure with nut. Tighten nut with screwdriver. Fig. 6.

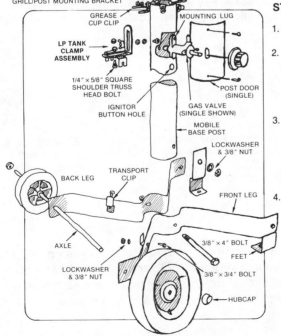

STEPS TO ASSEMBLE MOBILE BASE

1. Remove all parts from carton and check parts list.

2. Attach post to base legs using the 3/8″ × 4″ bolt, lockwasher and nut. In making this assembly position the base legs with transport clip holes (see illustration) to the left and valve access window to right front. Finger tighten only at this point.

3. Insert axle on the left side as illustrated. Position wheels with the hub extension facing to inside in contact with base legs, important: refer to illustartion to make sure this assembly is correct prior to attaching hub caps. Hub cabs cannot be easily removed once attached. Tap on hub caps to each end of axle.

4. Assemble the two transport clips and two base feet to inside of base legs as shown in illustration. All four parts attach using four 3/8″ × 3/4″ bolts, lockwashers and nuts with threads extended inward in all cases. Wrench tighten all bolts assembled to this point.

Figure 30. Assembly instructions.

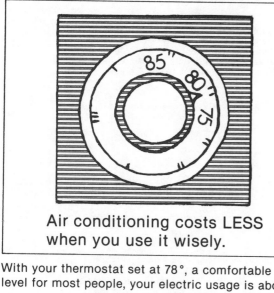

Air conditioning costs LESS when you use it wisely.

With your thermostat set at 78°, a comfortable level for most people, your electric usage is about:

9% less than at 77°
15% less than at 76°
21% less than at 75°
25% less than at 74°
29% less than at 73°
33% less than at 72°

To save money on your electric bill:

• If you have central air conditioning, keep your thermostat at 78°, the comfort setting.
• If you have window air conditioning, choose a moderate setting.
• Clean or replace filters frequently. A clogged filter makes a unit work harder.
• When you are going to be away from your home for a substantial part of the day, set the thermostat a few degrees higher than 78°. If you are going to be away for 24 hours or more, turn off air conditioning.

What is it you need to make your home warmer next winter?

Weather Stripping?

Storm Windows?

Attic Insulation?

Caulking?

If income in your household meets the following scale, you may be eligible for a government-sponsored Weatherization Program at no cost to you.

Size of Family Unit	Non-Farm Family	Farm Family
1	$ 4,738	$ 4,063
2	6,263	5,350
3	7,788	6,638
4	9,313	7,925
5	10,838	9,213
6	12,363	10,500

For family units with more than 6 members, add $1,525 for each additional member in a non-farm family and $1,288 for each additional member in a farm family.

Figure 31. Energy saving brochure.

needed services. Instructional activities should include locating the telephone numbers and calling for additional information. Experiences should be provided that furnish the individual with abundant experience in finding the variety of services he might need as an independent adult living in his own apartment or home.

4. Identifies services in catalogs and brochures and compares catalog prices with store prices. After determining all costs, he purchases the desired service in the most economical way.

| *Functional Essence* | Instructional plans should have as their functional essence the use of catalogs and brochures to compare prices found there to prices at the store. Instructional experiences should involve the review of publications from companies that conduct a catalog operation to determine the cost of services such as: |

a. rug cleaning;
b. insulation installation; and
c. reupholstery.

For each service hypothesized or needed, calculate relative costs.

5. Reviews promotion circulars, flyers, coupons, and store advertisements for price information. He then purchases needed services at the lowest price.

| *Functional Essence* | Instructional plans should have as their functional essence the use of advertisements and promotion circulars, flyers, and coupons to locate price information. Representative printed materials from the variety of stores in the general community should be used to plan contracts for service in hypothetical and actual situations. During this instructional plan, acquaint the individual with ways of checking the quality of services including recommendations of friends and relatives and consumer-oriented agencies such as the Better Business Bureau. |

6. When staying in a motel or hotel, reviews service information before obtaining the service he needs.

| *Functional Essence* | Instructional plans should have as their functional essence the obtaining of services as a motel or hotel guest. Provide experiences that review the various services available at a hotel or motel. Services that should be discussed include: |

a. laundry;
b. car rental; and
c. telephone rules and dialing instructions to obtain room service, wake-up calls, and long-distance operators.

Role play situations in which the individual plays the part of a guest at a hotel or motel and attempts to obtain various services. When there are forms to be completed such as a laundry checklist and car rental forms, instructional activities should develop skill in completing these forms.

7. Locates transportation schedules, selects an appropriate form of transportation from these schedules, and then plans trips according to time and budgetary constraints.

| *Functional Essence* | Instructional plans should have as their functional essence the location of transportation schedules and their use in planning trips. Trips to airports and bus and train depots should be scheduled not only to obtain printed schedules but also to review schedule bulletin boards, television monitors showing schedules, various areas such as information booths, ticket sales, and baggage check room. Activities should also involve determining the cost of using different forms of transportation and then making decisions in terms of time and budgetary constraints. Trips should be planned to diverse places to dramatize the influence of time in planning travel. |

8. Identifies information in store and building directories and uses this information to find desired locations.

| *Functional Essence* | Instructional plans should have as their functional essence the use of store and building directories to determine the location of desired items and offices. Trips should be scheduled to various stores and buildings to review directories. Prepare duplicate directories for instructional purposes in which the individual is expected to indicate where a specified item (store) or office (building) is. Go to a store and ask the |

Name _____

Room _____ Date _____

MON.	TUES.	WED.	THURS.	FRI.

No.	Dry Cleaning		Press only	Amount	
	Suits, Mens (2 pc)	$5.85	$4.50		
	Vests	1.50	1.00		
	Coats, Sport	3.75 up	2.50		
	Pants	3.00 up	2.50		
	Dresses	6.50 up	4.00		
	Suits, Lady	6.50 up	4.50 up		
	Skirts	4.50 up	3.00 up		
	Slacks, Lady	3.50 up	2.50 up		
	Sweaters, Shirts	3.50 up	2.50 up		
	Neckties	1.50 up	1.00		
	Raincoats & O'Coats	6.50 up	4.50 up		
	Blouses	4.00 up	2.50 up		
			TOTAL		

No.	Laundry			Amount	
	Shirts, Reg.		1.50		
	Shirts, Sport		1.75 up		
	Shirts, Knit		1.75		
	Pants (Flairs Extra)		3.00 up		
	Handkerchiefs		.45		
	Socks, pr.		.75		
	Undershirts		.75		
	Undershorts		.75		
	Pajama Pieces		1.00		
	Blouses		3.00 up		
			TOTAL		

Mark   Special Instructions

Figure 32.   Services available at a hotel/motel.

individual to find various items. Go to a building and ask the individual to lead you to an office and then ask him to deliver a message or package while you wait in the lobby.

9.   Identifies signs and rebuses found in community places that announce the cost of admission.

Functional Essence   Instructional plans should have as their functional essence the determination of cost of admission found in various community places including:

a.   movies;
b.   zoos;

c. ball parks;

d. museums;

e. state fairs;

f. amusement parks; and

g. wildlife parks.

Instructional experiences should focus on numerical amounts and on classes of tickets, i.e., "Adults" and "Children." Ask him to calculate the cost of admission for different patterns of attendees, e.g., three children and one adult or one child and two adults. In the case of ball parks and theaters, review the cost for different seat locations and, again, present calculation problems.

10. Compares his utility bills to meter readings in his home for accuracy and as a method of budgeting for future utility bills.

Functional Essence Instructional plans should have as their functional essence the verification of utility bills for payment *and* as a way of estimating future budget items. Instructional experiences should include reading gas, oil, water, and electric meters and identifying meter readings on sample bills. Describe to the individual the process he should follow in the verification of bills, i.e., checking the meter himself at the time of reading and recording that reading for future reference (when he receives the bill). Collect 12 consecutive monthly bills and demonstrate how to use averages (by season or by year) to make budgeting decisions.

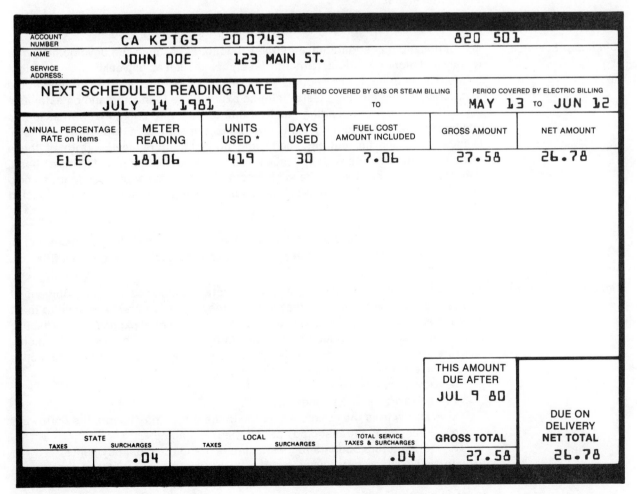

Figure 33. Verification of utility bills.

FINANCES

The individual:

1. Identifies the various coins and denominations of bills and uses these to pay for goods and services.

Functional Essence

Instructional plans should have as their functional essence the use of currency and coins to pay for goods and services. Sufficient instructional experience should be provided in the development of visual discrimination in identifying coins and currency. Numerals and pictures of presidents on bills should be reviewed as should coin features and words that indicate coin type. Various monetary exchanges should be engaged in to provide the individual sufficient practice in the use of cash.

2. Reviews his bank statements and deposit and withdrawal receipts or notations for accuracy.

Functional Essence

Instructional plans should have as their functional essence the checking of bank statements and deposit and withdrawal receipts for accuracy. Experiences should be provided in which the individual is expected to submit a withdrawal or deposit slip and then must check bank book notations and/or receipts obtained for accuracy. Once this skill is accomplished, instructional activities should center on verifying bank statements from collected withdrawal slips or cancelled checks and from deposit slips. Simulated statements, slips, and bank books may be used in early instructional stages.

3. Makes and continuously reviews a weekly and monthly budget.

Functional Essence

Instructional plans should have as their functional essence the development of a weekly and monthly budget. (Other time segments such as bi-weekly budgets might be more appropriate for individuals who are paid every other week.) Throughout the instructional program, emphasize relating expenditure to income and on establishing a priority order of spending needs within expenditure categories. An essential and integral part of budgeting is the development of strategies through which the individual assesses his current needs and projects future needs. Both of these elements require extensive experience and skill in keeping records of items on hand, items to be replaced, items to be supplemented. Activities should also feature unexpected shifts in priority expenditures requiring budget revisions and unexpected shifts in income.

4. Compares the various interest rates of banks and other lending agencies and institutions for buying on time and selects the one that best meets his financial needs.

Functional Essence

Instructional plans should have as their functional essence the development of awareness that there may be times when someone has to borrow money to meet unexpected drops in income and unanticipated but essential expenditures. Discuss the various places from which one can borrow money. Include banks, credit unions, store credit/installment plans, credit cards, and credit agencies. Instructional activities should emphasize the following elements:
   a. review credit terms;
   b. borrow only when necessary;
   c. borrow from the source where the interest rate most favors the borrower;
   d. arrange for a realistic pay back schedule; and
   e. revise future budgets to include interest and principal payments.
Explain that he may not always be able to borrow money at the cheapest rate because he does not meet the lending institution's requirements. In those cases, encourage him to seek the second lowest rate, etc.

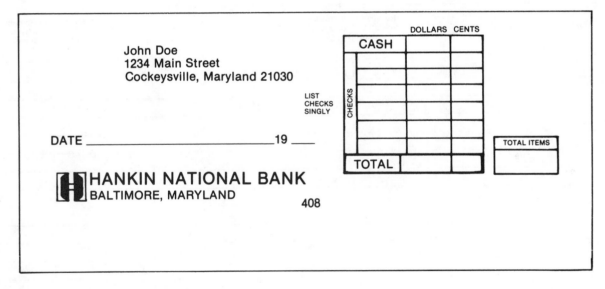

Figure 34. Verifying bank statements.

5. Establishes a savings program.

Functional Essence — Instructional plans should have as their functional essence the establishment of a savings program as a means of meeting unexpected expenditures or a drop in income and as a means of setting aside money for: large purchases; down payments on cars, appliances, and homes; travel and vacation plans; retirement funds; etc. Instructional activities should concentrate on the variety of savings-plan possibilities:

    a. purchase of savings bonds through payroll deductions;

    b. purchase of tax-sheltered annuities through payroll deductions;

    c. enrollment in a credit union with regular payroll deductions;

    d. enrollment in a credit union with optional payroll schedule;

    e. opening of a savings account in a commercial bank;

Plan for Family Spending

Income, set-asides, and expenses	Amount per month
Total income	$_____
Set-asides:	
Emergencies and future goals	$_____
Seasonal expenses	_____
Debt payments	_____
Regular monthly expenses:	
Rent or mortgage payment	$_____
Utilities	_____
Installment payments	_____
Other	_____
Total	_____
Day-to-day expenses:	
Food and beverages	$_____
Household operation and maintenance	_____
Furnishings and equipment	_____
Clothing	_____
Personal	_____
Transportation	_____
Medical care	_____
Recreation and education	_____
Gifts and contributions	_____
Total	_____
Total set-asides and expenses	$_____

Record of Your Expenses

Date	Item (or service) bought	Food and beverages	Household operation and maintenance	Furnishings and equipment	Clothing	Personal	Transportation	Medical care	Recreation and education	Gifts and contributions
		$	$	$	$	$	$	$	$	$
Total	xxxxxxxxxxxxxxx	$_____	$_____	$_____	$_____	$_____	$_____	$_____	$_____	$_____

Figure 35.   Forms for developing a budget.

f.   opening of a savings account in a savings and loan association; and

g.   opening a Christmas or Hannukah Club.

While providing experiences with these various savings options, be sure to review the advantages and disadvantages of each plan. Use appropriate brochures and pamphlets to do so. Further, with the existence of alternate savings plans available involving different interest rates depending on amount and length of deposit, sufficient time should be devoted to the advantages and disadvantages of these types of savings.

6. When he does not want to or cannot pay cash, selects an appropriate credit card and purchases goods and services that are within his projected budget and within credit limits.

Functional Essence Instructional plans should have as their functional essence the use of credit cards as an alternate means of paying for goods and services. Instructional activities should include experiences in:
   a. applying for a credit card;
   b. noting credit limits;
   c. keeping the credit card in a secure place;
   d. noting a number to call in case a card is lost or stolen; and
   e. using the credit card if the purchase is included in budget projections for the next bill period or the next several months. Be sure to point out interest rate penalties for not paying by the first bill date.

7. When he does not want to or cannot pay cash, draws a check to pay for goods and services.

Functional Essence Instructional plans should have as their functional essence the use of a personal check as an alternate means of paying for goods and services. Instructional activities should include:
   a. opening a checking account;
   b. depositing money or checks in that account;
   c. drawing, endorsing, and cashing a check made out to self;
   d. drawing a check to pay for goods and services;
   e. maintaining deposit and check usage records; and
   f. balancing a check book.
Emphasis should be placed on treating checks as carefully as cash and on avoiding check overdrafts.

8. Reviews warranties that accompany tools, materials, and other products. He fills them out and mails them back to the company.

Functional Essence Instructional plans should have as their functional essence the review of warranty cards and slips that accompany products before their purchase. Instructional objectives should feature an awareness of the importance of including warranty factors in the decision on whether to purchase the specific item. Also, experiences should include the review of the warranty card or slip for the purpose of completing it and mailing it back to the company.

9. Identifies information contained in his mortgage or lease to verify that he meets his obligations or to ensure that he obtains contracted-for services.

Functional Essence Instructional plans should have as their functional essence the thorough review of typical mortgages and leases to retrieve two essential sets of information:
   a. buyer or renter obligations and
   b. seller/bank or landlord obligations to the individual.
Once typical mortgage and lease contracts have been reviewed, when it does not invade the privacy of the individual, proceed to a study of his actual mortgage or lease.

10. Reviews the information on tax forms and arranges for them to be completed and filed on time.

Functional Essence Instructional plans should have as their functional essence the development of skills involved in meeting tax-filing requirements as specified by the federal government and local jurisdictions. Emphasis should be placed on seeking the advice and assistance of a tax consultant or service. Describe the various services including repre-

Account Number   NAME (print)

_____

Street
Address _____

City and State _____

Home Tel. _____

Bus. Ext. Tel. _____

Zip Code _____

Position _____
Division
or Dept. _____
Date
Employed _____

Date of
Birth _____
Soc. Sec.
Number _____
Spouse
First
Name_____

I hereby make application for membership in the B-V, Inc FEDERAL CREDIT UNION, *and agree to conform to its laws and amendments thereof and subscribe for at least one share ($5.00).*

Were you previously a member of
this credit Union? yes☐ no☐   Signature _____

(OVER)

This application approved by the Board of Directors, Executive Committee, or Membership Officer.

Date _____   Signed _____
                            (Membership Officer)

Refer to information sheet available from Credit Union office to decide whether you want a joint owner, a beneficiary, or both.

I.   In Trust for myself _____ and _____
                       (Print)   *(Print)*
    joint owners, balance at death to belong to the survivor, subject to the order of

    (EITHER) of the above, or (ONLY) _____
                                            (Print)
    Any or all of said joint owners may pledge all or any part of the shares in this account as collateral security for a loan or loans.
    I hereby designate the said joint owner as my beneficiary, unless differently designated below, to receive all sums of money paid by virtue of the terms of the Life Savings Plan to the credit union.
    I hereby reserve the right to change the beneficiary. Execution of a subsequent Designation of Beneficiary form shall constitute a change of beneficiary.

    WITNESS: Date _____

    _____   _____
                                     (Signature of Member)

    _____   _____
                                   (Signature of Joint Owner)

II. Beneficiary, if different than joint owner _____

C-137 _____ _____
       (Date)   *(Member's Signature)*   *(OVER)*

Figure 36. Credit union forms.

PAYROLL DEDUCTION   **FEDERAL CREDIT UNION**

The undersigned hereby understands that payroll deduction is not a requirement for a credit union loan, and I voluntarily choose payroll deduction as a method to repay my loan.

Deductions are a service provided by my employer and I agree to advise the Credit Union if deductions are nt made.

I hereby authorize the Payroll Department fo deduct from my check each pay day until otherwise notified.

Weekly_____Semi-Monthly_____

PRESENT payroll deduction is:

Weekly_____Semi-Monthly_____

CHANGE payroll deduction to:

Weekly_____Semi-Monthly_____

Effective Date _____

Account No._____

Soc. Sec. No. _____

_____   _____
Name-Please Print   Signature

Date _____

Withdrawal Application

_____

Date _____

Credit Union Account No. _____

I, _____, request a check for $_____
           (PRINT NAME)

Member's Signature_____

Address _____

_____ Zip _____

Telephone _____

_____

•FULL 90 DAY WARRANTY•

B-V Products Corporation warrants this product to be free from manufacturing defects in material or workmanship for a period of 90 days from date of purchase. This warranty does not apply to damages to the product resulting from misuse or abuse.

If the product is found to be defective during the warranty period, you should complete the Warranty Service Form (**see below**) and mail it together with the defective component part or unit (NOT THE ENTIRE SET) to:

B-V Products Corporation
Consumer Services Department
Post Office Box 00
Wood-Ridge, New Jersey 7075

We will repair or replace the component part or unit without charge.

To prevent damage in transit, the component part or unit should be packed securely.

This warranty gives you specific legal rights, and you may also have other rights which vary from state to state.

Figure 37. Warranty slip.

sentatives of the Internal Revenue Service. Encourage the individual to seek out reputable consultants or services based on the recommendations of relatives and friends.

11. Reviews mortgage statement to verify accuracy of charges.

Functional Essence

Instructional plans should have as their functional essence the encouragement of the individual to review monthly mortgage payments to verify the accuracy of charges. Instructional experiences should strongly emphasize reference to the original agreement and the filing of receipts for these payments as a record-keeping strategy and as a means of verifying the accuracy of future payments.

12. Reviews brochures, letters, and other written requests for fund-raising organizations and contributes to reputable charities according to his budgetary guidelines and personal preference.

Functional Essence

Instructional plans should have as their functional essence the development of skills in determining to which charitable organizations he would like to contribute. Instructional activities should focus on placing charitable contributions as a budget item *and* on determining whether the individual can afford to make donations based upon budget proportions. Further, stress the importance of selecting charities that are reputable. (Because the handicapped are more easily victimized by unscrupulous people, they must be given special instruction in avoiding "con" and other fast-talking artists of exploitation.)

13. Reviews brochures, letters, and other written information relevant to investment opportunities and interests in reputable enterprises according to his budgetary guidelines or personal preference.

Functional Essence

Instructional plans should have as their functional essence the review of brochures, letters, and other letters relevant to investment opportunities. Emphasis should be placed on seeking the advice and assistance of reputable investment counselors. Instructional activities should also stress the importance of investing only when one's budgeted needs are met and when there is sufficient savings available for emergency/unexpected expenditures. Throughout, encourage the individual to seek the advice of family and friends, especially in terms of recommending a skilled counselor. Each type of investment advertised in business sections of newspapers and magazines should be reviewed.

SAMPLE INSTRUCTIONAL PLAN

Topic Area __CONSUMER SKILLS-FUNCTIONAL READING__   Date ____5/26/80____

Teacher____Ms. Weaver____

Time Allotted ____25-30 minutes____

Individual(s) or Group Members Involved:
K. Simpson, B. Shapiro,
L. Richter, M. Csar,
P. Valetti, P. Robert

Special Notes or Precautions __Do not use 6 or 9 as an aisle number. P. Robert often__ __confuses these numberals and might fail to achieve the instructional__ objective because of this problem.

General Objective

The individual will function as a consumer of goods and services as independently and skillfully as possible by identifying words and other symbols.

Specific Objective (Food and Household Products - 2)

The individual consults his shopping list and finds desired items in a supermarket by using a store directory.

Instructional Objective

When given a ditto of a shopping list with labelled pictures of ten food items, the individuals will write down the aisle number of each item after referring to an especially prepared store directory chart showing only dairy, meat, and produce departments. They will do so with 100% accuaracy.

Materials and Equipment

1. Store directory chart
2. Five business size envelopes
3. Ten pictures of food items (dairy, meat, or produce)
4. Shopping list ditto (5 copies)

Motivating Activity

Tell the group that they are going to go on a practice shopping trip for a make-believe luncheon party and that they will be given a white envelope with two pictures of food items.

Instructional Procedures

1. Place a modified store directory on the chalkboard. This chart indicates the aisle number for only three departments: dairy, meat, and produce.
2. Review each work and accompanying aisle number. Discuss each department's category and the food items found there. Be sure to point out that the list is in alphabetical order. Assist the individuals in finding the aisle number.

3. Pass out the envelopes, reminding the individuals that they are getting an envelope with pictures of two food items. Instruct them to look at each picture and determine the department in which it is found. "When I call you, tell the group what food items you have, the departments in which you will find them, and the aisle number."
4. Call each individual in turn.
5. When each individual has responded, pass out a "Shopping List: Luncheon Party" ditto. The ditto will have pictures of ten food items found in the dairy, meat, and produce departments. Under each picture of these common foods, the name is written in manuscript.
6. Ask the individuals to find the aisle number for each item and to write down the number next to each item.
7. Go around the room giving assistance, encouragement, and reinforcement as warranted.

Individualized Reinforcement and
Reinforcement Schedules

Use verbal reinforcement (i.e., "You're doing nicely") as the lesson progresses. Do not reinforce P. Robert until he is completely successful.

Assessment Strategy

Observe each individual as he completes the task. Collect the papers of check the accuracy of his responses. Record the individual's performance on "The Consumer Skills: Functional Reading Checklist."

Follow-Up Activity/Objective

If the individuals achieve the objective, proceed to a similar instructional experience. This time, give the individuals a shopping list with the same food items as in this instructional plan, however, do not include the picture of the items, just the individual words; or give the individuals a shopping list with new food items from other departments of the supermarket.

Instructional Resources

Photographs or charts of store directories from local supermarkets.

Observations and Comments:

GENERAL OBJECTIVE: The individual will function as a consumer of goods and services as independently and skillfully as possible by performing diverse written tasks.

The individual:

1. Prepares a shopping list.

Functional Essence

Instructional plans should have as their functional essence the development of those cognitive and written skills involved in preparing a shopping list. These skills include:

    a. surveying food on hand;

    b. surveying household products on hand;

    c. projecting food needs for the week (or alternate established shopping interval);

    d. projecting household products needed for the immediate future;

    e. identifying drugs and medicine that need to be purchased or refilled;

    f. surveying clothing that has to be replaced and identifying new clothing needs;

    g. identifying furniture and appliance needs;

    h. determining income and establishing expenditure priorities within the categories included above and others such as fixed payments (e.g., mortgage or rent, interest payments, taxes), leisure activities expenses, cost of utilities and telephone, etc.; and

    i. finally, the development of a shopping list that is consonant with the individual's budget and reflects his needs and aspirations.

2. Orders needed goods and services.

Functional Essence

Instructional plans should have as their functional essence the development of skills in completing order forms to obtain needed materials and equipment and desired goods and services. Instructional activities should involve the completion of order forms found in:

    a. catalogs;

    b. newspapers;

    c. magazines;

    d. showrooms of department and discount stores; and

    e. mail-order brochures.

Ample experience should be provided in the various forms while simultaneously pointing out their commonalities in format and in requested information. Encourage the individual to examine the fine print to determine the conditions of the sale. When an actual situation arises, use that occasion for practice of the skill.

3. Writes letters of complaint relevant to consumer problems.

Functional Essence

Instructional plans should have as their functional essence the development of business letter skills with particular reference to the voicing of a complaint. Instructional activities should begin with hypothetical complaints relevant to inferior/malfunctioning products and to inferior/incomplete/incorrect services, e.g., the new lawn mower has never worked or the cabinets were installed in the wrong place and are crooked as well. For each hypothetical situation, assist the individual in following the letter format and in writing succinct, informative prose that communicates his emotional response to the failure of the seller to meet his obligations. When actual consumer complaints arise, assist the individual in composing a strong, clear

BILL TO:

Name of Institution
or Practice_____
Address _____
City _____
State _____ Zip Code _____

SHIP TO:

Name_____
Address _____
City _____ State _____ Zip _____
Attn: _____ Dept: _____

Purchase Order Number:		Date _____ 19_____			
TERMS: OPEN ACCOUNT: Pay invoice before 30 days are up. You pay shipping costs.					
Please SHIP the following items:					
Catalog No.	Product Description		Price	Quantity	Total
				Total	

Figure 38.   Catalog order form.

letter that has the potential power to have his complaints redressed. Write letters to all pertinent groups including:

    a.   government agencies;

    b.   businesses;

    c.   industry groups;

    d.   labor organizations; and

    e.   individual sellers or firms.

    4.   Writes letters requesting consumer information.

Functional Essence

Instructional plans should have as their functional essence the development of business-letter writing skills with particular reference to a letter that requests consumer information. Sample letters should be composed for submission to:

    a.   various governmental agencies, especially those whose function is in the consumer domain, e.g., Consumer Product Safety Commission;

    b.   businesses;

c. industry groups;
   d. labor organizations; and
   e. private consumer advocacy groups.
When an actual need arises, assist the individual in deciding what agency or organization is likely to be the most appropriate and is likely to respond rapidly. Throughout, emphasis should be placed on writing explicit letters that clearly delineate the request.

   5. Fills out the forms necessary to open savings and checking accounts.

Functional Essence   Instructional plans should have as their functional essence the completion of the actual forms used to open savings and checking accounts. Representational forms should be gathered and used during instructional experiences with the instructor providing guidance and assistance as necessary. If it is possible, arrange for the individual to open one or both of these accounts. Activities should always involve exploring the types of accounts available and identifying the ones that best meet the individual's financial requirements.

   6. Signs his name on the face of a check, endorses a check, and signs a charge plate and charge slips.

Functional Essence   Instructional plans should have as their functional essence the writing of the individual's legal signature as it appears:
   a. on a check on its bottom line and in the place of endorsement whenever he writes a personal check to himself to draw cash;
   b. on a check in the place of endorsement whenever he wishes to cash or deposit a check made out to his order;
   c. on a check on its bottom line when writing a check to pay for goods and services;
   d. on a charge plate; and
   e. on charge slips when he wishes to authorize payment.

   7. Writes a check to pay for goods and services.

Functional Essence   Instructional plans should have as their functional essence the development of skills in filling out a check to pay a bill. These skills include writing in the appropriate place:
   a. the day's date in numerals or in words and numbers;
   b. the name of the individual, company, or agency to whom the check is ordered;
   c. the amount of the check in numerals *and* in words;
   d. the writing of the individual's signature;
   e. the inclusion of pertinent additional information, e.g., the account number, the telephone number (on a phone bill); and
   f. lastly, the recording of the check number, date of check, and the name of the person, company, or agency to whom the check is written in the appropriate part of the record-keeping section of the check book.
Sufficient practice in all these aspects should be provided.

   8. Fills out deposit and withdrawal slips for banking purposes.

Functional Essence   Instructional plans should have as their functional essence the development of skills essential to the accurate filling out of deposit slips (savings and checking accounts) and withdrawal slips (savings accounts). Representative slips should be obtained, and the individual should be provided with sufficient practice in completing these slips for different hypothetical amounts. As soon as actual transactions can be incorporated into instructional plans, the added dimension of verifying the new

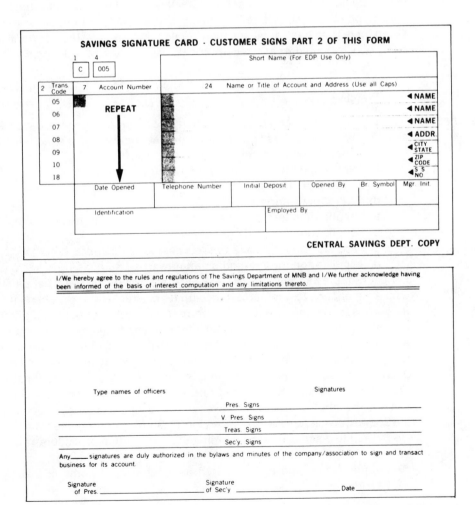

CHECKING ACCOUNT FORMS

SAVINGS SIGNATURE CARD · CUSTOMER SIGNS PART 2 OF THIS FORM

Figure 39. Forms for opening savings and checking accounts.

Figure 40. Writing a check.

amounts must be added. Verification of savings accounts requires the review of the bank slip as officially stamped and its later match to the bank statement while savings transactions (with a passbook) involve verifying entries in the bank book. Be sure to point out the different symbols and columns for deposits and withdrawal. When there is no bank book, the individual must treat the stamped bank receipt in the same way he would treat a receipt for a checking account deposit.

9.   Fills out various consumer-related application forms. (*See* Sample Instructional Plan.)

Functional Essence   Instructional plans should have as their functional essence the development of the skill in filling out various consumer-related application forms including:

    a.   application for a credit card;
    b.   application for a driver's permit and license;
    c.   a car registration form;
    d.   a product warranty form;
    e.   application forms for car, life, disability, and home/apartment insurance;
    f.   application for food stamps;
    g.   application for a bank or credit union loan; and
    h.   application for a refund on an unwanted purchase.

For each of the various applications or forms, the individual must be provided with ample experience to familiarize him with its existence, the key elements in the form, its purposes, its constraints, the information needed to complete, and sources of this information. This objective is an intensive and extensive one because it involves all the forms (other than order forms) that the individual might be exposed to as he functions in the market place. Thus, it will be necessary to develop a compendium of these forms as instructional materials for a variety of instructional experiences. Visits to various agencies where these forms are encountered should be beneficial as should visits from representatives of these agencies, e.g., a representative from the Social Service Agency to discuss food stamps and someone from the Motor Vehicle Bureau to discuss driver's permits and registration procedures and regulations.

10.   Signs papers and forms related to purchasing a home or leasing/renting an apartment.

Functional Essence   Instructional plans should have as their functional essence the development of skills involved in completing and signing papers and forms pertinent to purchasing a home or leasing/renting an apartment. Representative forms should be collected and used

IMPORTANT CHANGES in FOOD STAMPS can help

NEW AND IMPROVED

July 1, 1980 through
  December 31, 1980:
Revised eligibility levels
listed in this insert
could make you eligible
for Food Stamps or
increase your benefits

Number of Household Members

1	2	3	4
61	112	161	204

5	6	7	8
242	291	321	367

Page 5, Step 2
Budget Format

B. Subtract $70 standard deduction. This applies to all households.

C. Subtract dependent/child care cost necessary for a household to work. If this amount is more than $90, enter only $90 and do not calculate Steps 4 & 5. Instead, calculate adjusted income (Step 3) and put that figure in Step 6, Food Stamp Net Income.

Step 4

If dependent/child care cost (Step 2C) is less than $90, add together shelter expenses (rent, utilities, telephone). If dependent/child care cost is $90 or more, omit this step.

The combination of excess Shelter cost and dependent/child care cannot exceed $90. If the combination of these two deductions exceeds $90, only $90 will be used as the deduction.

Step 5

To calculate Food Stamp net income subtract excess shelter cost (maximum of $90) from your adjusted income.

Example 1, Page 6

The Burns family is a household of four with a public assistance check of $280.73. Their total monthly shelter expenses are $185.30. They have no Dependent/Child Care costs:

Step 1—Gross Monthly
  Income...................... $280
(All figures are rounded down, therefore $280.73 becomes $280.)

Step 2
  A. 20% of Earned Income $00
  B. Standard Deduction 70
  C. Dependent/Child Care
     Cost 00
Total deductions $70

Figure 41.   Sample food stamps information.

in mock real estate transactions. A visit from a real estate agent or broker should add a necessary dimension to the program. Throughout, the emphasis is not only on the mechanics of writing but on the judgments involved in participating effectively in these transactions. Emphasis, therefore, must be placed on assisting the individual in arriving at realistic and reasonable judgments as a preliminary to signing any contract.

11. Addresses packages when returning unwanted items or items needing repair to stores and businesses.

Functional Essence

Instructional plans should have as their functional essence the completion of a mailing address when sending unwanted items or items needing repair to stores and businesses. Experiences should include the construction or purchase of a mailer, the proper packaging of the item, the obtaining of insurance as necessary, and the writing act of addressing the package and placing the return address on the package. Also included should be the composition of a letter of explanation for the package either under separate cover or as part of the packing. Finally, the individual must select the postage class needed and either write it on the package or so inform the postal worker.

12. Draws up a weekly and monthly budget.

Functional Essence

Instructional plans should have as their functional essence the composing of a weekly and monthly budget based on:

   a. income and projected income;
   b. fixed expenses (e.g., rent/mortgage, interest on loans, taxes, utilities);
   c. food;
   d. clothing;
   e. household furniture and appliances;
   f. medical expenses;
   g. recreational expenses; and
   h. miscellaneous.

Instructional plans must deal with the actual economic or financial status of the individual if the plan promises to be of practical value to the individual. Instructional activities, therefore, must include a thorough assessment of current income and projected income, current assets and liabilities, and future needs. Future needs must be placed in a hierarchy according to expected priorities. Emphasis throughout must be placed on periodically reviewing the budget and modifying the budget *immediately* whenever significant changes occur in any of its dimensions, e.g., medical expenses, visitors from out of town, etc.

SAMPLE INSTRUCTIONAL PLAN

Topic Area CONSUMER SKILLS-FUNCTIONAL WRITING   Date _____ 5/9/81 _____

Teacher_____ Mr. Coldstream _____   Individual(s) or Group Members Involved:
                                         P. Kimm, F. Scarpa,
Time Allotted _____ 30 minutes _____   J. Jackson, A. Colt

Special Notes or Precautions _Be sure to inform the individuals only to fill out_
consumer-related forms that correspond to their financial status and
personal interests.

General Objective

   The individual will function as a consumer of goods and services
as independently and skillfully as possible by performing diverse
written tasks.

Specific Objective (9)

   The individual fills out various consumer-related application forms.

Instructional Objective

   When given a product warranty form, the individual will fill out
correctly his name, date of purchase, and place of purchase.

Materials and Equipment

   1. Product warranty form chart
   2. Product warranty forms

Motivating Activity

   Role play a hypothetical situation in which you bemoan the fact
that an appliance you purchased will not work, and you had forgotten
to fill out and mail in the warranty form.

Instructional Procedures

   1. Show the group members a chart of a representational product
       warranty form.
   2. Review the key words and phrases found there.
   3. Discuss the reasons for such a form and explain the terms of the
       warranty contract.
   4. Review the list of mailing addresses for repairs. Help the
       individuals find the nearest place.

Individualized Reinforcement and
Reinforcement Schedules

   Provide verbal praise for those individuals who fill out the
form correctly. Use the first one who fills out the form correctly
as a model to show the group.

Assessment Strategy

Collect the sample product warranty forms and check to see whether the individual has completed it accurately.

Follow-Up Activity/Objective

If the individual achieves the instructional objective, proceed to an instructional experience on filling out another consumer-related form, e.g., credit card, driver's permit and license, and insurance.

Instructional Resources

Contact businesses and industries and request they send you a sample of their warranty cards and forms.

Make an overhead transparency of a standard type form for instructional purposes.

Observations and Comments:

GENERAL OBJECTIVE: The individual will function as a consumer of goods and services as independently and skillfully as possible by performing necessary mathematical operations.

FOOD AND HOUSEHOLD PRODUCTS

The individual:
1. Buys desired food and household products after considering his quantity requirements and the unit price per each package size.

Functional Essence Instructional plans should have as their functional essence the calculation of the quantity of food needed for planned meals and snacks and the quantity of household products required to maintain the household. Instructional activities should involve the composition of a shopping list based on a combination of need and budget priorities. Experiences should also include converting portions needed into the size of package and/or number of packages needed. A further step is the decision to buy by container size in terms of unit price, quantity needed, storage capacity of the item, and storage facilities at home. Emphasis should be placed throughout on the various mathematical computations.

2. Buys desired food and household products where they are least expensive.

Functional Essence Instructional plans should have as their functional essence the development of comparative shopping skills. Instructional activities should feature the review of store hand-outs and advertisements as well as visits to stores to compare the cost of desired items. Prepare a sample shopping list and ask the individual to tally the cost of that list at each of the easily accessible stores and markets in his community. Be sure to be explicit in terms of brand and size for each listed item. Discuss the advantage of not only considering individual items but the total market basket especially in terms of the cost and time involved in traveling from one store to another. Encourage the individual to use a pocket calculator in tallying a shopping list.

3. Buys desired food and household products after considering the difference in price among brand, store, and generically labeled items and his budget and quality preferences.

Functional Essence Instructional plans should have as their functional essence the purchase of food and household items after considering the price and quality preferences. Arrange instructional activities in which the individual makes decisions on alternate brands of a household item by using them without knowing from which container each substance came. After using each item, identify the brand and then assist the person in deciding whether to buy a brand that costs more. Certainly, no such decision is involved when the preferred substance is the least expensive. When there are no taste preferences, help the individual to realize that the one with the cheapest price is the one to buy. Repeat these steps with various foods. From all of the instructional experiences, records should be kept so that the individual can refer to brand preferences before a shopping trip.

4. Buys the number of packages of desired food and household items when there is a savings for purchasing quantity and after considering his needs.

Functional Essence   Instructional plans should have as their functional essence the purchase of desired food and household items in quantity lots or sizes when:
    a.   there is a substantial savings;
    b.   there is money available from his budget;
    c.   when the item bought stores well; and
    d.   when he has storage space at home.
Shopping trips should be scheduled to examine factors a through d for each of many different items. Point out the relationship of unit price, when it is posted, to the determination of economy.

5. Buys the size and number of food packages needed for planned snacks and meals.

Functional Essence   Instructional plans should have as their functional essence the determination of the size and number of food packages needed for planned snacks and meals. Instructional activities must concentrate on translating the terms of recipes into portion sizes of food ingredients and items purchased that contain at least the portion size needed. If there is a food ingredient that is planned for several meals, assist the individual in computing the total quantity of that ingredient needed. Experiences should then be provided in which package-size figures are correlated with ingredient size needs. Sufficient experience should be provided in carrying out the various mathematical processes.

6. Weighs produce and other loose items on an estimate scale to arrive at a desired amount of food both in quantity and cost.

Functional Essence   Instructional plans should have as their functional essence the use of an estimate scale to approximate the weight of produce and other loose items. Instructional activities should involve the individual in weighing an assortment of items in different amounts: whole numbers, fractional parts, and mixed numbers. Conclude instructional activities by having him estimate the cost of the weighed items and verifying his estimate on the cash register and register receipt.

7. Estimates the cost of the food and household products in his shopping basket to determine whether he has sufficient money to pay the bill. (*See* Sample Instructional Plan.)

Functional Essence   Instructional plans should have as their functional essence the development of the skill of estimation. Instructional activities should focus on rounding out prices to the nearest half dollar and dollar and adding them up by dollar amounts. Also, experiences may be provided in rounding out prices to the nearest tens and combining items that approximate one dollar and then adding all one or more dollar combinations for an estimation. A third method is the use of a pocket calculator to add amounts rounded off to the nearest tens. Sufficient experience should be provided in rounding off numbers and in combining them through addition in dollar units. Actual shopping trips should always be scheduled.

8. Checks the price of each item purchased as it appears on the cash register.

Functional Essence   Instructional plans should have as their functional essence the development of the awareness that it is necessary to check each item rung up as it appears on the cash register. Instructional activities should, therefore, focus on matching numerals expressed in dollars and cents with their numeral counterparts. Instructional experiences should include the identification of price labels on goods purchased to price charts. Finally, instructional programs should involve matching price labels with the amounts shown on a cash register in the instructional area and then in a store.

9. Uses discount coupons to purchase desired food and household items, computing item cost with the discount.

Functional Essence Instructional plans should have as their functional essence the use of discount coupons and the computation of money saved. Discount coupons should be clipped from store hand-outs, newspapers, and magazines and collected from special mailings. Encourage the individual to collect those coupons for items he is likely to buy. Prepare a shopping list from a collection of coupons and ask the individual how much each item will cost with the discount. A double coupon day should be declared, and the individual asked to compute the cost of each discounted item. After practice sessions, proceed to actual shopping trips.

10. Pays for his order.

Functional Essence Instructional plans should have as their functional essence the use of:
    a. currency and coins;
    b. food stamps;
    c. a personal check; and
    d. a credit card
to pay for an order. Instructional activities should involve the identification of total price of an order on the cash register and/or receipt and the counting out of currency and coins and/or food stamps, the writing of a check, and the use of credit card with all its attendant steps. Experiences should be provided for each of these operations.

11. Counts his change and verifies its accuracy.

Functional Essence Instructional plans should have as their functional essence the counting of change received and the verification of its accuracy by checking change designations on the cash register and/or the market receipt. Instructional activities should involve the counting of change by either adding each coin and bill to amount spent or by adding the change and verifying its amount by matching it to the amount on the register or receipt. Experiences should also include checking the receipt for its accuracy.

12. Compares the accuracy of his market receipt with products purchased.

Functional Essence Instructional plans should have as their functional essence the matching of the price label on each item purchased to the prices appearing on the market receipt. Instructional activities should provide sufficient experience in matching prices on packages to charted prices. Actual shopping trips and market receipts should serve as instructional materials.

13. Puts exact amount of change in a vending machine or puts in more than exact change and verifies correctness of change received.

Functional Essence Instructional plans should have as their functional essence the use of coins to purchase items in a vending machine. Emphasis should be placed on the use of various coin combinations to insert exact change. After these experiences have been provided, activities should be scheduled in which the individual is expected to combine coins that are more than the exact amount and determine the change to be received. Actual vending machines should be used so that the individual may have the opportunity to verify accuracy of change.

14. Purchases snacks and meals while eating out.

Functional Essence Instructional plans should have as their functional essence the purchase of snacks and meals according to:
  a. food and dietary preferences;
  b. money on hand; and
  c. amount budgeted for meals.
Instructional programs should provide the individual with experience in ordering snacks and meals at various places including: fast-food places, cafeterias, diners, and other restaurants. At first, simulated experiences should be practiced as a prelude to actual eating-out experiences.

15. Leaves an appropriate tip at a restaurant where waitress or waiter service is provided.

Functional Essence Instructional plans should have as their functional essence the computation of an appropriate tip for served meals. In the beginning, a tip chart should be referred to in computing a tip. After the individual has sufficient experience, proceed to experiences in which the individual is expected to compute the tip from a simulated restaurant bill. Then continue by taking trips to restaurants where the individual is expected to compute the tip.

DRUGS AND MEDICINE

The individual:
1. Buys prescription and over-the-counter drugs where they are least expensive.

Functional Essence Instructional plans should have as their functional essence the development of skills in comparative shopping. Instructional activities should include visits to pharmacies and to stores with pharmacy departments to compare prices. Attention to newspaper and other advertisements should also lead to the keeping of records in which comparative prices of nearby stores are written. Simulated experiences may be provided in which the individual "buys" over-the-counter drugs and has prescriptions filled at the cheapest price.

2. Buys needed vitamins, minerals, medicines, and medications after considering the difference in price among name, store, and generic brands and his budget and quality preferences.

Functional Essence Instructional plans should have as their functional essence the individual's determination of the brand of vitamins, minerals, medicines, and medications he wishes to purchase after comparing the quality of various name, store, and generic brands. Throughout the various instructional experiences, attention must be directed toward the individual's budget. Because these various substances, however, cannot be freely tried as can food and household products, greater attention must be paid to difference in prices and the recommendations of relatives and friends.

3. Estimates the cost of desired items to determine whether he has sufficient funds to pay the bill.

Functional Essence Instructional plans should have as their functional essence the estimation of the cost of desired items by rounding costs to the nearest half dollar and dollar, by combining various items in terms of dollar amounts, and by using a pocket estimator. Provide the individual with experiences in estimating a variety of orders and using the several different approaches. Provide sufficient experience in simulated experiences before going on actual shopping trips.

4. Checks the prices that appear on the cash register against prices on items purchased.

Functional Essence   Instructional plans should have as their functional essence the matching of prices of items purchased against the prices appearing on the cash register. Compile a shopping basket and ring the items up on a cash register. In operating the register, make occasional mistakes and reward the individual for detecting these errors. After sufficient instructional practice, field trips should be taken to further refine and define the individual's skill.

5. Pays for his order.

Functional Essence   Instructional plans should have as their functional essence the use of coins, currency, a personal check, or credit card to pay for an order. Instructional activities should be provided in using each of these methods of payment in a variety of simulated purchases. Actual shopping trips should then be taken.

6. Counts his change and verifies its accuracy.

Functional Essence   Instructional plans should have as their functional essence the counting of change received to verify its accuracy. Various simulated shopping trips should be programmed. Some of these should involve giving the individual the incorrect amount of change. Praise the individual for finding errors. Once sufficient practice has been given, continue by scheduling actual shopping trips.

7. Compares the accuracy of his store receipt with products purchased.

Functional Essence   Instructional plans should have as their functional essence the matching of prices on labels to prices appearing on store receipts. Collect store receipts and match them to actual items. Place items and receipt in a bag; then ask the individual to verify the accuracy of the receipt. In some cases, place an incorrect receipt in a bag and reward the individual for detecting the error. Actual trips should then be arranged.

CLOTHING

The individual:
1. Buys desired clothing items that best meet his style, quality, color, and use preferences and needs where they are most economical.

Functional Essence   Instructional plans should have as their functional essence the purchase of desired clothing items that are most economical. Instructional activities should emphasize that consideration should be given to:
    a. style;
    b. fabric;
    c. quality;
    d. color; and
    e. intended use.
Activities should stress that comparison in prices must take into consideration approximately similar quality of fabric and workmanship. Also, include the impact of alteration costs in total cost. Provide sufficient experience in simulated behaviors and then in actual shopping trips.

2. Buys desired clothing items according to budgetary constraints.

Functional Essence   Instructional plans should have as their functional essence reference to the individual's budget in deciding whether to purchase a specific item of clothing. The key skill, thus, involves the creation of a realistic and reasonable budget. Activities should center not only on, "Can I afford this item?" but also on, "Can I afford a different one that is less expensive but, perhaps, not of the same quality?" Throughout all the activities, the emphasis should be placed on balancing needs, preferences, and money available.

3. Buys desired clothing items after reviewing various size designations on labels and/or tags.

Functional Essence   Instructional plans should have as their functional essence the identification of size of garments. Instructional activities should have as their goal the memorization by the individual of his various clothing sizes. The recall of sizes and their location on clothing labels are critical to his selecting garments that fit properly. In the beginning a size chart may be developed and then used as a means of reminding him. Be sure to include the concept that if he forgets a size to refer either to his chart or to ask a salesperson to measure him. Actual shopping trips should be included.

4. Computes the savings involved in buying sale items from the difference between current and former price as they appear on a price tag.

Functional Essence   Instructional plans should have as their functional essence the computation of savings accrued from buying a desired item that is on sale. Instructional activities should feature the idea that one does not buy an item solely because it is on sale, i.e., a sale item is only good if it is an item you want, can afford, and is more attractive to you because of its lowered price. Obtain a collection of sales tags that show the original and sale price. Use these tags as practice in subtraction. Visit a clothing store or clothing department in a store just before a scheduled sale and select desired items. Return to the store after the sale and try to locate these items. If a selected item is on sale, calculate the savings, and decide on the purchase.

5. Computes the price of a sale item by subtracting a percentage discount.

Functional Essence   Instructional plans should have as their functional essence the computation of a sale price by subtracting a percent discount. Instructional activities should be based on actual sales. Collect sale advertisements and demonstrate how to use a percentage or a fraction converted from a percentage to arrive at a sale price. Engage in before-and-after exercises in which you give a "before" price followed by a percentage sale and the individual computes the "after" or sale price. Visit shops during sales time to figure out sales prices when the store announces the original price and the percentage discount without quoting the sale price. Assist the individual, if necessary, in identifying the sale price.

6. Computes the total cost of a clothing item by including sales tax and cost of alterations whenever applicable.

Functional Essence   Instructional plans should have as their functional essence the computing of total cost of a clothing item. Instructional activities should involve the calculations involved in considering:
    a. a discount;
    b. cost of alterations; and
    c. sales tax.
Trips should be scheduled and items selected and alteration price lists should be referred to in estimating cost of garments. A simulated instructional store can be

then established in which total prices of clothing items are determined. Finally, actual trips should be scheduled in which the individual is to estimate cost and then verify total charges of a selected garment.

7. Checks the price of each item purchased, the sub-total, and the sales tax as they appear on the cash register and/or a sales slip.

Functional Essence
Instructional plans should have as their functional essence the verification of total cost of a purchase. Instructional activities should emphasize both the need for verification and the necessity to include in cost estimates any sales tax charges. For instructional purposes, collect a variety of old clothing, tag them, and set up a "Thrift Shop." In simulated activities, the individual should select several garments, and the person acting as cashier should prepare a sales slip or ring up the sale on a cash register. In some cases, the correct amounts should be tallied while in others mistakes should be made. Reward the individual for detecting errors in listing and in computation. Actual trips should follow these simulated practice sessions.

8. Pays for his purchase.

Functional Essence
Instructional plans should have as their functional essence the use of coins, currency, personal check, or credit card to pay for purchases. Instructional activities should involve experience in carrying out commercial transactions involving cash, check, or credit. After sufficient practice, trips should be planned in which the individual makes necessary purchases, as warranted by budgeted items and amounts, and pays for them in the several possible ways as appropriate to his financial status and style.

9. Counts his change and verifies its accuracy.

Functional Essence
Instructional plans should have as their functional essence the verification of change received when cash payments are made. Instructional activities should focus on the entire commercial transaction, i.e., the selection of items to be purchased, the estimation of whether they are affordable according to budgetary factors, the verification of the bill, the act of paying in cash, and the verification of change received. Sufficient experiences should be provided first in simulated transactions in the instructional area and then in actual ones in stores.

10. Takes his clothing to a dry cleaner who does satisfactory work and is the most economical.

Functional Essence
Instructional plans should have as their functional essence the development of skills in shopping comparatively for clothing-related services. Visit nearby dry cleaners to determine the cost of their various services. Charts should then be drawn up so that easy comparisons can be made. Identify the most economical place by type of service and then test the quality of that service by taking a garment for dry cleaning. When the garment is ready, inspect, with the individual's help, the garment for the success of the dry cleaning. If satisfactory, indicate this on the chart; if not, proceed to try each dry cleaner by going up the cost scale until satisfied with the quality of service. Indicate all decisions on the chart. Periodically review especially when there is new management and as prices change.

11. Takes his clothing for alterations to a tailor who does satisfactory work and is the most economical.

Functional Essence
Instructional plans should have as their functional essence the development of skills in locating a tailor who does satisfactory work and is the most economical. Visit nearby tailors to determine the cost of their various services. Charts should then be

drawn up so that ready comparisons can be made. Identify the most economical place by type of service and then test the quality of that service by taking a garment for alteration. When the garment is ready, inspect, with the individual's help, the garment for the success of the alterations. If satisfactory, indicate this on the chart; if not, proceed to try each tailor by going up the cost scale until satisfied with the quality of service. Indicate all decisions on the chart. Periodically review especially when there is new management, a new tailor, and as prices change.

12. Puts exact amount of change in a washer and dryer at a laundromat or apartment complex.

Functional Essence   Instructional plans should have as their functional essence the use of coins in the various combinations to activate a washer and a dryer at a laundromat or apartment complex. Instructional activities should focus on typical rates and the possible coin combinations. Because most machines, however, require not only exact change but exact coins to be inserted in starter slots, the task to be accomplished is determining costs of activating each type of machine, getting together the required coins for one or more loads, or obtaining change of bills, asking for the denomination and amounts of specific coins needed, and verifying the accuracy of change. Simulated experiences should be provided in abundance before actual visits to coin-operated washers and dryers.

FURNITURE AND APPLIANCES

The individual:
1. Buys desired furniture and appliances where they are most economical according to personal preferences and budgetary constraints.

Functional Essence   Instructional plans should have as their functional essence the identification of stores where specific individual items of furniture and appliances are most economical. Instructional activities should focus first on identifying desired brand and model of a particular item as a preliminary to reviewing advertisements and visiting various stores to determine where the best deal may be made. The time and cost of travel must be included in deliberations. Experiences should include visits to department, specialty, and discount stores. Activities should constantly focus on relating desired items to budgeted items and budgeted amounts. Whenever there are sources such as Consumer Union and *Consumer Reports* use their information to assist in identifying recommended brands and models.

2. Estimates the savings involved in buying sale items computing the difference between former and current price as they appear on a price tag.

Functional Essence   Instructional plans should have as their functional essence the encouragement of the individual to purchase desired items at sale prices. Instructional activities should concentrate on the development of computational skills involved in itemizing the amount of money saved in purchasing a desired item when it is on sale. Major emphasis, however, must always remain on comparative shopping because the regular price at a discount store may be less than the sale price at a non-discount store. Activities, thus, should concentrate on shopping for a desired item at the lowest possible price.

3. Computes the price of a sales item by subtracting a percentage discount.

Functional Essence   Instructional plans should have as their functional essence the computation of the sale price of an item when a percentage discount is announced and not computed by the store. Instructional activities should involve practice in taking percentage discounts or percentages converted into fractions from various list prices. Practice should be given in the most frequently occurring discounts: 10%, 20%, 25%, 33%, 40%, and 50%. After some of these simulated experiences, collect sales advertisements and use these for computational experiences. Actual trips should be taken to sales.

4. Estimates the total cost of an item by including sales tax and manufacturer's rebate whenever applicable.

Functional Essence   Instructional plans should have as their functional essence the development of those computational skills involved in delineating total cost of an item. These estimates include:
    a.   original price;
    b.   discount if applicable;
    c.   sales tax; and
    d.   manufacturer's rebate.
Instructional activities should include sufficient experience in computing total cost for a variety of different sale situations, i.e., rebate/non-rebate; discount/no discount. Actual shopping trips should be scheduled after sufficient simulated practice. Rebate coupons can be obtained from newspaper and magazine advertisements. These can be used in both simulated and actual transactions.

5. Checks the price of each item purchased and the sales tax as they appear on the cash register and/or sales slip.

Functional Essence   Instructional plans should have as their functional essence the checking of items purchased and the sales tax as they appear on the cash register and/or sales slip. Instructional activities should include simulated experiences in which the individual purchases items and the instructor rings it up on a cash register or writes up a sales slip. Errors should be made to provide the individual with practice in detecting errors. Reward the individual for uncovering mistakes. After sufficient practice, schedule actual trips.

6. Pays for his purchase.

Functional Essence   Instructional plans should have as their functional essence the use of coins, currency, a personal check, or credit card to pay for purchases. Instructional activities should involve experience in carrying out commercial transactions involving cash, check, or credit. After sufficient practice, trips should be planned in which the individual makes necessary purchases, as warranted by budgeted items and amounts, and pays for them in the several possible ways as appropriate to his financial status and style.

7. Buys on an installment plan if interest charges are reasonable (according to existing monetary conditions) and monthly payments are within his budget.

Functional Essence   Instructional plans should have as their functional essence the development of the awareness that it is possible to purchase needed items on an installment plan. The key concepts to be developed are that installment buying requires:
    a.   long-term budget planning and
    b.   shopping for the best possible terms.
Instructional activities should involve comparison shopping for terms and the revision of budgets to include required monthly payments. Before the individual purchases an item, review his budget and make the necessary modifications. If his budget would not meet this added expense, discourage its purchase.

8. Counts change received and verifies its accuracy.

Functional Essence   Instructional plans should have as their functional essence the verification of change received from a cash purchase. Instructional activities should feature a series of simulated transactions in which errors are made as well as correct change given. Reward the individual whenever he detects errors. Experiences should include various computations with a variety of bills, currency denominations, and coins.

9. Takes appliances to be repaired where work is done satisfactorily and where it is the most economical.

Functional Essence   Instructional plans should have as their functional essence the comparative shopping for the best prices for repairs to appliances. The key concept to be developed is that various estimates should be obtained before deciding on what store to take the item to be repaired. Include discussions of warrantees offered and judgments made about the effectiveness of previous work. Also, include descriptions of strategies for checking with consumer agencies such as the Better Business Bureau and for checking with family and friends. Provide simulation activities with getting estimates and with consulting authoritative and personal sources.

SERVICES IN THE HOME AND COMMUNITY

The individual:
1. Reviews his monthly bills and statements for accuracy and, after verification, pays his bills by the due date.

Functional Essence   Instructional plans should have as their functional essence the review of monthly bills and statements to verify their accuracy. Instructional activities should also include experiences in which the individual is expected to identify the due date. Ask the individual to bring in copies of his monthly statements (do not interfere with his privacy, however). Then ask him to bring in supporting evidence that the amounts due are correct, e.g., market receipts, records of long-distance phone calls, etc. Tell the individual to underline or circle the due date on each bill so that he will be alerted to pay by that date. Explain that failure to do so will result in the payment of fines.

2. Purchases needed services from reliable firms and individuals at the most economical cost.

Functional Essence   Instructional plans should have as their functional essence the development of comparative shopping skills in obtaining needed services. Instructional activities should concentrate on obtaining recommendations from both authoritative sources (e.g., the Better Business Bureau) and personal sources (e.g., neighbors, relatives, and friends). Also, experience should center on getting various estimates from business firms and reviewing terms and conditions of the contract including warranty elements and payment terms.

3. Plans and budgets for trips according to time and budgetary constraints.

Functional Essence   Instructional plans should have as their functional essence the planning of trips with emphasis placed on time needed and projected costs. Instructional activities should include the preparation of a time and cost budget for various hypothetical trips. Throughout, emphasize the alternate means of transportation, alternate lodging possibilities, alternate eating arrangements, etc. Alternate time and cost budgets should be drawn up for each hypothetical trip and the pros and cons of each should be thoroughly discussed before the selection of a particular plan. After sufficient practice, actual trips should then be planned.

4. Attends community and recreational events according to individual preferences as well as time and budgetary constraints.

Functional Essence   Instructional plans should have as their functional essence the identification of community and recreational events within the individual's resident and work environment. Instructional activities should be devoted to:
 a. identifying events of interest;
 b. estimating the cost of participating in these events; and
 c. estimating the time needed to be set aside to participate in each event.
Review the newspapers, advertisements, bulletin boards, correspondence, and other sources that announce the available events. For each announced event determine the individual's desire and time and financial ability to participate. Encourage realistic and reasonable participation.

5. Checks utility bills for accuracy and pays his bills by the due date.

Functional Essence   Instructional plans should have as their functional essence the verification of the accuracy of utility bills and their payment by the due date. Instructional activities should involve the reading of the various meters located in the house or apartment at the time of readings and the matching of these recorded readings to the measures on utility bills. In the case of telephone bills, encourage the individual to maintain a log of long-distance calls with dates and times in order to check later bills. Throughout, emphasize the consequences of not paying a bill by the due date, i.e., fines or termination of service.

Department of Education

American
Museum of
Natural
History

Central Park West at 79th St.
New York, N.Y. 10024

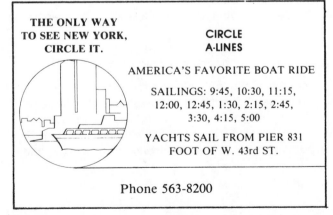

THE ONLY WAY TO SEE NEW YORK, CIRCLE IT.

**CIRCLE
A-LINES**

AMERICA'S FAVORITE BOAT RIDE

SAILINGS: 9:45, 10:30, 11:15,
12:00, 12:45, 1:30, 2:15, 2:45,
3:30, 4:15, 5:00

YACHTS SAIL FROM PIER 831
FOOT OF W. 43rd ST.

Phone 563-8200

July 26: 7:30 PM

THE GREAT GATSBY
Robert Redford
Mia Farrow

Figure 42. Identifying community and recreational events.

FINANCES

The individual:

1. Identifies the various coins and denominations of bills and uses these in commercial transactions.

Functional Essence
Instructional plans should have as their functional essence the identification and use of the various denominations of bills and coins in various business transactions. Instructional activities should provide the individual with sufficient experience in discriminating among these various denominations of money. Also, experiences should be given that reinforce their use in various interchanges of money.

2. Develops and maintains a weekly and monthly budget.

Functional Essence
Instructional plans should have as their functional essence the creation of a weekly and a monthly budget based on:
   a. income and projected income;
   b. fixed expenses (mortgage payments or rent, interest on loans, and installment buying);
   c. food;
   d. clothing;
   e. household furnishings and appliances;
   f. medical expenses;
   g. recreational expenses;
   h. emergency expenses; and
   i. miscellaneous.

Instructional plans must deal with the actual economic status of the individual if the plan is to be of practical value. Instructional activities, therefore, must include a thorough-going assessment of current and projected income, current assets and liabilities and future needs. Future needs must be placed in a hierarchy according to expected priorities. Emphasis throughout must be placed on periodically reviewing the budget and modifying the budget *immediately* whenever significant changes occur in any of its dimensions, e.g., medical expenses, visitors from out of town, a wedding, etc.

3. Deposits and withdraws money from a bank account according to saving plans and to meet special expenses.

Functional Essence
Instructional plans should have as their functional essence the depositing and withdrawing of money from a bank account. Instructional activities should provide the individual with abundant experience in filling out deposit and withdrawal slips. Collect sample slips from the various area banks for practice purposes. If possible, encourage the individual to set up a bank account, establish a savings plan, and to withdraw money only to meet special expenses.

4. Verifies the accuracy of bank, store, and other monthly statements.

Functional Essence
Instructional plans should have as their functional essence the verification of the accuracy of various financial statements. Throughout, the emphasis should be on maintaining accurate records so that statements can be verified or supported by collected evidence. Instructional activities should focus on developing a system of accurate financial record keeping. Assist the individual in setting up an effective and efficient system.

5. Compares the interest rates of banks and other lending institutions and buys on installment at prevailing rates when monthly payments are reasonably budgeted.

Functional Essence

Instructional plans should have as their functional essence comparative shopping for credit. Instructional activities should center on the various processes in obtaining a loan, including the comparison of rates of interest from the various banks in the community and from the store itself. Include the computation of monthly payments and the modification of the personal budget when an installment or other personal loan is obtained.

SAMPLE INSTRUCTIONAL PLAN

CONSUMER SKILLS-

Topic Area FUNCTIONAL MATHEMATICS   Date 5/15/80

Teacher Ms. Napier   Individual(s) or Group Members Involved:

Time Allotted 25-30 minutes

E. Maria, J. Goldsmith
G. Schiffman, P. Daniels,
M. Faillon, S. Laurence,
R. Cinders

Special Notes or Precautions For E. Maria, prepare a shopping list containing
pictures as well as words.

General Objective

   The individual will function as a consumer of goods and services
as independently and skillfully as possible by performing necessary
mathematical operations.

Specific Objective (Food and Household Products - 7)

   The individual estimates the cost of the food and household
products in his shopping basket to determine whether he has
sufficient money to pay the bill.

Instructional Objective

   After being given a billfold or purse with $5.00 and a shopping
list, the individuals will estimate the cost of their orders to
determine if they have sufficient funds. They will, on the first
trial, either proceed to the cashier if they have sufficient funds
or return an item if their funds are insufficient before proceeding
to the cashier.

Materials and Equipment

   1. Four purses and four billfolds
   2. Eight shopping lists (see note on E. Maria)
   3. Eight cardboard cartons (simulated shopping carts)
   4. Boxes, cans, and jars of food and household products
   5. A cash register

Motivating Activity

   Tell the group members that you had been embarrassed on a shopping
trip because, "I went through the checkout line, and I didn't have
enough money to pay the bill. I forgot to estimate my bill."

Instructional Procedures

   1. Show the group members a simulated shopping area and tell them they
       will be going shopping too. Because each will only have four or
       five items to buy, he will have to estimate in his head.
   2. Give each individual a shopping cart (e.g., a cardboard carton), a
       purse or billfold with $5.00, and a shopping list. Then ask each

in turn to go shopping and estimate the cost of his order.
Remind each to check the amount of money on hand.

Individualized Reinforcement and
Reinforcement Schedules

Provide a 15-minute break for beverage and snacks. P. Daniels has
difficulty adding and subtracting columns of numbers. Allow him
extra time and the use of a pencil and paper, and praise continually.

Assessment Strategy

Check each individual's estimate and observe if he returns an item
if his order exceeds $5.00. Record the individual's performance
on: "Consumer Skills: Functional Mathematics Checklist."

Follow-Up Activity/Objective

If the individuals achieve the objective, proceed to an instructional
experience in which they have larger shopping lists and must use a
pocket estimator or pocket calculator.

Instructional Resources

Chapter on Money (p. 176) and Consumer Skills (p. 217) from
Bender and Valletutti's Teaching the Moderately and Severely
Handicapped. Vol. III, University Park Press, 1976.

Observations and Comments:

chapter 6
WORK

Opportunities for employment range from those of a technical and highly skilled nature to those that can be learned from on-the-job training (OJT). The number of jobs and career fields is large and varied. State and federal job trends, however, as well as local employment markets rapidly change, making it difficult to predict the availability and exact type of job training programs most appropriate to specific individuals.

This section addresses the needs of individuals who lack basic work and on-the-job skills and provides generic occupational cluster information relevant to specific jobs or occupations. Clusters selected represent a sample of those found in society today.

Vocational readiness and job preparation programs currently in existence are often unrealistic and irrelevant. In addition to this problem, requirements for the same job may be totally different in one area of the country or even within the same state.

Vocational counselors, rehabilitation counselors, job placement interviewers, and employers have suggested that the best way of preparing an individual for work is through on-the-job training. They strongly suggest that academic information as well as training in interpersonal skills needed to interact successfully on a job should be taught as an integral part of a sound vocational program.

It is patently obvious that many individuals do not possess job-seeking skills. Although many have work skills and abilities, they often fail to obtain employment because they experience difficulty with the interview process and have problems in completing job application forms. The lack of these skills is especially critical whenever a small number of jobs are available in relation to the number of individuals seeking employment.

Ten individual occupational clusters were selected for discussion in this section. They do not represent all existing jobs nor do they address completely those jobs that are newly emerging as a result of technological advances. A major advantage of organizing occupations by clusters is that occupational tasks are identified on a broader basis. A strong advantage of the cluster concept is that the worker will become more employable if he generalizes acquired work skills to a variety of related jobs.

Basic work skills covered in this section include:

Applying for work
Getting ready for work
Going to work
Work rules
Interpersonal skills at work
Work breaks
Compensation for work

Also included are specific objectives for the ten major occupational clusters. Information in the areas of reading, writing, and mathematics are provided in:

1. Construction
2. Health Occupations
3. Graphics and Communication Media
4. Food Preparation and Service
5. Manufacturing
6. Clothing and Textile
7. Automotive and Power Service
8. Office and Business Occupations
9. Agriculture and Natural Resources
10. Distribution

Many related jobs and occupational descriptions are listed in the *Dictionary of Occupational Titles*, and readers may wish to consult this resource for specific information pertinent to their areas of interest. The following outline is provided for readers interested in those entry-level jobs commonly found in the clusters described in this section:

Construction
Construction Worker
Maintenance Person
Porter
Janitor
Carpenter
Carpenter's Helper
Insulation Worker
Cement Mason/Helper
Roofer
Bricklayer/Helper

Health Occupations
Nurse's Aide
Orderly
Home Health Aide
Physical Therapy Assistant
Occupational Therapy Assistant
Ambulance Attendant
Emergency Entrance Attendant
Hospital Maid
Child-Care Assistant
Janitor

Graphics and Communication Media
Book Binder
Bindery Machine Operator
Screen Printer/Maker
Plate Finisher
Photographer/Lithographer
Offset Press Operator
Printing Press Operator
Platen-Press Feeder
Compositor
Draftsman/Helper

Food Preparation and Service
Baker's Helper
Pastry Cook
Cook's Helper
Kitchen Helper
Host/Hostess
Waiter/Waitress
Bus Boy/Bus Girl
Tray-Line Worker

Manufacturing
Welder (and Repairer)
Welder (Arc and Spot)
Machinist
Production Machine Operator
Lathe Operator
Forming Machine Operator
Bench Grinder

Clothing and Textile
Launderer
Dry Cleaner
Marker
Spotter
Cleaner/Presser
Assembler
Seamstress/Seamster
Alteration Tailor
Drapery Operator/Hanger
Upholsterer/Automobile/Furniture
Upholsterer Helper

Automotive and Power Services
Automobile-service Mechanic/Helper
Muffler Installer
Auto-accessories Installer
New-car Ready Person
Service Station Attendant
Automobile Body Mechanic
Auto Painter/Sprayer
Motorcycle Mechanic
Power Saw Mechanic
Gasoline Engine Mechanic
Outboard-Motor Mechanic
Home Appliance Mechanic
Electrical Appliance Serviceman/Helper
Air Conditioning Mechanic (Commercial and Domestic)
Refrigeration Mechanic
Air Conditioning Installer/Domestic

Office and Business Occupations
Clerk (General Office)
Typist
File Clerk
Duplicating Machine Operator
Key Punch Operator
Calculator Operator
Inventory Worker
Receptionist
Appointment Coordinator

Agriculture and Natural Resources
Farm Equipment Operator (Heavy or Light)
Tractor Mechanic

Farm Machinery Set-up Person
Assembly Repairman
Greaser
Groundskeeper
Greenskeeper
Nursery Worker
Landscape Gardener
Floral Designer
Floral Salesperson
Forest-Fire Fighter
Park Caretaker
Seed-Core Picker
Logger
Park Worker

Distribution
Material Handler
Laborer (Stores)
Salesperson
Yard Person
Delivery Person
Clerk (Receiving Room)
Stock Person
Cashier
Bagger

Readers may wish to consult "Readings and Resources" at the end of this book for relevant information on preparing adolescents and adults for the world of work.

GENERAL OBJECTIVES

READING   The individual will function as a worker as independently and skillfully as possible by identifying words and other symbols.

WRITING   The individual will function as a worker as independently and skillfully as possible by performing diverse written tasks.

MATHEMATICS   The individual will function as a worker as independently and skillfully as possible by performing necessary mathematical operations.

FUNCTIONAL READING / INSTRUCTIONAL OBJECTIVES

GENERAL OBJECTIVE: The individual will function as a worker as independently and skillfully as possible by identifying words and other symbols.

LOOKING AND APPLYING FOR WORK

The individual:
1. Identifies the skills required in special job clusters after reviewing printed information booklets and brochures on:
    a. construction;
    b. health occupations;
    c. graphics and communication media;
    d. food preparation;
    e. manufacturing;
    f. clothing and textile services;
    g. automotive and power service;
    h. office and business occupations;
    i. agriculture/natural resources; and
    j. distribution.

Functional Essence   Instructional plans should have as their functional essence the review of booklets, pamphlets, and brochures for the purpose of finding key information to help the individual decide on a job cluster or clusters that interest him and for which he possesses essential prerequisites and basic skills.

2. Locates the help wanted section of newspapers and identifies job offerings appropriate to his interests, needs, and skills. (*See* Sample Instructional Plan.)

Functional Essence   Instructional plans should have as their functional essence the locating of the help wanted section of newspapers and the identification of appropriate job openings. Throughout the review of help wanted listings, emphasis should be placed on the analysis of the applicability of the job to the individual's interests, needs, and skills. In-depth discussions should also include other pertinent considerations such as distance from home, availability of public transportation, work hours, etc. Be sure to emphasize that the help wanted section is just one source of information on job openings. Review other sources including: personal contacts, state employment services, placement and counselor offices, bulletin boards, etc.

```
┌─────────────────────────────────────┐
│            GENERAL                   │
│          OFFICE CLERKS               │
│        KEYPUNCH OPERATOR             │
│            Part Time                 │
│ Immediate openings in our general    │
│ office and EDP depart-               │
│ ment. Aptitude for figures required. │
│ Must be available and                │
│ willing to work retail hours. Call   │
│ for appointment.                     │
│            363-1000                  │
│                                      │
│            BEVITZ                    │
│         FURNITURE CO.                │
│         9500 Deereco Rd.             │
│   Equal Opportunity Employer M/F     │
└─────────────────────────────────────┘
```

HELP WANTED
DOMESTIC (422)

BUTLER-HOUSEMAN Ref. Exp., Wages $110 week. Must have car. Call Mrs Johnson 547-5411 bet 9 am & 12 noon

COMPANION (live-in), retired, for elderly working widow (apt). Refs 844-1243 4-6 or aft 8 PM

COMPANION WANTED light housekeeping for man with broken hip. Call 425-5990

COMPANION to live-in, mature, rec refs. Minimum 1 yr exp. Gen duties, cooking, child care. 40 hr wk. $3.10/hr, free rm/board. Bring copy of ad to Md. State Employment, 1300 N Eutaw

POSITION WANTED
DOMESTIC (432)

COMPANION—elderly, Exp. Live-in 5-6 days, Drive. 564-0934.

LADY des. 5 days wk., refs. 548-9855.

NURSING AIDE wishes care of elderly, refs. 655-9685.

BABYSITTERS &
CHILD CARD (442)

BABYSITTER needed Rosedale, Ros Ridge Apts. days. Call 345-8756 aft 6

LICENSED DAY CARE MOTHER Will watch Pre school toddlers in my home. 564-9807.

WTD Depen. daycare for 8 yr old boy. Sparks are. 435-9876

Figure 43. Help wanted ads.

3. Identifies common abbreviations found in the help wanted section of newspapers and relates them to his interests, needs, and skills.

Functional Essence Instructional plans should have as their functional essence the identification of common abbreviations found in help wanted ads with the purpose of clarifying the job specifications, employment conditions, and employee benefits listed there. Throughout, the emphasis should focus on the questions, "Does this job interest me?" "Does this job meet my various needs?" and "Am I qualified for the job?" These three questions shape most instructional plans that deal with job-seeking skill development.

4. Locates occupational cluster information found on: business bulletin boards, in work pamphlets, at state and local job banks, and at employment agencies. He selects an occupational cluster or clusters of interest.

A.M.	= morning	sal.	= salary
P.M.	= afternoon and evening	exc.	= excellent
hrs.	= hours	comm.	= commission
Mon.	= Monday	w/	= with
Tues.	= Tuesday	w/sales	= with sales
Wed.	= Wednesday	w/stds.	= with standards
Thurs.	= Thrusday	pd.	= paid
Fri.	= Friday	refs.	= references
wk.	= week	pos.	= position
wkly	= weekly	mfr.	= manufacturer
mo.	= month	oppt.	= opportunity
eves.	= evenings	co.	= company
yr.	= year	mgr.	= manager
mgmt	= management	exp.	= experience
ass't	= assistant	exp'd	= experienced
thru	= through	dept.	= department
pref.	= preferred	sts.	= streets
bldgs.	= buildings	equip.	= equipment
dntwn.	= downtown	lic.	= license
transp.	= transportation	appt	= appointment
gen.	= general	nec.	= necessary
estab.	= established	perm.	= permanent
temp.	= temporary	avail.	= available

Figure 44.   Help wanted abbreviations.

Functional Essence
Instructional plans should have as their functional essence the locating and reviewing of occupational cluster information found from a variety of sources. The emphasis throughout these many instructional experiences must be on assisting the individual to identify a cluster or clusters of interest with the goal of initiating further inquiry to help the individual focus on developing his skills to increase his marketability.

5.   Obtains a job application form and identifies key words which request personal data information including: name, address, phone number, social security number, and birth date.

Functional Essence
Instructional plans should have as their functional essence the development of reading skills necessary to complete a job application. Key sight vocabulary should be reviewed using a variety of actual job application forms. Application forms for jobs in the individual's selected occupational cluster(s) should be given priority.

6.   Upon being hired, obtains and reviews all job related brochures and forms including: medical insurance, pension information, holiday schedules, and other components in an employee benefit package.

Functional Essence
Instructional plans should have as their functional essence the facilitation of the individual's informed selection of employee benefit components as well as a sophisticated awareness of employee benefits that apply to all workers. Topics covered should include:
   a.   medical insurance;
   b.   dental insurance;
   c.   life insurance;
   d.   accident and disability insurance;
   e.   worker's compensation;

f.   vacation days;
g.   sick leave;
h.   pension plans; and
i.   tuition reimbursement.

Throughout, the emphasis is on finding information and then interpreting it from the individual's own perspective.

INSTRUCTIONS—READ CAREFULLY

1. PLEASE READ BOTH SIDES OF THIS APPLICATION CAREFULLY.

2. FILL IN ALL SPACES BELOW AND SIGN BOTH SPACES ON THE OTHER SIDE OF THIS CARD. PRINT OR TYPE ALL INFORMATION. AN INCOMPLETE APPLICATION MUST BE RETURNED AND WILL USUALLY RESULT IN A DELAY IN MEMBERSHIP.

3. If you are applying for a change of coverage (change from Individual to Family membership, etc.), enter your present membership number and the membership number of any dependents who are already members in the spaces provided. If the change is requested because of marriage, give the date of marriage.

4. List all eligible members of your family, that is, spouse and unmarried children under 19, including those who will become 19 during the current calendar year, and unmarried dependent children over age 19 who are mentally retarded or physically handicapped. Enrollment must be in accordance with family and marital status. A Widow(er), or a divorced or separated applicant with one unmarried child under 19, (including one who will become 19 during the current calendar year) should apply for parent and chid membership.

5. BE SURE TO CHECK COVERAGE DESIRED.

6. DATE and SIGN this card in the two spaces provided and give it to your employer.

	(Membership Number)	B/C—Eff. Date—B/S	B/C—Orig.—B/S
PLEASE PRINT	DO NOT WRITE ABOVE THIS LINE—FOR OFFICE USE ONLY		**PLEASE PRINT**

Your Last Name	First Name Initial	Your Social Security No.

Your Address—Number and Street	City-State-Zip Code	Home Phone No.	Your Date of Birth

Marital Status: ☐ Single   ☐ Married   ☐ Widowed   ☐ Divorced   ☐ Separated

SEX: ☐ Male   ☐ Female _____

Date of Marriage	Date Employed	Firm Name of Employer	Group No.

CHECK
COVERAGE DESIRED: ☐ INDIVIDUAL   ☐ PARENT-CHILD   ☐ HUSB.-WIFE   ☐ FAMILY

Please indicate the name of any other Health Insurance, with which you have coverage: **Policy No.** _____

Name of Insurance _____   **Employer or Group** _____

DEPENDENTS:	List All Eligible Family Members. See Paragraph 4 Above.		BIRTHDATE		
RELATIONSHIP	FIRST NAME	INITIAL	Month	Day	Year
SPOUSE M☐ F☐					
SON ☐ DAUGHTER ☐					
SON ☐ DAUGHTER ☐					
SON ☐ DAUGHTER ☐					

If covered, by Maryland Plan or other Blue Cross and/or Blue Shield Plan?	
City and State	Membership Number

Figure 45.   Sample benefit plan information.

PAY ROLL DEDUCTION AUTHORIZATION

(THIS AUTHORIZATION CARD TO BE RETAINED BY THE EMPLOYER)

☐ NEW MEMBERSHIP ☐ CHANGE OF COVERAGE ☐ TRANSFER

CHECK BLUE CROSS-	☐ INDIVIDUAL	☐ HUSBAND-WIFE
BLUE SHIELD		
COVERAGE DESIRED	☐ PARENT-CHILD	☐ FAMILY

I hereby authorize my employer to deduct, in advance, each month from wages due me, such amount as may be necessary to pay the subscription charges for the type of Coverage checked above and to remit this amount to Blue Cross of Maryland, Inc., when due. The subscription charges shall be as set forth in the current announcement of Blue Cross of Maryland, Inc., or such revision thereof as may be hereafter approved by the State Insurance Department of Maryland.

_____   SIGN
                            HERE _____
Date   Subscriber's Signature, DO NOT PRINT

Blue Cross Blue Shield of Maryland

700 East Joppa Road
Baltimore, Maryland 21204

I hereby apply for myself and on behalf of the dependents, if any, listed hereon for the type of subscription agreement(s) as checked on the reverse side hereof. This application is subject to acceptance, and if accepted, to the waiting periods, exclusions and all other provisions contained in such subscription agreement(s). I agree to pay the current charges for these agreement(s) and authorize my employer, when applicable, to deduct such charges from my pay and remit them to you when due.

I further agree that any physician, hospital or other provider of service that has made a diagnosis, rendered treatment or provided service in connection with any illness for which hospital, medical or other health care benefit is sought under this membership is authorized to furnish you, upon request, full information and records or copies relating to the diagnosis treatment, or care rendered me or my family, if any, listed hereon. Such information is to be held confidential.

I have carefully read both sides of this subscription application and agree to the terms specified hereon. The foregoing statements are complete, true and correctly recorded, and are representations made to induce the issuance of, and form part of the consideration for the subscription agreement(s) for which I have applied.

Date _____   _____
                                 Subscriber's Signature (Do Not Print)

1.13.1 (2-79)   **TURN OVER**

Figure 45. Continued

BLUE CROSS AND BLUE SHIELD BENEFITS

Eligibility Provision

You are eligible to enroll during the first 60 days after reporting for work. During this period your coverage will become effective on the date you complete your enrollment card.

Membership Card

After enrollment under this program, you will receive a membership card showing your name, your membership number, and the effective date of your eligibility for benefits. This card serves to identify you and your eligible dependents. Always present it to the hospital at the time of admission or to your physician when requesting care.

Change of Family Status

You must notify Blue Cross of Maryland immediately if there is a change in your family status such as marriage, birth of a child, the marriage of any of your children, death of spouse, or divorce.

If you marry after your enrollment under this program, you should immediately apply for "Family" membership which provides maternity benefits after a waiting period of eight months. Failure to apply has the effect of increasing the waiting period.

Newborn children will be added as Members under a "Family" membership effective the date of birth. They will be eligible for Blue Cross and Blue Shield benefits from the date of birth with the exception that normal nursery care allowed under maternity benefits will not be counted in determining the newborn's duration of benefits as a Member.

Eligible Dependents

You may apply to include the following dependents as Members in this program:

Your spouse, who has not yet become 65 years of age, and unmarried children. Such children shall include (1) a blood descendent of the first degree, (2) a legally adopted child (including a child living with the adopting parents during the period of probation), (3) a stepchild residing in your household, (4) a child permanently residing in the household of which you are the head and actually being supported solely by you, provided you are related to the child by blood or marriage or are the child's legal guardian, (5) an unmarried child (as defined) until the end of the calendar year in which such child reaches age 19, (6) an unmarried child (as defined), who is a full-time student and dependent upon you for support, until the end of the

Figure 45. Continued

The individual:

1. Uses a calendar to identify work days and holidays when he does not have to work.

Functional Essence

Instructional plans should have as their functional essence the use of the calendar in determining whether the individual must report for work. Be sure to include the necessity of calling in on work days when one is too ill to work. Instructional activities, in certain instances, should involve marking off work holidays on a wall and/or individual calendar. Whenever applicable, the printed holiday schedule should be used in marking the calendar.

2. Follows a daily wake-up schedule that makes it possible for him to wash, dress, and groom himself and be ready for work.

Functional Essence

Instructional plans should have as their functional essence the determination *first* of the optimal wake-up time before engaging in the *second* act of setting the alarm clock. Determination of the optimal time of wake-up involves various estimates including time for:

   a. bathroom needs;
   b. washing and dressing;
   c. preparing and eating breakfast;
   d. taking vitamins, medicines, and medications;
   e. cleaning up;
   f. grooming;
   g. traveling to work; and
   h. allowing some leeway.

Once optimal time needed is estimated, instructional experiences should concentrate on assisting the individual in setting an alarm clock to a time reading that is equal to work reporting time minus estimated time needed from wake-up to arrival at work. Sufficient time must be spent on identifying time by the hour, half hour, and other intervals on clocks and watches.

3. Identifies time by the hour, half hour, and other intervals on clocks and watches to be prepared to leave for work on time.

Functional Essence

Instructional plans should have as their functional essence the encouraging of the individual to check the time periodically as he gets ready for work to determine whether he is proceeding within time estimations. Various activities should be planned where variations in the tempo should be made by the individual based on varying expenditures of time and on changes in travel conditions, e.g., snow, road repairs, detours, etc.

4. Selects the type of clothing needed from a specially prepared work-clothing list for specific jobs, e.g., construction worker, gardener, and foundry worker.

Functional Essence

Instructional plans should have as their functional essence the preparation and use of a work clothing list to correspond to his actual or selected job. The emphasis is on familiarizing the individual with specific types of work clothes.

5. Uses toiletries and grooming aids according to the directions appearing on equipment, printed on labels, and found in instructional booklets.

Functional Essence

Instructional plans should have as their functional essence the proper use of various toiletries and grooming aids according to directions appearing on equipment, printed on labels, and found in instructional booklets. Grooming aids and toiletries should be appropriate to the individual's needs and taste preferences. Experiences might include electric grooming aids such as a hair blower and a shaver. Toiletries should always include a deodorant and any facial medications. Optional toiletries and grooming aids should be introduced while being careful to stress that their use is a matter of individual health, taste, and budgetary factors.

6. Prepares a nutritious breakfast from recipes and other written sources.

Functional Essence Instructional plans should have as their functional essence the preparation of a nutritious breakfast from written recipes. The individual should be encouraged to collect favorite recipes for later use. Because breakfast is often less elaborate than other meals, emphasis could be placed on memorizing simple recipes and meal combinations.

GOING TO WORK

The individual:
1. Meets buses, car pools, and shuttle services after reviewing written departure schedules.

Functional Essence Instructional plans should have as their functional essence the estimating of time needed to get to the vehicle that will transport the individual to work. Whenever appropriate, departure schedules should be reviewed and the time of getting ready for work monitored by reference to watches and clocks. This will ensure getting to the transportation vehicle on time.

2. Pays the correct fare on a taxi meter when using a taxi (in special instances) to go to work and tips the driver appropriately.

Functional Essence Instructional plans should have as their functional essence the review of the taxi meter's reading and the computation of a suitable tip. Special emphasis should be placed on the special occasions when a taxi should be used to get to work, e.g., lateness or the individual's car has broken down. Throughout, stress should be placed on the relative cost of the various forms of transportation. Be sure to make clear that not all costs are obvious, e.g., depreciation on the car and cost of insurance.

3. Takes the correct bus to work using numeral and destination signs on public buses.

Functional Essence Instructional plans should have as their functional essence the signaling for a bus to stop. This skill is especially important when several different buses pick up passengers at the same stop. Instructional experiences should also include finding a bus at a terminal where placards announce the bus number and destination. Particular attention should be directed toward the actual bus line the individual takes to work. All other nearby bus lines should be reviewed because there is always a possibility that the individual will change jobs in the future.

4. Selects alternate routes to get to work.

Functional Essence Instructional plans should have as their functional essence the identification of alternate travel routes in case of unusual conditions. Instructional activities should include a study and review of bus and subway maps when applicable. Hypothetical situations should be posed in which the individual is expected to select a reasonable alternate route. Whenever an actual situation arises, encourage the individual to plot an alternate travel route.

5. Who drives to work, obeys traffic signs and signals and follows prescribed routes.

Functional Essence   Instructional plans should have as their functional essence the preparation of the individual for safe driving. To accomplish this objective, representative traffic signs and signals should be employed to acquaint the individual with the concept or meaning underlying each sign/signal. Part of the various instructional experiences should involve identifying street name signs and highway exit and entrance signs that label various points along the prescribed travel route. Trips should be taken to identify the various important signs found along the route. From these trips a map should be drawn and then used to help familiarize the individual with the route.

6. Locates the building or plant in which he works by street signs and address designations on buildings.

Functional Essence   Instructional plans should have as their functional essence the use of street signs and address designations on buildings to locate his place of work. Once the individual's occupational cluster or clusters preferences have been identified, trips to various places of work within these job clusters should be taken. If it is not feasible to go to each building or plant, simulated trips should be taken utilizing specially prepared maps or pictures of prospective job sites. Before the individual starts a job or travels to a new job, review the key signs found on the travel route including street signs and building addresses.

7. Obeys signs on entrance doors leading to the work place.

Functional Essence   Instructional plans should have as their functional essence the identification of signs that indicate the manner of opening doorways (e.g., "Push," "Pull," and "One Way"). Practice on this task may be obtained throughout the community because all public buildings are work sites for people and potential work sites for the individual.

8. Operates the buttons on self-service elevators and goes to the exact location of his job.

Functional Essence   Instructional plans should have as their functional essence the following skills:
    a. pressing the appropriate call button ("Up" or "Down");
    b. pressing the floor button;
    c. using other buttons and switches as appropriate, e.g., "Open Door," "Close Door," "Alarm," and "Emergency"; and
    d. using the emergency telephone.
Throughout the instructional activities, be sure to point out that the special buttons and switches must be used *only* under specific conditions. Also, clarify the use of the emergency telephone. When applicable, point to the emergency number appearing on the phone enclosure or nearby wall.

WORK RULES

The individual:
1. Locates the number of his employer or employer representative in his personal telephone directory and calls that person if unable to report to work or when he is going to be late.

Functional Essence   Instructional plans should have as their functional essence the individual's recognition that it is his responsibility to call his employer or employer representative when he is going to be late or absent. The physical and cognitive act of locating the number and dialing it is secondary to the awareness that a telephone call should be made. Instructional experiences should also be devoted to exploring legitimate reasons for missing a day's work, e.g., death in the family, personal illness, illness of a family member for whom the individual is responsible, and court appearance.

2. Follows directions on the timeclock and timecard and verifies his timecard after punching in and out to make sure it has been correctly stamped.

Functional Essence   Instructional plans should have as their functional essence the correct use of the timecard and timeclock as the method of verifying time on the job. Encourage the individual to check his watch against the timeclock and make any necessary adjustments aimed at getting to work by the time on the timeclock.

3. Identifies work clothing, shop coats, and other personal items by name tags and labels.

Functional Essence   Instructional plans should have as their functional essence the selection and storage of personal items used on the job. Instructional experiences should include the attaching of name tags and labels on items to be used on the job. Also, provide activities in which the individual is expected to replace deteriorating and illegible name tags and labels. Stress security factors in keeping personal items in a secure place such as a locker.

4. Obeys health rules pertinent to his job.

Functional Essence   Instructional plans should have as their functional essence the development of behaviors that will contribute to the individual's own health and the health of others. Signs such as "Employees must wash their hands before leaving" must be brought to the individual's attention. Discuss the health reasons for each rule, e.g., "You should wear your plastic gloves while handling food that others will eat. If not, people who eat the food you handled with your hands might get sick." A trip or trips should be taken to a business site where there are posters and signs cautioning healthy behavior. Each sign encountered should be discussed with emphasis placed on consequences of noncompliance.

5. Obeys those safety rules pertinent to his job.

Functional Essence   Instructional plans should have as their functional essence the development of behaviors that will contribute to the individual's own safety and the safety of others. Special equipment should be demonstrated and attention directed toward directions on the equipment and on equipment packages. Instructional activities should include the identification of emergency power switches. Take a trip or trips to business sites where there are posters and signs cautioning safe behavior. Each sign encountered should be discussed with emphasis placed on the consequences which may result from not following its directions.

6. Follows the directions and safety instructions on flammable and other dangerous substances with which he works.

Functional Essence   Instructional plans should have as their functional essence the development of safe behaviors in the handling of corrosive and toxic substances. Special attention should be directed toward warning words appearing on the labels and packages of dangerous substances. Throughout, instructional experiences should concentrate on the safe use of corrosive and toxic elements. Attention should be paid to maintaining proper ventilation at all times.

7. Follows posted directions and routing signs for fire escape procedures and uses them during a fire emergency and fire drill.

Functional Essence Instructional plans should have as their functional essence the preparation of the individual for a fire or any other emergency in which the premises needs to be vacated. Routing signs should be reviewed and posted directions studied and carried out in periodic drills.

8. Follows the operating and safety instructions for electric tools, appliances, and machinery he uses on his job.

Functional Essence Instructional plans should have as their functional essence the development of safe behaviors in operating electric tools, appliances, and machinery. Special attention should be directed to accompanying brochures and pamphlets to locate words of warning and caution. Whenever feasible, the safe use of equipment such as lathes, drill presses, shapers, planers, and table saws should be demonstrated and the individual supervised in their use as appropriate to his interests, needs, and skills.

9. Locates signs leading to his supervisor, nurse, or other significant person's office and goes there when necessary.

Functional Essence Instructional plans should have as their functional essence the development of skill in finding the location of the offices of significant persons on the job. Furthermore, the emphasis must first be placed on the reasons for seeking the attention of each of the key personnel at the business site. Channels of communication and approaches to effective communication must be continuously stressed. Locating a specific office must remain secondary to an understanding of the circumstances under which one would seek that office.

INTERPERSONAL SKILLS AT WORK

The individual:
1. Reviews work memos and when appropriate shares key information found on them with fellow workers.

Functional Essence Instructional plans should have as their functional essence encouraging the individual to review work memos for information of importance. Instructional plans should include experiences that motivate the individual to share key information of interest to his co-workers. Samples of representative memos should be distributed and reviewed. Key ideas should be underlined and discussed. Be sure to point out instances where fellow workers who have not read the memo should be informed. Throughout, differentiate between personal correspondence and memos that are generally distributed.

2. Selects a personal label or rebus and puts it on his personal property.

Functional Essence Instructional plans should have as their functional essence the identification of job-related personal property that needs to be secure. Once such job-related personal property is identified, assist the individual in preparing personal labels and in attaching them to his property.

3. Leaves his personal belongings, food, or special work articles in his own locker or other assigned storage area.

Functional Essence	Instructional plans should have as their functional essence the securing of personal items. Engage in discussions in which the individual is acquainted with the fact that security is necessary because there are people who steal. Once the concept of the need for security is established, then activities should be scheduled that aid the individual in identifying his locker or storage area from words, numerals, or rebuses affixed there.

4. Follows the posted rules and/or procedures for returning tools and unused materials to tool rooms or sheds.

Functional Essence	Instructional plans should have as their functional essence stressing the concept that tools and unused materials must be returned to appropriate places. Instructional experiences should be devoted to reviewing posted rules that are frequently found on tool room and shed doors. When silhouettes are used as clues to correct tool replacement, demonstrate the silhouette's correspondence to the actual tools.

5. On a voluntary basis, participates in work or sports pools by selecting numbers or names of specific teams or individuals.

Functional Essence	Instructional plans should have as their functional essence acquainting the individual with the office pool. Explain that participation is optional and depends on one's budget and attitude toward gambling. Assist the individual in understanding how these pools work. If he decides not to participate, help him to refuse in a way that does not antagonize his co-workers who do participate.

6. On a voluntary basis, takes his turn in treating fellow workers to coffee and/or snacks as is the customary practice of a work group.

Functional Essence	Instructional plans should have as their functional essence the development of the concept that co-workers and friends, at times, will treat each other to coffee and/or snacks *and* that if you accept the treats paid for by others you must take a turn. Explain the consequences of accepting treats continuously without contributing your share.

WORK BREAKS

The individual:
1. Locates restrooms, telephones, exits, and entrances, snack bars, and cafeterias by signs designating these areas.

Functional Essence	Instructional plans should have as their functional essence the identification of areas on the building or plant that may be used during work breaks. Preliminary to identifying these areas must be the development of an awareness of the nature of work breaks. Be sure to emphasize when a work break is appropriate and the appropriate length of breaks. Indicate that it is the individual's responsibility to find out the employer's work break policy.

2. Operates vending machines as desired during breaks and other appropriate times.

Functional Essence	Instructional plans should have as their functional essence the selection of coins needed to operate a vending machine to obtain desired items. Also, experiences must be provided in which the individual does not have the exact change and must use more than the exact change and then verify the correctness of the change. Throughout, stress that the use of vending machines should be restricted to work breaks or emergency situations.

3. Looks through magazines and newspapers and reviews bulletin boards during leisure breaks.

Functional Essence   Instructional plans should have as their functional essence the use of reading materials as a recreational activity during leisure breaks. Instructional experiences should involve exposing the individual to popular magazines and area newspapers. Throughout these explorations of popular reading materials, the individual should be encouraged to find newspapers and magazines and sections of these that interest him. Explain further that there are frequently items of interest on a bulletin board. Prepare a bulletin board with clippings of interest from newspapers and magazines. Point out the relationship between the bulletin board clippings and magazine and newspaper articles.

COMPENSATION FOR WORK

The individual:
1. Checks the gross amount of his paycheck and compares it to time worked and rate of pay.

Functional Essence   Instructional plans should have as their functional essence the identification of key numbers and terms on his paycheck so that he may compute the accuracy of his gross pay.

2. Locates the specific categories of gross pay, deduction information, and net pay and verifies that they are correct.

Functional Essence   Instructional plans should have as their functional essence the identification of key numbers and terms related to deductions to compute the accuracy of his net pay.

3. Opens a savings account in a credit union or bank.

Functional Essence   Instructional plans should have as their functional essence the development of a plan of savings as part of his individual budget.

4. Opens a checking account and utilizes it for depositing a portion of his salary for paying bills.

Functional Essence   Instructional plans should have as their functional essence the opening of a checking account for the purpose of paying bills that are more conveniently and economically paid by mail and/or when a cancelled check is needed as a receipt. Throughout the instructional experiences, the relationship between money deposited less bank charges, if any, and amount of money available for writing checks, should be stressed.

JOB CLUSTER SKILLS
Construction

The individual:
1. Reviews scales and markings on measurement, leveling, and layout tools while performing construction work.

Functional Essence   Instructional plans should have as their functional essence the skillful and safe use of the most common measurement, leveling, and layout tools used in construction work. Included are:

a. measurement tools (tape and folding ruler);

b. leveling tools (level and plumb bob); and

c. layout tool (square).

Instructional experiences should be devoted to monitoring performance by observing the scales and markings on these tools. Throughout all the activities with these tools, dual emphasis must be on safety and accuracy of measurement.

2. Follows directions involving linear, square, and cubic measurement of materials for building purposes.

Functional Essence   Instructional plans should have as their functional essence the observing of directions involving different dimensions of measurement, including

a. linear (the measuring of wood);

b. square (the measuring of square footing for laying floors and carpeting and for putting up tiled ceilings); and

c. cubic (the filling of forms with cement).

Throughout all the instructional experiences with linear, square, and cubic measurement, dual emphasis must be placed on safety and accuracy of measurement.

3. Identifies specifications and size information from floor plans.

Functional Essence   Instructional plans should have as their functional essence the conversion of data on linear and square measures found in floor plans into work specifications. All instructional experiences, except for an introductory few, should be devoted to implementing these plans in a work activity.

4. Identifies common lumber sizes and grades for construction projects.

Functional Essence   Instructional plans should have as their functional essence the identification of common lumber sizes and the selection of a specified size or grade as required by a specific work task. Instructional activities should also include the selection of lumber according to:

a. strength;

b. durability;

c. availability;

d. appearance; and

e. work budget.

Instructional activities should consist of a series of work problems that the individual is expected to solve in terms of both size and grade. Problems specify work conditions, desired work outcomes, and monetary and other constraints. In each case, the individual is expected to select the lumber needed for a work task.

5. Identifies appropriate nail, screw, and fastener sizes for construction projects.

Functional Essence   Instructional plans should have as their functional essence the identification of nail, screw, and fastener size appropriate to the type of material being joined in a specific work assignment. Instructional activities should consist of a series of work problems that the individual is expected to solve in terms of size of fasteners needed.

6. Reviews maintenance schedule.

Functional Essence   Instructional plans should have as their functional essence the periodic review of equipment and machinery maintenance schedules. Instructional experiences should emphasize the chart/checklist nature of maintenance schedules. Degree of use and the passage of time should both be stressed as critical elements in monitoring a chart/checklist. Be sure to stress the importance of recording, i.e., making entries whenever a maintenance task is carried out.

7. Follows the mixing directions on concrete and mortar bags.

Functional Essence Instructional plans should have as their functional essence identifying and following directions found on concrete and mortar bags to mix these substances as needed for work assignments. Cement can be mixed for *x* minutes while specific types of mortar can be mixed for a longer or shorter time. Each of these tasks offer the opportunity to assist the individual in reviewing mixing directions and in activating these preparation recommendations.

8. Reviews master stud layout plan before erecting studs.

Functional Essence Instructional plans should have as their functional essence the review of master stud layout plans, paying particular attention to:
    a.   the number of studs referred by codes;
    b.   the type of support referred; and
    c.   the work budget.
As each stud layout plan is reviewed, the individual should be expected to discuss the reason for constructing them preliminary to actually performing the task.

Health Occupations

The individual:
1. Reviews patients' charts for pertinent information.

Functional Essence Instructional plans should have as their functional essence the development of the individual's reading skills with particular attention to the identification of key words such as: "temperature," "medications," and "allergies."

2. Reviews linen and supply inventories.

Functional Essence Instructional plans should have as their functional essence the development of those skills involved in conducting an inventory. Basically, the individual must be able to compare numbers of various items on hand with the numbers of various items as recorded on a master chart. Throughout the instructional activities, attention should be directed toward counting and tallying skills and placing numbers in appropriate columns. In all charting activities, the individual must be able to read column headings and designations accurately.

3. Takes temperature of patients.

Functional Essence Instructional plans should have as their functional essence the reading of a thermometer. As part of the instructional experiences, assist the individual in recording temperature readings in the patient's chart. Other areas of instruction should include:
    a.   preparing the thermometer for use;
    b.   differentiation of type;
    c.   insertion;
    d.   waiting for a specified time;
    e.   shaking the thermometer down; and
    f.   storing it.

4. Identifies prescribed medicines in the medicine cabinet.

Functional Essence Instructional plans should have as their functional essence the identification of medicines by labels by matching them to medication names appearing in patients' charts. Sample charts should be given to the individual with medicines and dosages specified there. Show the individual how to match the listing with the names on labels.

Graphics and Communication Media

Functional Essence

The individual:

1. Follows directions for operating darkroom equipment.

Instructional plans should have as their functional essence the effective use of the following items:
   a. a printer;
   b. an enlarger;
   c. a copy camera;
   d. a timer;
   e. a paper cutter; and
   f. a dryer.
Emphasis throughout should be on the adjustments to be made in the various components of each piece of equipment.

2. Reviews the printer's measuring system before setting type.

Functional Essence

Instructional plans should have as their functional essence the development of skill in premeasuring a line as a preliminary to setting up a line of type.

3. Selects correct settings on light meter during picture taking.

Functional Essence

Instructional plans should have as their functional essence the setting of a light meter according to directions found on the instrument or in its instructional booklet. Cameras with built-in light meters should also be included in this experience.

Food Preparation and Service

The individual:

1. Reviews food, supplies, and utensil inventories for ordering purposes.

Functional Essence

Instructional plans should have as their functional essence the development of those skills involved in conducting an inventory. Basically, the individual must be able to compare numbers of various items on hand with the numbers of various items as recorded on a master chart. Throughout the instructional activities, attention should be directed toward counting and tallying skills and placing numbers in appropriate columns. In all charting activities, the individual must be able to read column headings and designations.

2. Selects and carries out recipes.

Functional Essence

Instructional plans should have as their functional essence the selection of recipes for a meal followed by implementation of their directions. An essential part of learning experiences should be identification of key terms for cooking processes, abbreviations for units of measurement, and words that indicate the sequence of events. Instructional activities should involve both the cognitive and social processes essential to the selection of appropriate recipes and the cognitive and motor skills essential to carrying out the recipes.

Pineapple-Crowned Fruit Pie

This three-layer fresh fruit pie topped with pineapple sauce takes first prize—

1¼ cups crushed
  graham crackers
¼ cup sugar
6 tablespoons butter
  or margarine,
  melted

2 medium bananas,
  sliced
Lemon juice
2 cups fresh straw-
  berries, sliced, *or*
  other fresh fruit,
  sliced

2 teaspoons
  cornstarch
1 20-ounce can
  crushed pineapple
1 teaspoon vanilla
⅓ cup chopped
  walnuts

Combine crushed graham crackers and sugar; stir in melted butter or margarine till well blended. Press mixture evenly in a 9-inch pie plate, forming a high edge. Dip banana slices in lemon juice; arrange in a layer in piecrust. Top with sliced strawberries or desired fresh fruit. In saucepan blend cornstarch into **undrained** pineapple. Cook and stir over medium heat till thickened and bubbly; cook 1 minute longer. Add vanilla. Spoon hot pineapple mixture over top of pie. Chill several hours before serving, sprinkle with the nuts.

Cheryl Hiltebeitel, Richmond, Va.

Figure 46.   Selecting recipes.

3. Locates and follows directions on labels for preparing foods and beverages.

Functional Essence   Instructional plans should have as their functional essence the preparation of foods and beverages from directions on labels. Instructional activities should concentrate on the collection of packages with recipes printed on them. Assist the individual in reviewing the recipes and in preparing the food or beverage. The selection of appropriate and nutritious foods and beverages that are within the individual's budget must always remain central to the objective.

4. Reviews the day's menu to assist customers and to record orders.

Functional Essence   Instructional plans should have as their functional essence the work task of reviewing the daily menu so that the individual may serve as a waiter or counterperson in a snack bar, cafeteria, or restaurant. Instructional activities may begin with simulated waiter-customer scenes using actual menus to practice under supervision in an actual work experience.

5. Reviews checks of customers.

Functional Essence   Instructional plans should have as their functional essence the preparation and verification of a customer's check for a snack or meal. Instructional activities should feature the writing of customers' orders based on the reading of the printed menu for item names and prices. The verification process involves the same task of reading the menu and matching it to the written order form. Instructional activities may begin with simulated waiter-customer scenes using actual menus to practice under supervision in an actual work experience.

6. Operates a cash register.

Functional Essence   Instructional plans should have as their functional essence the operation of a cash register in a restaurant or cafeteria. Throughout the instructional sequence, the emphasis is on identifying and punching the keys that correspond to the amounts appearing on the customers' checks, plus any tax. With modern cash registers, the identification of amount paid must also be punched in so that the amount of change is recorded. In this case, the amount of change must be read by the individual and then counted out. (*See* the section "Functional Reading in the Home" for additional kitchen objectives and activities.)

Manufacturing

The individual:

1. Identifies markings on measuring rules and related tools including micrometers and calipers.

Functional Essence

Instructional plans should have as their functional essence the safe use of measuring tools to check the length, width, or circumference of items such as bearings, spindles, axles, and spheres.

2. Follows readings on gauges and vernier measuring tools.

Functional Essence

Instructional plans should have as their functional essence the use of gauges and vernier measuring tools to check to verify that objects are in line and to measure for accuracy.

3. Reviews directions for operating machinery typically found in manufacturing occupations.

Functional Essence

Instructional plans should have as their functional essence the safe and effective operation of typical machinery found in manufacturing occupations. Instructional experiences should review the written directions and the operation of machinery, including:

    a. a shaper;
    b. a milling machine;
    c. a planer;
    d. a table and radial arm saw;
    e. a jointer;
    f. a lathe; and
    g. a drill press.

Throughout the experiences, the emphasis must always be on safety first then on effectiveness and efficiency.

4. Follows a schedule for lubricating machinery and equipment.

Functional Essence

Instructional plans should have as their functional essence the review of written schedules or charts that indicate the times of lubrication for machines and equipment. Samples of such charts should be used in early instructional activities. Once actual equipment is used, the individual should be encouraged to check machinery and equipment periodically to determine whether they are approaching the time for a lubrication.

5. Follows blueprints and plans.

Functional Essence

Instructional plans should have as their functional essence the conversion of data included in plans (schematic, pictorial, or perspective types) and blueprints (representational) into work tasks. Throughout work activities, the individual should be encouraged to refer to plans or blueprints for guidance and for checking on the accuracy of his performance.

6. Identifies industrial safety signs and observes their precautions.

Functional Essence

Instructional plans should have as their functional essence development of the individual's awareness of the existence of safety signs. Instructional activities should expose the individual to actual safety signs he is likely to encounter in a typical manufacturing setting. In each case, the reasons for the warning should be discussed and the consequences of ignoring the rules should be explored. The individual should be rewarded for working safely.

Clothing and Textiles

The individual:
1. Follows the measurements for adjusting cuffs and sleeves.

Functional Essence

Instructional plans should have as their functional essence the following of work orders for adjusting cuffs and sleeves. Particular attention must be paid to reading units of measurement on work orders and on measuring tapes.

2. Reviews measurements for cutting fabrics.

Functional Essence

Instructional plans should have as their functional essence the following of work orders for cutting fabric. Particular attention must be paid to reading units of measurement on work orders and on measuring tapes.

3. Reviews clothing inventories.

Functional Essence

Instructional plans should have as their functional essence the development of inventorying skills including the tallying and computing of stock on hand. The individual should be provided with experience involving the use of an inventory chart with particular reference to clothing type, manufacturer, style number, color, and size designations. Inventory charts must be thoroughly reviewed before their actual use.

4. Checks clothing invoices.

Functional Essence

Instructional plans should have as their functional essence the development of inventorying skills involved in checking clothing invoices against incoming orders. The essential skill is checking size and style number designations on labels against packing invoices while attending to color differences. Another element is the checking of billed invoices against packing invoices.

5. Follows measurements for shortening or lengthening articles of clothing.

Functional Essence

Instructional plans should have as their functional essence the following of work orders for altering clothes. Experiences should include letting out and taking in waistlines, hiplines, bustlines, etc. Additionally, the individual should have experiences with different kinds of fabrics.

6. Follows measurements for altering clothing.

Functional Essence

Instructional plans should have as their functional essence the following of work orders for altering clothes. Experiences should include letting out and taking in waistlines, hiplines, bustlines, etc. Additionally, the individual should have experiences with different kinds of fabrics.

Automotive and Power Service

The individual:
1. Follows a lubrication schedule.

Functional Essence

Instructional plans should have as their functional essence the review of written schedules or charts that indicate when a vehicle needs to be lubricated. Samples of such charts should be available in early instructional activities. Assist the individual in identifying mileage driven on the odometer and in determining whether the vehicle should receive a lubrication.

2. Reviews amount of money needed for damage repairs.

Functional Essence   Instructional plans should have as their functional essence the review of estimated costs for the repair of damages to a vehicle. This skill involves the reading of key automotive terms and money amounts. Sample repair estimates and bills should be used to develop the specialized sight vocabulary of automotive terms.

3. Follows the directions on work orders.

Functional Essence   Instructional plans should have as their functional essence the development of skills in following work orders. In the preliminary stages sample directions that are typically found on automotive and power service work orders should be used. Each direction should be read aloud, analyzed, and then carried out. All three steps must be carried out if the functional essence is to be realized. After the more typical work orders are reviewed, less representational ones should be introduced.

4. Follows an automotive diagnostic checklist.

Functional Essence   Instructional plans should have as their functional essence the review of a diagnostic checklist as a form of work order. Instructional activities should commence with short and simple checklists and gradually be increased with more tasks and then with more difficult (in terms of difficulty level of reading) tasks.

5. Reviews the information obtained from gauges and equipment.

Functional Essence   Instructional plans should have as their functional essence the functional use of information obtained from gauges and equipment, e.g., the air gauge indicates air pressure of 26 pounds and the individual adds 2 pounds of pressure to bring the air pressure to the recommended standard.

6. Reviews refrigerant temperature and quantity to see if adjustment or replacement is needed.

Functional Essence   Instructional plans should have as their functional essence the reading of temperatures in appliances or equipment (air conditioner) using refrigeration. When an appliance appears to be operating inefficiently instruction should be provided on how to make necessary changes or adjustments.

**Office and
Business
Occupations**

The individual:
1. Follows the directions on work orders.

Functional Essence   Instructional plans should have as their functional essence following directions in work orders. Sample work orders should be prepared to cover the range of tasks typical of the several office and business occupations. Assist the individual in reviewing and carrying out the tasks specified in the work order. After sufficient practice, provide the individual with work orders and encourage him to comply without your assistance.

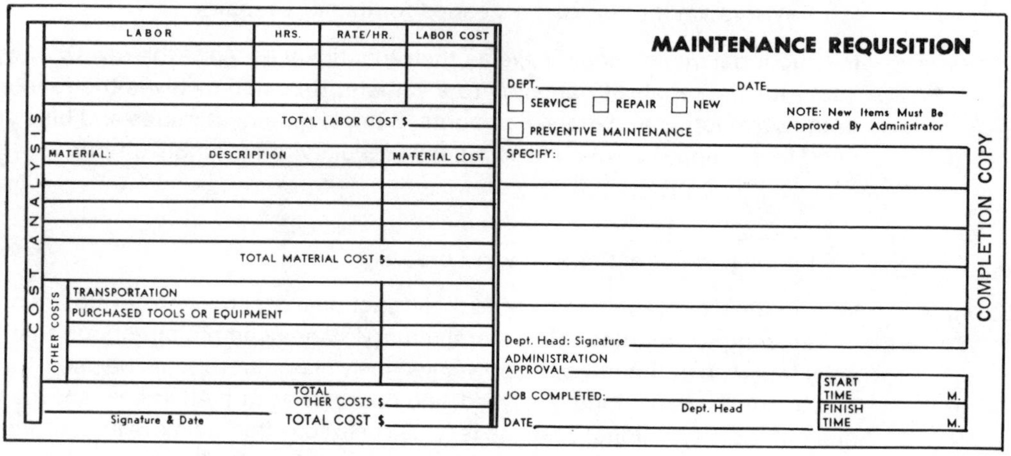

MAINTENANCE REQUISITION

COST ANALYSIS

LABOR	HRS.	RATE/HR.	LABOR COST
TOTAL LABOR COST $			

MATERIAL:	DESCRIPTION	MATERIAL COST
TOTAL MATERIAL COST $		

OTHER COSTS		
	TRANSPORTATION	
	PURCHASED TOOLS OR EQUIPMENT	
	TOTAL OTHER COSTS $	

Signature & Date TOTAL COST $

DEPT. DATE

☐ SERVICE ☐ REPAIR ☐ NEW

☐ PREVENTIVE MAINTENANCE

NOTE: New Items Must Be Approved By Administrator

SPECIFY:

Dept. Head: Signature

ADMINISTRATION APPROVAL

JOB COMPLETED: Dept. Head

DATE

START TIME M.

FINISH TIME M.

COMPLETION COPY

Figure 47. Sample work order form.

2. Files correspondence, memos, and other documents according to an established filing system.

Functional Essence

Instructional plans should have as their functional essence the development of filing skills, including:

a. selecting the category, letter, or symbol, under which an item should be filed;
b. finding the appropriate drawer;
c. finding the correct folder; and
d. making up new folders as needed.

Instructional plans should include alphabetizing skill development.

3. Locates correspondence, memos, and other documents stored in files.

Functional Essence

Instructional plans should have as their functional essence the locating of filed items according to probable category, probable file drawer, probable folder, and probable place in folder. In the beginning stages, start with simple categories and more recently stored documents. Further, this objective should follow closely the activities in item 2, i.e., the items filed away as part of objective 2 should then be retrieved by the individual in the activities subsumed in this objective.

4. Orders office materials and supplies using interoffice requisitions.

Functional Essence

Instructional plans should have as their functional essence the review of interoffice requisition forms as a precursor to ordering office supplies and materials. Instructional experiences should focus on the importance of inventorying supplies and materials and anticipating the need for more before the supply runs out. The requisition form should be reviewed as another chart or checklist to be filled out when appropriate.

5. Orders office materials and supplies from appropriate catalogs.

Functional Essence

Instructional plans should have as their functional essence the inventorying of supplies and materials and the anticipation of the need for more before the supply runs out. Furthermore, various catalogs should be reviewed from a comparative shopping viewpoint. Questions of quality, amount, size, and price should be raised before selecting the company and selecting the item. Sample order forms should be studied for their language content.

6. Follows the directions for operating electronic calculators.

Functional Essence Instructional plans should have as their functional essence the review of written directions and diagrams found in printed instructions and booklets that accompany electronic calculators. Instructional experiences should include the matching of words, numerals, and other symbols found on diagrams and in written instructions to the same words, numerals, and other symbols found on the calculator itself. Once the individual is able to identify the buttons on the calculator, simple computations must be carried out.

OFFICE SUPPLIES REQUISITION
ORDER BY UNIT PACK SHOWN

ORDERED BY BY:	EXT.	COST CENTER
APPROVED BY:		DATE
DEPT. OR FLOOR		RECEIVED BY:

CODE	QUANTITY NO. OF UNITS	UNIT PACK	CHECK IF COMPLETE	DESCRIPTION
1100		EACH		BINDERS, 3 RING, 1" BLACK
1105		EACH		BOOK, COMPOSITION, SPIRAL, 11x8.5
1110		EACH		BOOK, COMPOSITION, 9.75x7.5
1115		EACH		BOOK, STENO, GREGG RULED
1120		EACH		BOX, FILE, FOR 1M CARDS 3x5
1200		PACK		CARDS, INDEX, 3x5 PLAIN, 100/Pk.
1205		PACK		CARDS, INDEX, 3x5 RULED, 100/Pk.
1210		PACK		CARDS, INDEX, 4x6 PLAIN, 100/Pk.
1215		PACK		CARDS, INDEX, 4x6 RULED, 100/Pk.
1220		PACK		CARDS, INDEX, 5x8 PLAIN, 100/Pk.
1221		PACK		CARDS, INDEX, 5x8 RULED, 100/Pk.
1225		EACH		CASSETTES. DICTATING, 30 MIN., 3M
1230		EACH		CASSETTES, DICTATING, 60 MIN, 3M
1235		EACH		CASSETTES, DICTATING, 90 MIN, 3M
1240		EACH		CASSETTES. DICTATING, 120 MIN, Bud
1245		BTL		CEMENT, RUBBER, 4 OZ. CARTER
1250		BOX		CLIPS, #1 GEM PAPER, 100/Bx.
1255		EACH		CLIPBOARD, LETTER SIZE

Figure 48. Interoffice requisition form.

7. Follows the directions for operating photographic duplicating machines and produces a specified number of papers and documents.

Functional Essence   Instructional plans should have as their functional essence the review of written directions and diagrams found in printed instructions and booklets that accompany photographic duplicating machines. Instructional experiences should include the matching of words, numerals, and other symbols found in the instructions with the same words, numerals, and other symbols found on the machine itself. Once the individual is able to identify the various dials and buttons, the production of copies should proceed. Various sizes of documents and varying numbers of copies should be ordered from the individual. Assistance may be offered in the early stages.

8. Reviews and fills customer orders.

Functional Essence   Instructional plans should have as their functional essence the review of customer orders for the purpose of filling them. A functional vocabulary list should be developed featuring the names of items sold by the company. Throughout, the reading of numbers must be reviewed and reinforced. Sample order forms should be used in initial instructional experiences. Later on actual orders should be filled whenever feasible.

9. Reviews purchasing and invoice documents.

Functional Essence   Instructional plans should have as their functional essence the review of purchasing and invoice documents for accuracy. Sample purchase and invoice forms should be used with explanations provided for each aspect of these forms. Assist the individual in comparing purchase and invoice forms with company price lists. The company's price list should be reviewed in detail before working with purchasing and invoice documents.

10. Reviews sales and billings for accounts receivable.

Functional Essence   Instructional plans should have as their functional essence the review of sales and billings for the purpose of entering the amounts viewed by date, customer name, customer address, and billing or invoice number. As part of this objective, a sample page of an accounts receivable ledger must be provided so that the individual may be shown the correspondence between the bill/invoice and the format of the accounts receivable ledger. Instructional activities must conclude with either the posting of entries in accounts receivable or the verification of entries made by others.

11. Uses the correct denomination of stamps to mail correspondence and packages.

Functional Essence   Instructional plans should have as their functional essence the selection of stamps necessary for mailing correspondence and packages. A significant part of this objective is the identification of:
   a. type of mail/package;
   b. weight of mail/package; and
   c. value of stamps required for type of mail and weight of letter/package.
A part of the instructional activities, therefore, must involve weighing letters and packages and consulting postage rate charts. Letter scales and package scales should be reviewed by using sample letters and packages. After the individual masters the task with sample items, proceed to the mailing of actual letters and packages. Review domestic and international rates as well. Be sure to assist the individual in selecting various combinations of stamps as appropriate.

YOUR INVOICE NUMBER	DATE	AMOUNT	REFERENCE NUMBER	OUR PURCHASE ORDER NO.

SUBJECT INVOICE IS NOT BEING PAID FOR THE REASON(S) CHECKED BELOW —

☐ We require _____INVOICE COPIES.
☐ INVOICE enclosed RECEIVED IN ERROR.
☐ We are RETURNING attached invoice.
☐ PURCHASE ORDER NO. incorrect or missing.
☐ PRICE ☐ TERMS ☐ DISCOUNT
   ☐ do not agree with quotation.
☐ Please forward CORRECTED INVOICE or CREDIT MEMO
   for following reason:
   ( ) Quantity incorrect.   ( ) Extension incorrect.
   ( ) Should be F.O.B. destination. ( ) Unit price incorrect.
   ( ) Material wrong or defective.
☐ SALES TAX not applicable. Exemption No. is _____.

☐ We have no record of RECEIVING INVOICE
   NO. _____ shown on your statement.
   Please send duplicate invoice.
☐ Signed proof of delivery required.
☐ Copy of Bill of Lading required.
☐ We have no record of transaction covered
   by your invoice, supply date of shipment,
   proof of delivery, and name of person
   placing order.

☐ See your Salesman _____.
☐ Other: See REMARKS below.

Remarks

SIGNED

Reply

DATE   SIGNED

Figure 49. Purchasing and invoice documents.

12. Uses a postage meter.

Functional Essence   Instructional plans should have as their functional essence the same elements as described in 11 above with the added dimension of the operation of the postage meter. The operation of a postage meter requires the identification of number amounts on dials corresponding to postage rates found on postage charts.

13. Locates telephone numbers and addresses of clients and prospective clients.

Functional Essence   Instructional plans should have as their functional essence the location of telephone numbers and addresses of clients through alphabetizing skills in:
    a. a rolladex;
    b. a business telephone directory;
    c. an index file; and
    d. a telephone directory.
The individual should be provided with instructional experiences in the finding of names in each of the above places.

14. Makes telephone calls.

Instructional plans should have as their functional essence the making of telephone calls as required by the business operation. Simulated telephone calls should be made to:

    a. order supplies and materials;

    b. speak to an individual whose order is ready to be picked up or shipped;

    c. return a customer's call;

    d. speak to a customer whose bill is past due;

    e. announce a sale;

    f. inform a customer that new stock or merchandise has arrived; and

    g. answer an inquiry that is better handled over the telephone.

Emphasis should be placed throughout on not making personal calls unless absolutely necessary.

15. Sorts incoming mail.

Functional Essence Instructional plans should have as their functional essence the separation of incoming mail by departments and/or by individuals. Instructional activities should involve the use of mail slots or cubby holes and the consequent matching of the name on correspondence with the name on the mail slot. Experiences may also include mail delivery to the department or individuals involved.

16. Sorts interoffice and outgoing mail.

Functional Essence Instructional plans should have as their functional essence the sorting of outgoing and interoffice mail into separate piles. Instructional experiences should be geared to assisting the individual in identifying clues as to each type of mail, e.g., type of envelope, nature of address, completeness of address, and the name of an internal person and/or department.

Agriculture and Natural Resources

The individual:

1. Reviews a planting schedule before planting trees, flowers, and shrubs.

Functional Essence Instructional plans should have as their functional essence the review of planting schedules as a preliminary step in planting. A functional vocabulary list of common trees, flowers, and shrubs should be developed and reviewed with the individual as should the names of the seasons. Once the planting schedule chart is introduced, plantings should be done according to the recommendations found on the chart.

2. Follows a schedule for watering plants and shrubs.

Functional Essence Instructional plans should have as their functional essence the following of a posted schedule. Functional vocabulary words involving time of day and other time designations, e.g., once a week, should be reviewed. Rebuses or pictures of the plant or shrub may be used whenever needed. Be sure to include activities in which the individual is expected to water sufficiently without overwatering. Add to the schedule relevant directions on supplying plants and shrubs with food.

3. Follows a schedule for caring for livestock and other animals.

Functional Essence Instructional plans should have as their functional essence the review of a posted schedule of care for livestock and other animals. Schedules should include feeding, watering, cleaning, exercising, health check-ups, collection of eggs and milk as appropriate, and preparation for marketing or for direct use as a food source. Each type of activity should be entered into whenever feasible with emphasis placed on the observation of scheduled events.

4. Follows a service and lubricating schedule for farm machinery.

Functional Essence   Instructional plans should have as their functional essence the observation of service and lubrication schedules. Sample schedules should be reviewed, the nature of the task discussed, and the task carried out or referred out as scheduled.

5. Follows directions for operating equipment and machinery.

Functional Essence   Instructional plans should have as their functional essence the review of operating manuals for equipment and machinery. Diagrams should especially be studied with emphasis on the words and other symbols found there and to the actual parts in the equipment and machinery. Whenever practical, verbal mediation should precede actual operation, i.e., saying what is to be done before doing it. While verbal mediation may help some, it may confuse others. Therefore, take into consideration the personality characteristic of the individual before encouraging verbal mediation.

Distribution

The individual:
1. Follows the directions in work orders.

Functional Essence   Instructional plans should have as their functional essence the observance of work orders. Sample work orders that call for typical work assignments should be reviewed. Assist the individual in carrying out written instructions whenever necessary. Reinforce independent efforts.

2. Follows a transportation rate scale.

Functional Essence   Instructional plans should have as their functional essence the review of transportation rate charts. Activities should be provided that assist the individual in selecting the appropriate carrier in terms of quality of service, speed of service, and cost of service.

3. Reviews inventories.

Functional Essence   Instructional plans should have as their functional essence the development of skills involved in conducting an inventory of stock on hand. Activities should center on tallying and computing and then recording data on specially prepared inventory sheets or charts.

4. Reviews stock orders to verify accuracy.

Functional Essence   Instructional plans should have as their functional essence the review of orders for the purpose of verifying their accuracy with particular reference to stock number, sizes, colors, quantity and other pertinent dimensions of the objects ordered. Simulated orders should be filled. Be sure to encourage the individual to double check the order.

5. Reviews the weight of a shipment of goods.

Functional Essence   Instructional plans should have as their functional essence the use of a scale to arrive at the postage needed for shipping goods. Packages of various sizes and weights should be included in instructional experiences. Assist the individual in his reading of transportation rate charts.

6. Follows markings on measurement and layout tools.

Functional Essence

Instructional plans should have as their functional essence the observation of markings on measurement and layout tools. These markings should be used to make decisions about the amount of material to be used, its size and to provide information required for a specific job.

7. Reviews sales checks.

Functional Essence

Instructional plans should have as their functional essence the review of sales checks to make sure that the customer has been billed the correct amount for all items purchased. Remind the individual to recheck each item against its listing. Be sure to include the use of a sales tax chart as appropriate.

8. Reviews costs of goods or services and participates in sales transactions.

Functional Essence

Instructional plans should have as their functional essence the proper billing, computing of cost, including sales tax, the acceptance of cash, credit, and check as appropriate, the use of a cash register, and the giving of change. Be sure to review the proper procedures to follow in the acceptance of checks and of credit cards.

SAMPLE INSTRUCTIONAL PLAN

Topic Area __WORK-FUNCTIONAL READING__   Date ___4/13/80___

Teacher ___Ms. Simms___   Individual(s) or Group Members Involved:
A. Shallali, P. Cohen
Time Allotted ___30-40 minutes___   T. Nitti, J. McGerk

Special Notes or Precautions __J. McGerk has a significant visual problem and needs__ __a special magnifier for close visual work.__

General Objective

The individual will function as a worker as independently and skillfully as possible by identifying words and other symbols.

Specific Objective (Looking and Applying for Work - 2)

The individual locates the help wanted section of newspapers and identifies job offerings appropriate to his interests, needs, and skills.

Instructional Objective

When given a job category, the individual, using a local newspaper, will locate at least three different available jobs in that category.

Materials and Equipment

Copies of local newspapers

Motivating Activity

Discuss with the group those jobs of interest and those jobs for which they are qualified. Write down the job categories identified, adding those that are pertinent but not identified by the individuals.

Instructional Procedures

1. Pass out the "Help Wanted" section of the same newspaper to each member of the group.
2. Assist each individual in finding the job categories discussed in the motivating activity.
3. Ask the members of the group to identify job categories not mentioned previously.
4. Pass out complete editions of different local newspapers and ask each individual to locate at least three different jobs listed according to a specified category.

Individualized Reinforcement and Reinforcement Schedules

For each correct response visually praise the individual by making a notation on a chalkboard that his response was correct. For J. McGerk provide verbal praise. Allow those individuals who complete activity independently and correctly to write in an IF (independent functioning) on their activity checklist.

Assessment Strategy

Check the individual's responses to make certain that he has correctly identified job listings by the assigned category. Reward the individual's response on the "Work: Functional Reading Checklist."

Follow-Up Activity/Objective

If the individual achieves the instructional objective, proceed to an instructional experience in which the individual is expected to identify other sources of information on job openings.

Instructional Resources

Bulletion boards in stores advertising job openings
Job bank flyers

Observations and Comments:

GENERAL OBJECTIVE: The individual will function as a worker as independently and skillfully as possible by performing diverse written tasks.

The individual:

1. Completes all required job-related forms including: work permit, social security application, employment application, and tax-withholding forms.

Functional Essence

Instructional plans should have as their functional essence the development of those writing skills required to complete job-related forms, including: work permit, social security application, employment application, and tax-withholding forms. Specific skills include:

a. printing his name;
b. printing his address;
c. writing his telephone number;
d. writing his social security number;
e. writing the numerals of his birth date;
f. writing the numerals of his age;
g. writing the date of application;
h. indicating his sex;
i. indicating his marital status;
j. indicating his dependents;
k. indicating his military status and background;
l. listing previous employment background information;
m. listing educational background information; and
n. signing his name.

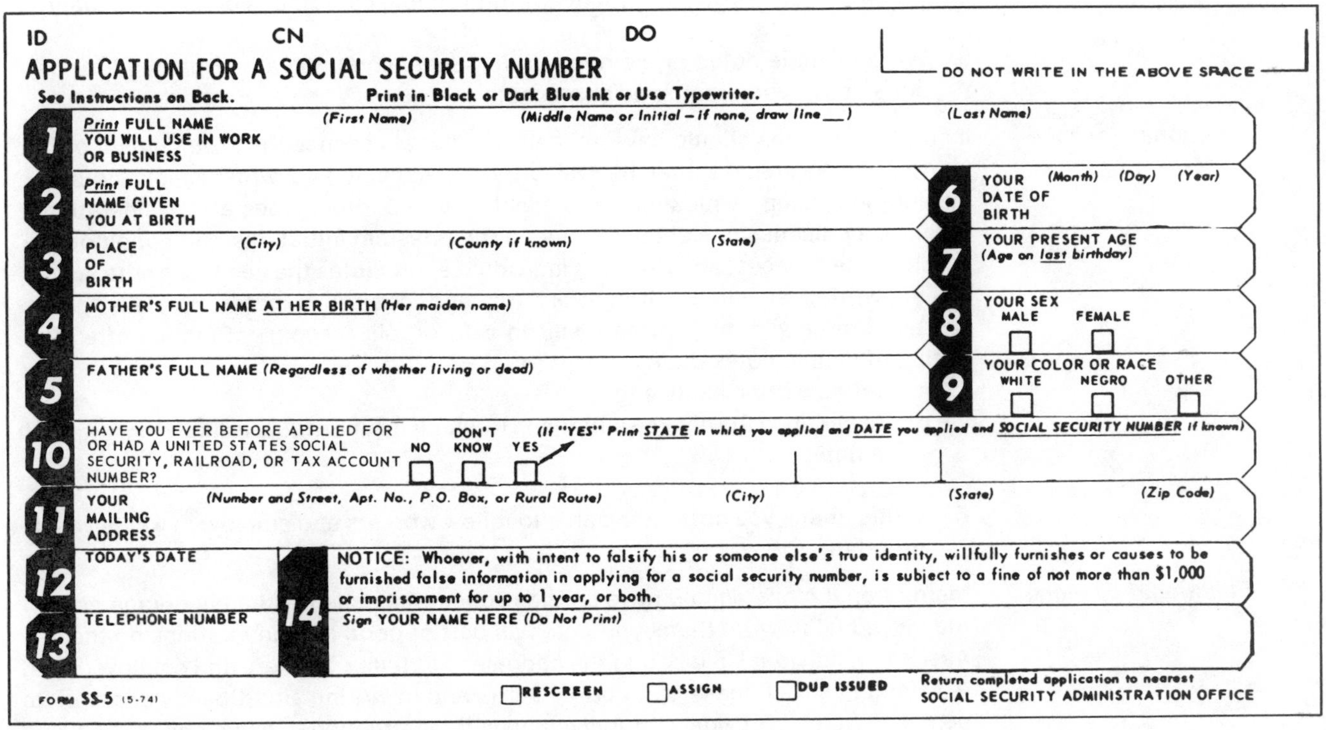

ID CN DO

DO NOT WRITE IN THE ABOVE SPACE

APPLICATION FOR A SOCIAL SECURITY NUMBER

See Instructions on Back. Print in Black or Dark Blue Ink or Use Typewriter.

1 Print FULL NAME YOU WILL USE IN WORK OR BUSINESS (First Name) (Middle Name or Initial – if none, draw line ___) (Last Name)

2 Print FULL NAME GIVEN YOU AT BIRTH

6 YOUR DATE OF BIRTH (Month) (Day) (Year)

3 PLACE OF BIRTH (City) (County if known) (State)

7 YOUR PRESENT AGE (Age on last birthday)

4 MOTHER'S FULL NAME AT HER BIRTH (Her maiden name)

8 YOUR SEX MALE FEMALE

5 FATHER'S FULL NAME (Regardless of whether living or dead)

9 YOUR COLOR OR RACE WHITE NEGRO OTHER

10 HAVE YOU EVER BEFORE APPLIED FOR OR HAD A UNITED STATES SOCIAL SECURITY, RAILROAD, OR TAX ACCOUNT NUMBER? NO DON'T KNOW YES (If "YES" Print STATE in which you applied and DATE you applied and SOCIAL SECURITY NUMBER if known)

11 YOUR MAILING ADDRESS (Number and Street, Apt. No., P.O. Box, or Rural Route) (City) (State) (Zip Code)

12 TODAY'S DATE

14 NOTICE: Whoever, with intent to falsify his or someone else's true identity, willfully furnishes or causes to be furnished false information in applying for a social security number, is subject to a fine of not more than $1,000 or imprisonment for up to 1 year, or both.

13 TELEPHONE NUMBER

Sign YOUR NAME HERE (Do Not Print)

FORM SS-5 (5-74) RESCREEN ASSIGN DUP ISSUED Return completed application to nearest SOCIAL SECURITY ADMINISTRATION OFFICE

Figure 50. Sample job-related form (social security).

2. Completes all desired optional job-related forms.

Functional Essence Instructional plans should have as their functional essence the development of those writing skills required to complete all desired optional job-related forms. Instructional experiences should be provided in completing representational forms such as:

    a. medical insurance;
    b. dental insurance;
    c. retirement plans;
    d. credit union forms;
    e. vacation schedule requests; and
    f. sick-leave requests.

3. Prepares name tags and labels for his work clothing, shop coats, and other personal items.

Functional Essence Instructional plans should have as their functional essence the preparation of name tags and labels to be attached to work clothing and other job-related personal items. Assist the individual in deciding upon an appropriate, easily identified, and clearly individual label. Individuals with common names may need to add a nickname or rebus. Individuals with reading and writing problems may have to design or select individualized rebuses.

4. Writes simple notes to place in employees' suggestion box.

Functional Essence Instructional plans should have as their functional essence the encouragement of the individual to make *constructive* suggestions to improve production and/or working conditions. Sufficient instructional time should be devoted to assisting the individual in distinguishing between constructive and petty, nasty, threatening, and personally endangering notes. Once the individual appreciates the *positive* nature of suggestions, then provide instructional activities that assist him in writing simple, direct, and diplomatic notes. Practice writing simple paragraphs or notes frequently.

5. Writes simple notes or memoranda to supervisors indicating the need for personal leave and other special requests.

Functional Essence Instructional plans should have as their functional essence the development of the individual's awareness that he will often be expected to write simple notes or memoranda when requesting personal leave and other special considerations. Preliminary discussions should focus on the possible situations and conditions in which a note is necessary. Once the individual appreciates the need for a note, assist him in writing succinct, straightforward, and courteous notes. Explain that a courteous note will more often result in a favorable response. Practice often the writing of simple notes in an attempt to:

    a. refine writing skills and
    b. experience the diverse situations in which the individual is likely to write such a note.

6. Writes thank you notes and cards to fellow workers and employers whenever appropriate.

Functional Essence Instructional plans should have as their functional essence the encouragement of the individual to write thank you notes as part of good human relations on the job. Assist the individual in locating the addresses of fellow workers and employers and in selecting situationally appropriate cards and in writing situationally appropriate personal notes. Provide the individual with instructional experiences involving writing thank you notes and cards for the following different occasions:

a. having received a gift for a birth;
b. having received a gift for an engagement;
c. having received a gift at a shower;
d. having received a gift for a marriage;
e. having received a gift for an anniversary;
f. having been provided support or a gift during personal illness or recuperation;
g. having been provided support, personal donation, charitable donation, a plant, floral arrangement, or a mass card during times of bereavement.

Assist the individual with addressing the envelope, writing the return address, and signing his name at the end of the message.

7. Writes congratulatory cards on happy occasions to fellow workers. (*See* Sample Instructional Plan.)

Functional Essence Instructional plans should have as their functional essence the encouragement of the individual to send congratulatory cards to fellow workers as part of good human relations on the job. Assist the individual in locating the addresses of fellow workers and in selecting situationally appropriate cards. Take a trip to card stores to identify card categories and display signs. Review the types of cards available. Provide the individual with instructional experiences in sending congratulatory cards on such happy occasions as:
a. the birth of a child;
b. an engagement;
c. a marriage;
d. an award or other special recognition or achievement;
e. a move into a new home or apartment;
f. an anniversary;
g. graduation from high school or college;
h. a baptism or christening;
i. a confirmation or bar mitzvah; or
j. retirement.

Assist the individual with addressing the envelope, writing the return address, and signing his name at the end of the message as needed.

8. Writes get-well cards to fellow workers who are hospitalized or who have been ill for a significant length of time.

Functional Essence Instructional plans should have as their functional essence the encouragement of the individual to send get well cards to fellow workers as part of good human relations. Take trips to card stores to identify the get-well card section. Review the cards on display there. Discuss when a get-well card should be sent. Include in your discussion, length of illness, severity of illness, and hospitalization as the major criteria for sending get-well cards. Review hypothetical illnesses and role play the decision-making process, e.g., "I don't need to send Jack a get-well card for his sinus headaches, but I will have to send him a card when he goes to the hospital to have his nasal polyps removed." Assist the individual with addressing the envelope, writing the return address, and signing his name at the end of the message, as needed.

9. Writes sympathy cards to fellow workers who have suffered the loss of a family member.

Functional Essence Instructional plans should have as their functional essence the encouragement of the individual to send sympathy cards to fellow workers who have suffered the loss of a family member. Take trips to card stores to identify the sympathy card section. Review the cards on display there. Discuss the fact that many sympathy cards are written from a religious viewpoint and that one must know something about a person's religious feelings and/or religious affiliation if one chooses a religious or denominational card. Emphasize that it is better to avoid deeply religious or sectarian cards when unsure of the person's feelings or religious beliefs. Assist the individual with addressing the envelope, writing the return address, and signing his name at the end of the message as needed.

JOB CLUSTER SKILLS
Construction

The individual:
1. Records completed maintenance activities.

Functional Essence Instructional plans should have as their functional essence the inculcation of the need to record important events that are part of the individual's job specification. Give the individual a maintenance schedule and encourage him to record the completion of each task as he finishes it. Practice with different job assignments and different forms.

2. Orders appropriate size lumber and hardware for a specific job.

Functional Essence Instructional plans should have as their functional essence the completion of an order form with particular reference to accuracy of quantity, size, and catalog or style number designations. Practice with different order forms and different quantities, types, and sizes of materials.

3. Records measurements of materials.

Functional Essence Instructional plans should have as their functional essence the inculcation of the need to record measurements of materials being used. Provide the individual with a variety of materials to be measured and with forms for recording this information. Supervise the individual as he measures and then records. Provide whatever assistance is needed.

4. Records amount of supplies and materials on hand.

Functional Essence Instructional plans should have as their functional essence the inculcation of the idea that it is important to have a record of supplies and materials on hand. Assist him in inventorying skills and in tallying and computing stock on hand. Demonstrate with inventory forms where entries should be made. Observe the individual as he conducts an inventory and records the results. Be sure to emphasize that inventories must be conducted periodically because they naturally change with use.

Health Occupations

The individual:
1. Records amount of liquid consumed during a day or a specified period of time.

Functional Essence Instructional plans should have as their functional essence the measurement and recording of the amount of liquid consumed by a patient during a specified time period. Instructional experiences should include the measuring of different sizes of glasses and the computing of total amounts. Also, instructional experiences should include the filling of a container with a liquid, drinking some of the liquid, and measuring the amount left in the container to arrive at the amount consumed. After a variety of such measuring *and* recording experiences in simulated experiences, proceed to instructional activities in which actual amounts of liquid are consumed dur-

PLEASE USE PEEL-OFF LABEL FROM BACK COVER OR PRINT NAME AND ADDRESS EXACTLY AS IT APPEARS.		If you want this order shipped to another person or to a different address give directions here.

SOLD TO

PRINT NAME _____
First _____ Middle _____ Last

STREET ADDRESS _____

CITY _____

STATE _____ ZIP _____

IF DIFFERENT SHIP TO

PRINT NAME _____
First _____ Middle _____ Last

STREET ADDRESS _____

ROUTE _____ BOX _____

CITY/STATE _____ ZIP _____

IMPORTANT: My telephone number is: Home ( ) _____ Work ( ) _____

OFFICE USE ONLY	HOW MANY	MODEL NUMBER	CAT. PAGE	ITEM DESCRIPTION	TYPE OF WOOD	WEIGHT	PRICE EACH	TOTAL PRICE	OFFICE USE ONLY EXT. CK.
					TOTAL WEIGHT				

ENGRAVED NAME PLATE, Print clearly. Max. 18 letters. Leave open box for spaces. **$6.95 EA. P.P.**

ABBREVIATION CODE

- ✔ or X Shipped
- B/O If you paid by cash or check we are holding your order and will ship as soon as possible. If you paid by credit card the items back-ordered will be charged when shipped.
- D/S Deop shipped directly to you from the manufacturer.
- P/C Price change—see current catalog.
- N/L/A No longer available. Refund will follow.
- C/I Cannot identify item requested. Please reorder.
- D/U Money due us—please remit.
- C/R The information you requested will be forwarded.

☐ Check or Money Order

Amount $ _____

☐ Charge to Credit Card below
Check One
☐ VISA   ☐ AMERICAN EXPRESS
☐ MASTER CHARGE-INTER BANK #

Enter Credit Card number in boxes provided.

Exp. Date _____

Signature _____

TOTAL FOR GOODS		
5% SALES TAX MASS. Residents only		
SHIPPING & HANDLING CHARGES See Chart page 9		
TOTAL AMOUNT		

Shipped Via:	UPS☐	PP☐	TRUCK☐
Dated Shipped	Assembled By	Packed By	No. of Pkgs.

5140

SORRY:
NO C.O.D.s ACCEPTED.

▶ **Please do not write in shaded areas.**

Figure 51.   Order form.

ing a specified time. Review checking with a watch or clock to determine time of measurement. Also, review the method and place of recording the information, i.e., the place on the patient's chart. Caution the individual to report any unusual patterns of consumption immediately.

(SHIP TO US UNLESS INDICATED BELOW.)

S
I
P
P
L
I
E
R

S
H
I
P

T
O

DATE	DATE WANTED	SHIP VIA	F.O.B.	TAX EXEMPT	TERMS
				CHARGE TAX	

QUANTITY	RECEIVED	DESCRIPTION	UNIT PRICE	AMOUNT

Figure 51. Continued

2. Records temperature of patients.

Functional Essence   Instructional plans should have as their functional essence the measurement and recording of a patient's temperature at specified times of the day. Review with the individual, the times of day when the patient's temperature should be taken. Assist the individual in using his watch or a clock to determine the approximate time when the temperature should be taken. Demonstrate the physical/cognitive processes involved in selecting a sterile thermometer, inserting it, waiting an appropriate amount of time, reading the thermometer, recording the temperature in the patient's chart, shaking down the thermometer, and sterilizing it once again. Assist the individual as he develops each of the skills. Be sure that the individual records the temperature in the appropriate place on the chart paying particular attention to date and time of reading. Caution the individual to report any marked deviations or alarming readings immediately.

3. Records pulses of patients.

Functional Essence   Instructional plans should have as their functional essence the measurement and recording of a patient's pulse rate at specified times of the day. Review with the individual, the times of the day when the patient's pulse should be taken. (Typically, it is at the same time as temperature taking. If this is so, be sure to discuss these tasks as occurring as part of a general patient check-up schedule.) Assist the individual in using a watch with a second hand to determine pulse rate. Review the method and place the recording pulse rate information on the patient's chart. Caution the individual to report any alarming rate immediately.

4. Records blood pressure of patients.

Functional Essence   Instructional plans should have as their functional essence the measurement and recording of a patient's blood pressure at a specified time of the day. Review the times of the day when the patient's blood pressure should be taken. Demonstrate how to perform the various tasks in obtaining a blood pressure reading including: placing the band around the patient's arm, pumping it up, and listening with a stethoscope to the beat while watching the dropping mercury in the blood pressure gauge. Review the method and place of recording blood pressure readings on the patient's chart. Caution the individual to report any unusual or alarming reading immediately. Some newer equipment, i.e., digital readouts, may necessitate modifying the above procedure, and in this case, follow the directions outlined in the instrument information booklet.

5. Notes pertinent observations in medical charts.

Functional Essence   Instructional plans should have as their functional essence the development of observation skills in the individual so that he will record significant observations in the patient's chart. Review the possible items that might be included:
    a. unusual bowel or bladder activities;
    b. unusual sleeping/waking patterns;
    c. somatic complaints;
    d. increased or loss of appetite;
    e. unusual visual aspects such as changes in skin color; and
    f. unusual behaviors.
Demonstrate how to record these observations as simply as possible, merely as a *report* without interpretation.

Graphics and Communication Media

The individual:
1. Uses drafting equipment.

Functional Essence   Instructional plans should have as their functional essence the use of drafting equipment to draw or lay out building plans. Instructional experiences should include the use of a scale, divider, protractor, compass, and templates, to draw lines, curves, circles, and other forms according to specified measurements.

2. Follows a work order and checks off completed tasks.

Functional Essence   Instructional plans should have as their functional essence the completion of order forms for graphics and media supplies. A specialized vocabulary list should be introduced to the individual so that he may recognize these words on order forms. Special attention should be paid to paper size, film speed, film type, silk screen and offset, and related printing material. Whenever appropriate, remind the individual to consult pamphlets, brochures, and written instructions for insights into the specifics of ordering for particular equipment and for special tasks. As part of instructional activities relate the ordering of supplies and materials to inventory and budget.

3.   Prints letters and numerals on paper, cards, posters and charts.

Functional Essence   Instructional plans should have as their functional essence the neat, stylistic, and artistic reproduction or copying of letters and numerals on papers, cards, posters, and charts. Instructional activities should feature lettering activities including the introduction of different graphic styles. Once lettering skills are developed, provide the individual with assignments involving the creation of cards, posters, and charts for public use, display, and sale.

4.   Prepares work orders.

Functional Essence   Instructional plans should have as their functional essence the preparation of work orders for others. Instructional activities should begin with the preparation of mock work orders typical of occupations in graphics and communication media. Review typical work orders in detail and then ask the individual to prepare work orders based on negotiated contracts. Prepare simulated written contracts and/or give simulated verbal contracts over the telephone or in person. Observe the individual as he prepares a work order that reflects the contract. Provide assistance and direction as needed.

Food Preparation and Service

The individual:
1.   Records for ordering and inventory purposes the amount of food, supplies, and utensils needed for serving meals.

Functional Essence   Instructional plans should have as their functional essence the recording of food, supplies, and utensils needed for serving meals as a guide to items to be ordered and to estimating the most efficacious time of ordering. As part of instructional experiences, discuss the relationship between recipe specifications and estimated number of servings as a means for determining quantity of food needed. Also, include evaluations of previous needs as a guide to future orders/needs.

2.   Follows a work order and checks off completed tasks.

Functional Essence   Instructional plans should have as their functional essence the inculcation of the idea that as a work order is carried out, the worker must check off completed tasks noting any unusual or noteworthy factors. Instructional activities should include actual work order assignments prepared on work order forms that contain places for check-off and for comments.

3.   Prepares checks for meals ordered.

Functional Essence   Instructional plans should have as their functional essence the recording of individual meal orders and the computation of the final check including tax as applicable. Instructional experiences, in the initial stages, should use menus and check forms in simulated waiter-customer relationships. Whenever practical, provide the individual with actual waiting-on-tables experiences.

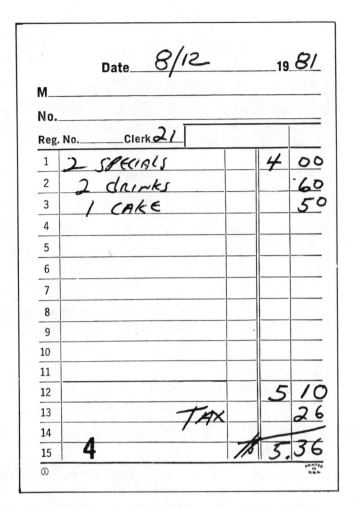

Figure 52. Preparing checks for meals ordered.

Manufacturing

The individual:

1. Records when he has lubricated machinery and equipment.

Functional Essence   Instructional plans should have as their functional essence the stressing of reporting important events that are part of the individual's job description. As an example, give the individual a lubrication schedule and encourage him to record the completion of the task as soon as he is finished. Use actual lubrication charts during this experience.

2. Records the linear, square, or cubic amount of materials needed for a given project.

Functional Essence   Instructional plans should have as their functional essence the recording of amounts of materials needed to carry out a work project. Instructional activities should involve the individual in measuring then recording linear, square, or cubic amounts of specific substances or materials. Observe the individual in both the measuring and recording processes. Reward as appropriate.

**Clothing and
Textiles**

The individual:

1. Records or marks cuff and sleeve measurements for alterations.

Functional Essence

Instructional plans should have as their functional essence stressing the need to record cuff and sleeve measurements before alterations. Pants and jackets should be fitted and marked and/or pinned and then altered.

2. Records measurements for waistline, hip line, and bustline alterations.

Functional Essence

Instructional plans should have as their functional essence emphasis on the need to measure and then record individual measurements for the purpose of altering clothes. Practice should be given with both men and women's clothing.

3. Prepares invoices.

Functional Essence

Instructional plans should have as their functional essence the preparation of invoices for items shipped and for accounts due. Instructional experiences should include preparing invoices from:
    a. packing slips;
    b. sales slips; and
    c. accounts receivable entries.
Standard invoices should be collected and should serve as the forms to be used for instructional purposes.

4. Records inventories.

Functional Essence

Instructional plans should have as their functional essence emphasis that the taking of an inventory involves not only tallying and computing stock on hand but on accurately recording the quantity of each item according to size, color, fabric, style, style number, manufacturer, and all other pertinent identifying designations. Instructional activities should consist of using a clothing inventory form to determine stock.

5. Writes sales slips.

Functional Essence

Instructional plans should have as their functional essence the development of those skills involved in writing a sales slip. These skills include taking relevant information off the labels of garments, indicating the number of items, specifying the article, recording the prices, and totaling the accumulated cost including tax as applicable. Sample sales slips including charge slips should be collected and used as an instructional tool in developing sales-slip writing skills in the individual.

6. Writes customer pick-up receipts.

Functional Essence

Instructional plans should have as their functional essence the development of skills involved in preparing a customer pick-up receipt. Instructional experiences should include writing these receipts under the following circumstances:
    a. customer has placed a deposit as part of a lay-away purchase;
    b. customer has placed a deposit for an item to be ordered; and
    c. customer has placed a deposit or paid in full for items needing alteration.
Practice each of the above in simulated and real situations whenever possible.

Great Dane

Cleaners

Shirt Launderers

X 8937

THE FINEST IN
DRY CLEANING AND
LAUNDERING

Expert Tailoring

Phone 251-9000

Date .... 198____

Name ________________________________

Address ________________________________

MON	TUE	WED	THU	FRI	SAT	AM	PM
	TROUSERS						
	M. SUITS						
	COATS						
	SHIRTS						
	JACKETS						
	DRESSES Plain Fancy BELTS						
	SKIRTS Plain Fancy						
	L. SUITS						
	BLOUSES						
	COATS						
	LAUNDRY						
				TOTAL			

Figure 53. Customer pick up receipt.

Automotive and Power Service

The individual:

1. Orders a replacement part.

Functional Essence

Instructional plans should have as their functional essence the ordering of a replacement part when the individual finds a defective part in the course of his work assignment. Standard order forms should be used to develop skill in ordering accurately.

2. Orders lubrication materials according to a specific schedule.

Functional Essence

Instructional plans should have as their functional essence the observation of a specified schedule as the first step in completing an order form. Instructional experiences should include acquainting the individual with typical forms for ordering lubrication materials.

3. Records amount of money needed for damage repairs.

Functional Essence   Instructional plans should have as their functional essence the recording of money needed for damage repairs. The recording of repair amounts must follow the inventorying of damage, the estimation of subcomponent repair costs, including parts and labor, and the computation of the total cost. Instructional activities should provide experiences in all of the above aspects incorporating reading, writing, and mathematics.

4. Record refrigerant temperature and quantity.

Functional Essence   Instructional plans should have as their functional essence the recording of refrigerant temperature to determine whether adjustment or replacement is needed. Instructional activities should include the presentation of information in which the individual is expected to make decisions on replacement or adjustment dependent upon hypothetical temperature readings.

5. Writes out a maintenance schedule label and affixes it to the car.

Functional Essence   Instructional plans should have as their functional essence the inculcation of the idea that the individual mechanic must record on a maintenance schedule all work completed. Emphasis should be placed on the writing out and affixing of the label as a vital part of the work assignment in addition to the mechanical work.

6. Completes an automotive diagnostic checklist.

Functional Essence   Instructional plans should have as their functional essence the completion of an automotive diagnostic checklist as a related and essential part of carrying out a diagnostic survey. Instructional experiences should include the interaction between work ordered and work completed and the reporting of work completed through a checklist format.

7. Prepares customer bills.

Functional Essence   Instructional plans should have as their functional essence the development of writing skills involved in translating work orders into customer bills when the work is completed. Experiences should be provided in which the individual specifies various costs (parts and labor) and totals the bill as required. Current supply catalogs and price lists should be supplied so that the cost of parts reflect current prices. Assist the individual in locating the price for the specific parts replaced. Encourage him to use a calculator to verify his computations.

8. Fills out charge slips

Functional Essence   Instructional plans should have as their functional essence the development of skills involved in filling out charge slips. Preliminary experiences should be related to translating customer bills into charge slip notations. Activities should also be carried out in which the individual records the gas pump price reading onto the charge slip. (Note: In some places the reading must be doubled if the price of gas is $1.00 or more per gallon.) Simulated and actual billing should be carried out whenever possible through the mechanism of the charge slip. Remind the individual to match the charge slip with the charge plate's label and then to return the charge card to the customer.

**Office and
Business Occupations**

The individual:
1. Orders office materials and supplies using interoffice requisitions.

Functional Essence
Instructional plans should have as their functional essence the development of skills in filling out an interoffice requisition. Instructional experiences should first be devoted to encouraging the individual to periodically check to determine materials and supplies on hand so that requisitions are completed before their depletion. Once this behavior is reinforced, activities involving analyzing typical requisition forms should be scheduled. After this, the individual should be expected to fill several of these forms to order different supplies on several separate occasions. Remind the individual to keep a copy of each requisition so that he can check off items as they are received.

2. Orders office materials and supplies from appropriate catalogs using order forms.

Functional Essence
Instructional plans should have as their functional essence the completion of order forms found in supply catalogs. Instructional experiences should first emphasize the importance of anticipating supply and material needs. Second, the focus should be on comparison shopping using several catalogs. Consideration here should be given to item quality, item price, delivery time, billing polices, and policies vis-a-vis replacement of defective materials in deciding on which catalog to use. Finally, activities should stress the actual filling in of the order form. Practice sessions using a variety of catalogs should precede actual orders.

3. Makes tabs for file folders.

Functional Essence
Instructional plans should have as their functional essence the typing or printing of label tags for file folders. Instructional activities should begin with the preparation of tabs from a prepared list. Once this activity is mastered, proceed to experiences where the individual must decide whether a new file folder is needed and then prepare a name tab, e.g., a new customer requires a file folder.

4. Schedules appointments.

Functional Essence
Instructional plans should have as their functional essence the use of an appointment book to schedule appointments for self or others. Instructional experiences should begin with simulated phone conversations in which people (e.g., customers, job applicants, etc.) request appointments. Show the individual how to use an appointment book to record the appointment by day, date, and time designations.

5. Types or prints addresses and address labels.

Functional Essence
Instructional plans should have as their functional essence the typing or printing of addresses and address labels on correspondence and packages. Instructional experiences should begin by asking the individual to address or make address labels from a prepared list. Further activities should include addressing from a business telephone directory. Additional activities should involve the preparation of individual pieces of correspondence or packages from work orders, memos, and typed correspondence.

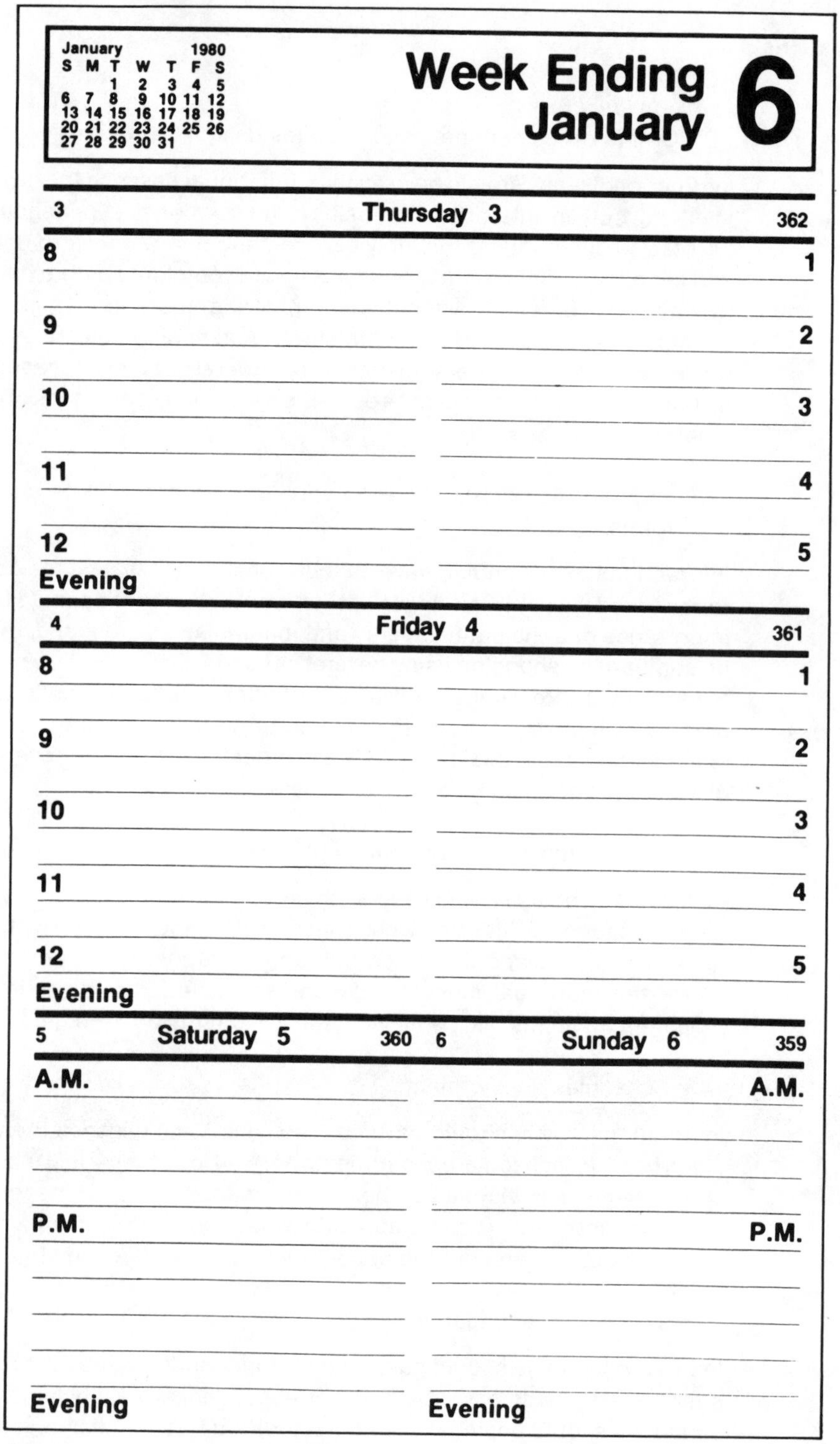

Figure 54. Sample appointment book page.

6. Types memos and simple correspondence.

Functional Essence Instructional plans should have as their functional essence the development of basic typing skills so that the individual will be able to type memos and simple correspondence when supplied with a model. Special attention should be given to matters of format, spacing, and other business letter and memo conventions.

CONTENTS: MERCHANDISE
POSTMASTER: THIS PARCEL
MAY BE OPENED FOR POSTAL
INSPECTION IF NECESSARY.
RETURN POSTAGE GUARANTEED.

FROM _____
_____

TO _____
_____
_____

FROM _____
_____
_____

PARCEL POST

CONTENTS: MERCHANDISE

RETURN REQUESTED

TO _____
_____
_____
_____

Figure 55.   Sample address labels.

7.   Develops and/or adds to a business address and telephone list or directory.

Functional Essence   Instructional plans should have as their functional essence the development of an office telephone/address list, including its ongoing maintenance through additions and deletions as appropriate. Instructional experiences should be provided whereby the individual is expected to use:

    a.   correspondence;
    b.   requests and orders;
    c.   salespersons' cards;
    d.   invoices and bills;
    e.   advertisements and flyers; and
    f.   regular telephone calls

to make up or add to a telephone/address list or directory. In the initial stages assist the individual in the decision making process. Review alphabetizing skills as needed.

8.   Records simple phone messages.

Functional Essence   Instructional plans should have as their functional essence the use of a telephone message pad to record phone messages. Show the individual a copy of a telephone message pad and demonstrate its use. Using a tele-trainer, give him various messages and check to determine whether he has taken the message correctly.

```
┌─────────────────────────────────────────────────────────────┐
│  Quick-Note                        Date_____19____       │
│  ─────────────────────────────────────────────────────────   │
│  To ──────────────────────────────────────────────────────   │
│  Subject ─────────────────────────────────────────────────   │
│  ─────────────────────────────────────────────────────────   │
│  ─────────────────────────────────────────────────────────   │
│  ─────────────────────────────────────────────────────────   │
│  ─────────────────────────────────────────────────────────   │
│  ─────────────────────────────────────────────────────────   │
│              From ────────────────────────────────────────   │
│  ─────────────────────────────────────────────────────────   │
└─────────────────────────────────────────────────────────────┘
```

Figure 56.   Short memo form.

Whenever possible, involve the individual in actual message-taking situations. Throughout the experiences, remind him to confirm the accuracy of the message as he takes it, with particular reference to the accuracy of the call-back number and the spelling of the person's name.

9.   Operates electronic calculators and records answers.

Functional Essence   Instructional plans should have as their functional essence the accurate operation of an electronic calculator with special emphasis placed on recording answers on appropriate forms or papers. Remind the individual to check his recorded answer with the number on the calculator before cancelling it.

10.   Records customers' orders.

Functional Essence   Instructional plans should have as their functional essence the taking of customers' orders:
   a.   over the phone;
   b.   in person when an item must be ordered; and
   c.   in person when the order form has to be routed to someone else for filling.
Instructional experiences should include all of the above situations. It may be necessary to develop a functional reading-writing list appropriate to the individual's business or business area of interest. Sample order forms should be collected and the individual given orders that he must record on these forms.

11.   Prepares purchasing and invoice documents.

Functional Essence   Instructional plans should have as their functional essence the development of skills in preparing purchasing and invoice documents. Instructional experiences should feature sample purchasing and invoice forms. Review these forms with the individual specifying headings and other words and symbols found on them. Assign the individual the task of completing these forms for specific hypothetical orders.

```
To _____

Date_____Time_____


              WHILE YOU WERE OUT


M _____

of _____

Phone _____
       Area Code    Number    Extension

  ┌──────────────────┬──────────────────┬──┐
  │ TELEPHONED       │ PLEASE CALL      │  │
  ├──────────────────┼──────────────────┼──┤
  │ CALLED TO SEE YOU│ WILL CALL AGAIN  │  │
  ├──────────────────┼──────────────────┼──┤
  │ WANTS TO SEE YOU │ URGENT           │  │
  └──────────┬───────┴──────────────┬───┴──┘
             │ RETURNED YOUR CALL   │
             └──────────────────────┘

Message _____
_____
_____
_____
_____

              Operator
```

Figure 57.   Telephone message form.

12.   Records bills in accounts receivable.

Functional Essence   Instructional plans should have as their functional essence the posting of billings in accounts receivable. Show the individual the accounts receivable ledger. Demonstrate sample postings while pointing out the relationship between the content of bills and the written notations in the ledger. After sufficient explanation and demonstration, present the individual with bills to post. Assist as necessary.

13.   Records amount of petty cash available for reimbursement purposes.

Functional Essence   Instructional plans should have as their functional essence the maintenance of a petty cash fund. Throughout the instructional experiences, stress the need for keeping the money secure and in keeping accurate records. Show the individual how to maintain a petty cash ledger with particular attention to names, purposes, dates, and amounts reimbursed. As part of the instructional sequence, encourage the individual to collect receipts, as required by company policy, for each reimbursement.

Agriculture and Natural Resources

The individual:
1.   Orders general supplies from catalogs.

Functional Essence   Instructional plans should have as their functional essence the review of catalogs for the purpose of ordering needed supplies. Effective consumerism should be the key factor in selecting the catalog and then the item to be order. Once decisions about from whom and what to order have been made, then the act of completing order forms should be undertaken. Use sample order forms for instructional programming, paying particular attention to item number, size, material, color, price, and quantity designations.

2. Orders parts for hydraulic and lubricating systems when needed.

Functional Essence   Instructional plans should have as their functional essence the review of specialty catalogs for the purpose of ordering parts for hydraulic and lubricating systems. Sophisticated consumerism should be the key factor in selecting the catalog and then the item to be ordered. Once decisions of cost, from whom, and what to order have been made, then the act of completing order forms should be undertaken. Use sample forms paying particular attention to size, material, and other differentiating factors.

3. Records amount of water and fertilizer used during a specified time period.

Functional Essence   Instructional plans should have as their functional essence the development of monitoring skills involved in maintaining an inventory of water and fertilizer used. Initial stocks (or in the case of water, meter readings) must be recorded and periodic measurements or readings taken. Instructional experiences should include reference to a schedule and a calendar and should involve the measuring of new levels to be subtracted from the previous scheduled reading.

4. Prepares inventories of equipment and supplies.

Functional Essence   Instructional plans should have as their functional essence the development of tallying and computing skills involved in conducting an inventory. Use sample inventory forms appropriate to agricultural/natural resources as the essential instructional material. Conduct inventories whenever possible.

5. Maintains a checklist of procedures in caring for livestock and maintaining crops.

Functional Essence   Instructional plans should have as their functional essence the development of skills involved in following a checklist work order. Prepare sample work checklists for the individual to carry out. Explain the reasons for the schedule. Monitor the individual to determine whether he completes each task recording completion as he proceeds. Move on to checklist work orders that are to be carried out over time. Assist the individual in using a calendar and watches/clocks as a way of self-monitoring his activities.

Distribution

The individual:
1. Records inventories.

Functional Essence   Instructional plans should have as their functional essence the development of inventorying skills including tallying and computing. Encourage the individual to keep a running record of materials, supplies, and equipment on hand. Throughout, emphasize the reasons for conducting an inventory, e.g., planning for reorders.

2. Orders specified stock according to size, shape, and number of items.

Functional Essence   Instructional plans should have as their functional essence the completion of order forms to order new stock or replenish stock based on shifting needs and demands.

Sample order forms should be used with particular concentration on size, shape, and quantity.

3. Records the weight of a shipment of goods.

Functional Essence Instructional plans should have as their functional essence the use of a scale to measure the weight of a shipment of goods. Throughout instructional activities, the individual must be continuously encouraged to record the scale readings as they are obtained. Sample packages may be used in the beginning to provide the individual with practice, but, whenever possible, packages that need to be mailed should be used.

4. Prepares shipping labels.

Functional Essence Instructional plans should have as their functional essence the preparation of shipping labels from work orders.

5. Writes sales checks.

Functional Essence Instructional plans should have as their functional essence the writing of sales checks from in-person and telephone orders. Role playing and simulated phone calls should be used to give the individual the practice needed for writing sales checks in actual situations.

6. Records information derived from balancing cash fund and cash register.

Functional Essence Instructional plans should have as their functional essence the verification of cash funds with cash register notations. Cash receipts and cash register notations should be recorded in a special ledger. Assist the individual in the following:
   a. counting cash receipts;
   b. recording the cash fund;
   c. recording the cash register notation;
   d. balancing the two figures; and
   e. turning over the cash fund to the person authorized to receive it.
If coupons are part of this transaction, include it in the instructional experience.

7. Prepares invoices.

Functional Essence Instructional plans should have as their functional essence the preparation of invoices based upon customer orders. Instructional activities should feature the use of typical invoice forms to be completed by the individual from phoned-in, written, and in-person orders.

8. Prepares work orders.

Functional Essence Instructional plans should have as their functional essence the development of skills in preparing work orders. This skill should consist primarily of converting oral instructions and conceptualized plans into written instructions. Activities should include work requests by customers that the individual must write down for a fellow worker to carry through.

SAMPLE INSTRUCTIONAL PLAN

Topic Area WORK-FUNCTIONAL WRITING   Date 3/3/80

Teacher Ms. Morris

Individual(s) or Group Members Involved:
J. Jameson, P. Entwit,
C. Brown, J. Rubenstein,
B. Porterhouse

Time Allotted 20-30 minutes

Special Notes or Precautions None

General Objective

The individual will function as a worker as independently and skillfully as possible by performing diverse written tasks.

Specific Objective (7)

The individual writes congratulatory cards on happy occasions to fellow workers.

Instructional Objective

When given five hypothetical situations such as an engagement, a marriage, a move into a new home or apartment, graduation, and an anniversary, the individual will select an appropriate card for each occasion and will correctly address the envelope, write the return address, and sign his name.

Materials and Equipment

Sample greeting cards that offer congratulations

Motivating Activity

Show the group a collage made from the pictures appearing on greeting cards. Explain that these cards originally brought people happiness when they were received and are now bringing joy in their recycled use in an attractive collage.

Instructional Procedures

1. Explain that good human relations on the job is helped by sending congratulatory cards to co-workers on happy occasions.
2. Ask the group to identify happy occasions. List these occasions on the chalkboard.
3. Show the individuals samples of each of the types of cards enumerated.
4. Review addressing envelopes, writing return addresses, and signing one's name to the message.
5. Give each individual five hypothetical situations and ask him to find appropriate greeting cards from card boxes and then prepare them for mailing to hypothetical or real co-workers.

Individualized Reinforcement and
Reinforcement Schedules

Reinforce individuals with verbal praise for correctly completing activity. When appropriate, allow individuals to tell you of a happy occasion coming up and give them a card or cards which they can fill out and mail.

Assessment Strategy

Collect the cards to determine whether each individual has selected the appropriate card for the hypothesized occasion and accurately prepared it for mailing.

Follow-Up Activity/Objective

If the individual achieves the instructional objective, proceed to Specific Objective #8, "The individual writes get-well cards to fellow workers who are hospitalized or who have been ill for a significant length of time."

Instructional Resources

Old greeting cards
A catalog of greeting cards
A visit to a greeting card store or section of a supermarket

Observations and Comments:

GENERAL OBJECTIVE: The individual will function as a worker as independently and skillfully as possible by performing necessary mathematical operations.

The individual:

1. Sets an alarm clock for the desired wake-up time.

Functional Essence

Instructional plans should have as their functional essence the selection of the hour or part of an hour that corresponds to the time he has predetermined is the desired wake-up time. Instructional activities in the beginning stages should involve setting the alarm for a variety of times. After a desired time is determined, experiences should focus on setting that time.

2. Follows a daily wake-up schedule from his estimation of the time needed to leave home for work.

Functional Essence

Instructional plans should have as their functional essence the development of skill in estimating time. Instructional experiences should involve the carrying out of all the necessary activities in preparation for leaving the home. These activities should be timed and repeated several times to arrive at an average time. Encourage the individual to add 10–15 minutes of leeway time. Emphasize that departure time is based on travel time.

3. Prepares a nutritious breakfast from recipes and other sources.

Functional Essence

Instructional plans should have as their functional essence the following of recipes and other sources with particular attention paid to measurement skills. Instructional experiences should concentrate on the use of measuring spoons and cups. Various recipes should be tried to provide experiences in using different units of measurement.

4. Leaves his home with sufficient time to arrive at work on time.

Functional Essence

Instructional plans should have as their functional essence the estimation of time needed to travel to work so that time can be subtracted from the hour he is to report to work to find the sensible departure time. Emphasize that estimates of time needed should be changed in consideration of weather conditions and traffic patterns.

5. Pays the correct fare on a taxi meter when using a taxi to go to work, including a tip as appropriate.

Functional Essence

Instructional plans should have as their functional essence the selection of currency and coins to pay a taxi fare. Instructional activities must also include the computation of an appropriate tip and the addition of that sum to the payment. Experiences should include both the paying of the exact amount as well as the payment of a greater sum so that change can be verified.

6. Puts correct amount of change in a pay telephone.

Functional Essence

Instructional plans should have as their functional essence the selection of coins needed to make a telephone call. Experiences should include the use of pay telephones in which no coins are needed to call the operator, to call emergency numbers, or to call information. Practice both local and long distance calls in simulations so that the individual has experience in selecting different sums.

7. Puts correct amount of change in a parking meter.

Functional Essence   Instructional plans should have as their functional essence the selection of coins needed to secure a parking meter for a required amount of time. Practice with various meters that have different cost requirements and different time allotments.

8. Puts exact amount of change in a vending machine or puts in more than exact change and verifies correctness of change received.

Functional Essence   Instructional plans should have as their functional essence the selection of coins to activate a vending machine. Instructional activities should include situations in which exact change is used and other situations in which more than exact change is used. The latter activity involves the individual in the computing of the correctness of change received.

9. Checks the gross amount of his paycheck and compares it to time worked and rate of pay.

Functional Essence   Instructional plans should have as their functional essence the computing of the accuracy of the gross pay notation on his paycheck. Instructional activities should involve the multiplication of time worked with the rate of pay. Experiences with different rates and different time segments should be provided so that computational skills may be sharpened.

10. Checks the net amount of his paycheck and compares it to gross pay less deductions. (*See* Sample Instructional Plan.)

Functional Essence   Instructional plans should have as their functional essence the computing of the accuracy of the net pay notation on his paycheck. Instructional activities should involve the addition of all deducted amounts followed by the subtraction of deductions from gross pay to verify the correctness of the net pay. Experiences with different gross amounts and different deductions should be provided so that computational skills may be sharpened.

11. Fills out deposit slips correctly when depositing checks.

Functional Essence   Instructional plans should have as their functional essence the accurate filling out of bank deposit slips. Instructional experiences should involve the subtraction of amount deposited from the net amount of a paycheck or other check to arrive at the correct amount of cash received. Experiences with different amounts to be deposited from different face amounts of checks should be provided so that computational skills can be practiced and reinforced.

12. Counts out an asked-for number of objects as requested by a co-worker.

Functional Essence   Instructional plans should have as their functional essence the developing of counting skills in response to requested amounts. Instructional activities should focus on simulated experiences in which a co-worker asks the individual to count out and present to him a requested number of objects.

13. Counts out a predetermined number of objects.

Functional Essence   Instructional plans should have as their functional essence the counting out of specified numbers of objects and placing them into an envelope or other container. Instructional activities should focus on counting out objects such as in an assembly line task. Practice with different amounts to sharpen counting skills.

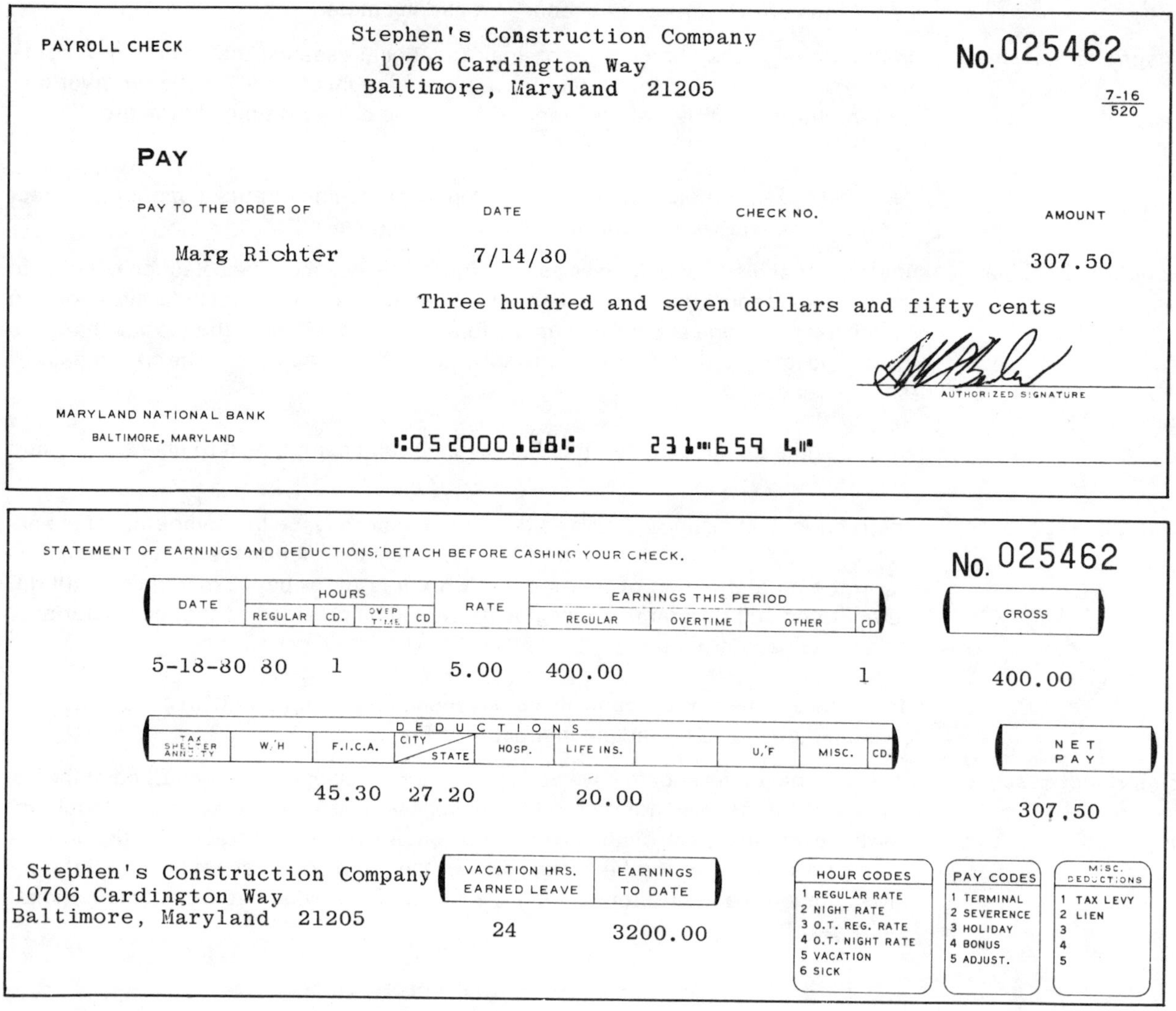

PAYROLL CHECK

Stephen's Construction Company
10706 Cardington Way
Baltimore, Maryland 21205

No. 025462

7-16
520

PAY

PAY TO THE ORDER OF	DATE	CHECK NO.	AMOUNT
Marg Richter	7/14/80		307.50

Three hundred and seven dollars and fifty cents

AUTHORIZED SIGNATURE

MARYLAND NATIONAL BANK
BALTIMORE, MARYLAND

⑆052000168⑆ 231⑈659 4⑈

STATEMENT OF EARNINGS AND DEDUCTIONS, DETACH BEFORE CASHING YOUR CHECK.

No. 025462

DATE	HOURS				RATE	EARNINGS THIS PERIOD				GROSS
	REGULAR	CD.	OVER TIME	CD		REGULAR	OVERTIME	OTHER	CD	
5-18-80	80	1			5.00	400.00			1	400.00

DEDUCTIONS										NET PAY
TAX SHELTER ANNUITY	W/H	F.I.C.A.	CITY / STATE	HOSP.	LIFE INS.		U/F	MISC.	CD.	
		45.30	27.20		20.00					307.50

Stephen's Construction Company
10706 Cardington Way
Baltimore, Maryland 21205

VACATION HRS. EARNED LEAVE	EARNINGS TO DATE
24	3200.00

HOUR CODES	PAY CODES	MISC. DEDUCTIONS
1 REGULAR RATE	1 TERMINAL	1 TAX LEVY
2 NIGHT RATE	2 SEVERENCE	2 LIEN
3 O.T. REG. RATE	3 HOLIDAY	3
4 O.T. NIGHT RATE	4 BONUS	4
5 VACATION	5 ADJUST.	5
6 SICK		

Figure 58. Pay check and stub information.

14. Constructs objects by measuring and cutting required lengths and widths.

Functional Essence

Instructional plans should have as their functional essence the developing of measuring skills for cutting various substances according to specified lengths and widths. Instructional experiences should include both work with different measurements and with different materials.

JOB CLUSTER SKILLS
Construction

The individual:

1. Uses measurement, leveling, and layout tools while performing construction work.

Functional Essence

Instructional experiences should have as their functional essence the development of measurement skills in using the following:

a. measuring tools (tape, scale, and other measuring tools);
b. layout tools (square and folding rule, and other layout tools); and

c. leveling tools (level and plumb bob, and other leveling instruments). Instructional activities should include experiences in using each tool in a variety of tasks.

2. Utilizes linear, square, and cubic measures of materials for building purposes.

Functional Essence   Instructional plans should have as their functional essence the determination of specified linear, square, and cubic measures as required by specific work tasks. Instructional activities should provide experience with each type of measure in diverse construction tasks.

3. Locates specifications and size information from floor plans.

Functional Essence   Instructional plans should have as their functional essence the location and interpretation of specifications as represented on floor plans. Instructional experiences should include floor plans in various scales.

4. Selects common lumber sizes in amounts needed and grade for construction projects.

Functional Essence   Instructional plans should have as their functional essence the selection of lumber by size and grade and amount for specified work assignments. Instructional experiences should concentrate on presenting the individual with various work orders involving the selection of the lumber needed for the task.

5. Selects appropriate nail, screw, and fastener sizes for construction projects.

Functional Essence   Instructional plans should have as their functional essence the selection of nails, screws, and fasteners for fastening tasks in construction projects. Instructional experiences should concentrate on presenting the individual with various work orders involving the selection of the appropriate fastener in its appropriate size.

6. Counts out necessary hardware for a specific job.

Functional Essence   Instructional plans should have as their functional essence the development of counting skills as required by specific jobs. Instructional activities should provide the individual with experiences in counting out different types of hardware. Sample work plans and orders should be used to give the individual experiences with different amounts.

7. Schedules maintenance activities.

Functional Essence   Instructional plans should have as their functional essence the observance of maintenance schedules. Instructional activities should require the consideration of time and use factors in developing maintenance schedules.

8. Mixes concrete and mortar according to directions.

Functional Essence   Instructional plans should have as their functional essence the following of directions for mixing concrete and mortar. Special attention should be paid to various combinations of ingredients as they might be used on construction tasks.

9. Places studs according to a master stud layout plan.

Functional Essence   Instructional plans should have as their functional essence the accurate placement of studs according to the space and position specifications on a master stud layout plan. Various plans should be presented to provide the individual with a wide range of experiences.

SELECTING LUMBER

Air-dried (AD)

Indicates that the lumber has been dried in the open for a required period of time.

Board foot (bd.ft.)

Is the unit of measurement by which most yard and cabinet lumber is sold. A piece of lumber which measures 1 inch thick, 12 inches wide, and 12 inches long is defined as a board foot.

Clear (clr.)

Means that the material is clear of knots, stains, blemishes, and other unsound features.

Common (comm.)

Along with select, is one of the grades of softwood. Common grade is a general utility type of lumber and is graded further into grades No. 1 to No. 5, with No. 1 common being better than No. 5 common.

First and Seconds (FAS)

Is a combined term indicating the highest grade of hardwood. It is graded further into No. 1 common and No. 2 common.

Softwood (sftwd.)

Is used to indicate softwood such as pine, fir, and spruce.

Hardwood (hdwd.)

Is used to indicated such lumber as maple, birch, oak, etc.

Kiln-dried (KD)

Means that the lumber has been dried under controlled conditions in a kiln.

Random lengths (r.l.)

Is a term often used in ordering hardwood.

Random Widths (r.w.)

Is often used in ordering hardwood.

Rough (rgh.)

Indicates that the lumber has not been planed.

Surfaced two sides (S2S)

Means that the surfaces are planed and that the edges are rough.

Surfaced four sides (S4S)

Indicates that all four sides of the board have been surfaced.

Select (sel.)

Is one of the terms used in grading softwood. Select is the highest quality of softwood and is subgraded into A, B, C, and D, with A being the highest grade.

SPECIES	COLOR OF HEARTWOOD	TYPE OF FIGURE		EASE OF WORKING HANDTOOLS	GRAIN	STRENGTH	HARDNESS	WEIGHT
		PLAIN-SAWED	QUARTER-SAWED					
Ash	grayish brown	conspicuous growth ring	distinct growth ring	difficult	open	medium	medium	medium
Birch	reddish brown	faint growth ring	wavy	difficult	close	strong	hard	heavy
Cedar	brown to red	faint growth ring	streaked	medium	close	medium	medium	light
Cherry	reddish brown	faint growth ring	burl	difficult	close	strong	hard	medium
Chestnut....	grayish brown	conspicuous growth ring	distinct growth ring	easy	open	medium	medium	light
Cypress	yellowish brown	conspicuous growth ring	distinct growth ring	medium	close	medium	soft	light
Elm	grayish brown	distinct growth ring	faint growth ring	difficult	open	strong	hard	medium
Gum, red	reddish brown	faint growth ring	distinct	medium	close	medium	medium	medium
Hickory	pale brown	distinct growth ring	faint	difficult	open	strong	hard	heavy
Magnolia ...	yellowish brown	faint growth ring	none	medium	close	strong	medium	medium
Mahogany ..	reddish brown	faint growth ring	faint growth ring	medium	open	strong	medium	medium
Maple	light brown	faint growth ring	curly and wavy	medium	close	strong	hard	heavy
Oak	grayish brown	conspicuous growth ring	pronounced flake grain	difficult	open	strong	hard	heavy
Pine, white ..	light brown	faint growth ring	none	easy	close	medium	soft	light
Pine, yellow .	reddish brown	conspicuous growth ring	distinct growth ring	difficult	close	strong	medium	medium
Poplar, yellow	yellowish brown	faint growth ring	none	easy	close	medium	soft	light
Redwood ...	deep reddish brown	distinct growth ring	faint growth ring	medium	close	weak	soft	light
Walnut	chocolate brown	distinct growth ring	distinct wavy, curly crotch	medium	open	strong	hard	medium

Figure 59.   Charts for selecting lumber.

SCREW SIZES AND DRILL SIZES FOR DRILLING SHANK HOLES AND PILOT HOLES

Screw Gauge		Shank Clearance Hole		Pilot Hole for Hard Wood			Pilot Hole for Soft Wood			Flat- and Oval-head Diameters Nearest Fraction	No. of Auger Bit to Counterbore for Head
Size	Decimal Dimension	Drill No. or Letter	Nearest Fraction	Hole Size	Nearest Fraction	Nearest Drill No.	Hole Size	Nearest Fraction	Nearest Drill No.		
2	.086"	42	3/32"	.052"	3/64"+	55	.035"	1/32"+	65	11/64"	3
3	.099"	37	7/64"−	.063"	1/16"+	52	.042"	3/64"−	58	13/64"	4
4	.112"	32	7/64"+	.070"	5/64"−	50	.050"	3/64"+	55	7/32"	4
5	.125"	30	1/8"+	.082"	5/64"+	45	.057"	1/16"−	53	1/4"	4
6	.138"	27	9/64"+	.093"	3/32"	42	.062"	1/16"	52	9/32"	5
7	.151"	22	5/32"	.106"	7/64"−	36	.066"	1/16"+	51	19/64"	5
8	.164"	18	11/64"−	.116"	7/64"+	32	.076"	5/64"−	48	21/64"	6
9	.177"	14	3/16"−	.128"	1/8"+	30	.082"	5/64"+	45	23/64"	6
10	.190"	10	3/16"+	.140"	9/64"	28	.088"	3/32"−	43	3/8"	6
12	.216"	2	7/32"+	.152"	5/32"−	24	.102"	7/64"−	38	7/16"	7
14	.242"	D	1/4"−	.166"	11/64"−	19	.116"	7/64"+	32	31/64"	8
16	.268"	I	17/64"+	.189"	3/16"+	12	.132"	1/8"+	29	17/32"	9
18	.294"	N	5/16"−	.209"	13/64"+	4	.145"	9/64"+	26	19/32"	10

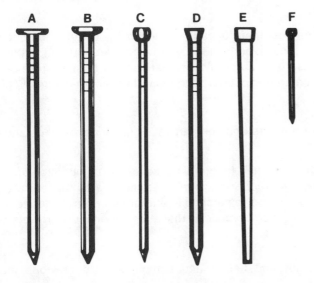

SIZE (PENNY)	LENGTH (INCHES)
2	1
3	1 1/4
4	1 1/2
5	1 3/4
6	2
7	2 1/4
8	2 1/2
10	3
12	3 1/4
16	3 1/2
20	4

Types of Nails. A—Box nail; B—Common nail;
C—Finishing nail; D—Casing nail;
E—Cut nail; F—Wire brad.

Figure 60.   Charts for selecting nails and screws.

Health Occupations

The individual:

1. Counts hospital linens and other supplies needed for daily use.

Functional Essence   Instructional plans should have as their functional essence the development of counting skills in the collection of needed linen and other hospital supplies as required by work orders. Instructional experiences should feature various work orders requiring differing amounts and types of linen and other supplies to be counted out.

2. Measures amount of liquid consumed during a day or specific period of time.

Functional Essence   Instructional plans should have as their functional essence the measurement of liquids consumed by a patient during a specified time. Various measures must be taken, including size of glasses and cups and quantities of liquid in varying sizes of containers. Instructional activities should include totaling amounts of beverage consumed and subtracting any amounts of liquid remaining in containers. Attention must also be directed toward using watches and clocks to measure the passage of time.

3. Takes temperatures of patients and compares it to previous readings and to normal rates.

Functional Essence   Instructional plans should have as their functional essence the comparison of consecutive temperature readings. Instructional experiences should also feature the reporting of significant variations to persons in authority. Comparisons to normal temperature should also be made so that alarming or unusual readings will be reported immediately.

4. Takes pulses of patients and compares them to previous readings and to normal rates.

Functional Essence   Instructional plans should have as their functional essence the comparison of consecutive pulse rates. Instructional experiences should also feature the reporting of significant variations to persons in authority. Comparisons to normal pulse rates should also be made so that alarming or unusual rates will be reported immediately.

5. Takes blood pressure of patients and compares it to previous readings and to normal levels.

Functional Essence   Instructional plans should have as their functional essence the comparison of consecutive blood pressure levels. Instructional experiences should also concentrate on the reporting of significant variations to persons in authority. Comparisons to normal blood pressure levels should also be made so that alarming or unusual levels will be reported immediately.

6. Measures patient's weight and height and compares it to previous measurements.

Functional Essence   Instructional plans should have as their functional essence the comparison of patient's weight and height with previous measurements. Unusual or rapid gain or loss of weight should be reported immediately. Instructional activities should involve the frequent use of scales and measuring devices on a variety of people.

The individual:
1. Determines size of copy required for printing.

Functional Essence   Instructional plans should have as their functional essence the selection of size of copy before setting up for printing. Once copy size is selected, a proof print should be made of the material followed by a printing run.

2. Binds pads of paper according to size and number of sheets.

Functional Essence   Instructional plans should have as their functional essence the selection of pads of paper by size as a preliminary to counting out a specified number of pads for binding. Instructional activities should include the use of various sizes of pads, different types of binding, and differing quantities in each pack.

3. Cuts paper according to specifications.

Functional Essence   Instructional plans should have as their functional essence the setting of size measures on a paper cutter to cut paper according to prescribed work orders. Instructional activities should involve setting the measures for different paper sizes as requested in work orders. Care must be taken in working with a sharp-edged instrument when determining the amount of paper to be cut.

4. Operates darkroom equipment according to directions.

Functional Essence   Instructional plans should have as their functional essence the operation of the following darkroom equipment:
    a. printer and/or enlarger;
    b. copy camera; and
    c. timer.
In all activities, emphasis should be placed on various measurements and the calculations involved in modifying settings as required by the type of photographic task.

5. Uses the printer's measuring system while setting type.

Functional Essence   Instructional plans should have as their functional essence the use of the printer's measuring system to set type. Instructional activities should include experiences with the different styles and sizes of type.

6. Determines correct settings on light meters during picture taking.

Functional Essence   Instructional plans should have as their functional essence the selection of settings of cameras based on light meter readings and information in instruction brochures and pamphlets. Instructional activities should include different settings on the camera using different film and under diverse light conditions. Cameras with built-in light meters and accompanying flash systems should also be included in this instructional experience.

7. Uses drafting equipment while preparing drawings.

Functional Essence   Instructional plans should have as their functional essence the use of drafting equipment in the preparation of drawings. These tools should include:
    a. scale;
    b. divider;

    c. compass;
    d. T-square; and
    e. templates.

Food Preparation and Service

The individual:
1. Inventories food, supplies, and utensils needed for serving meals.

Functional Essence   Instructional plans should have as their functional essence the development of tallying and computing skills in conducting inventories.

2. Weighs and measures ingredients for cooking.

Functional Essence   Instructional plans should have as their functional essence the use of food scales, measuring cups, and measuring spoons. Instructional activities should feature a variety of recipes.

3. Prepares beverages according to measurements on labels.

Functional Essence   Instructional plans should have as their functional essence the use of measuring cups and spoons in preparing beverages. Instructional activities should include a variety of recipes and the making of beverages from frozen concentrates, powders, syrups, etc. Use of special measuring cups often contained in beverage powders should also be included in the instructional experience.

4. Portions pies and desserts to serve at meals.

Functional Essence   Instructional plans should have as their functional essence the portioning of pies and other desserts in fractional parts. Instructional activities should involve various foods to be apportioned for different numbers of servings. Various sizes should be used in instructional programming.

5. Operates a cash register.

Functional Essence   Instructional plans should have as their functional essence the matching of numbers on bills and food items to keys on cash registers. Instructional activities should concentrate on the issuing of change whether or not the amount of change is recorded on the cash register. Different totals and different amounts of money paid by the customer should be used in simulations and actual transactions.

6. Prepares checks for meals ordered.

Functional Essence   Instructional plans should have as their functional essence the preparation of checks by copying numbers on menus, totaling costs, and computing taxes as appropriate. Instructional activities should involve different practice menus and different simulated meal orders. If it is not confusing to the individual, refer to different tax rates found in different cities and states.

Manufacturing

The individual:
1. Uses measuring rules and related tools, including micrometers and calipers.

Functional Essence   Instructional plans should have as their functional essence the development of measuring skills as related to the use of rules, micrometers, and calipers. Instructional experiences should be provided in measuring the following:

    a.   thickness;
    b.   depth;
    c.   breadth;
    d.   circumference; and
    e.   length.

These measurements are made to decide whether parts need to be replaced because of wear or incompatibility.

2.   Selects and uses layout tools.

Functional Essence   Instructional plans should have as their functional essence the use of various layout tools in developing plans or specifications. Point out that layout tools are specially designed for preciseness and need to be handled very carefully.

3.   Follows and uses readings on gauges.

Functional Essence   Instructional plans should have as their functional essence the use of readings on gauges to make adjustments, e.g., adding air to a tire to bring it up to a desired level of air pressure. In each case, the emphasis should be placed on the mathematical computations needed to make adjustments to desired levels of hardness, depth, thickness, etc. levels.

4.   Uses vernier measuring tools.

Functional Essence   Instructional plans should have as their functional essence the use of vernier measuring tools to measure thickness of machine parts, and breadth of openings. Throughout, the emphasis must be on using the readings to make decisions on specified tolerance levels.

5.   Operates machinery requiring depth or thickness adjustments.

Functional Essence   Instructional plans should have as their functional essence the setting of machinery requiring depth or thickness adjustments based on mathematical calculations. Instructional activities should provide experiences with such machinery as:

    a.   a shaper;
    b.   a jointer;
    c.   a milling machine;
    d.   a table saw;
    e.   a radial arm saw;
    f.   a drill press; and
    g.   a band saw.

Point out that there are often fellow workers called set-up persons who will set the machinery up and all the individual has to do is operate it.

6.   Lubricates machinery and equipment according to a time schedule.

Functional Essence   Instructional plans should have as their functional essence the reading of service manuals, factory specifications, and instructional booklets to determine maintenance and lubrications schedules. The individual then must observe a specified passage of time or numbers on machinery gauges that record revolutions or hours of use in planning for maintenance and lubrication.

7.   Cuts stock with hand and power tools according to blueprints and plans.

Functional Essence   Instructional plans should have as their functional essence the reading of dimensions, angles, and radii from blueprints and plans and the subsequent calculation of settings for cutting stock. Instructional activities should include experiences with:

    a. hand tools (rip and crosscut saws, coping saws, hack saws) and

    b. power tools (shaper, milling machine, table saw, radial arm saw, lathe, drill press, etc.).

Include experiences designed to choose different tools for different stock.

8.   Determines linear, square or cubic amount of materials needed for a given project.

Functional Essence   Instructional plans should have as their functional essence the purchasing of supplies and materials in the most economical dimensions for the specified purposes, thus minimizing waste. Instructional activities must focus on the dimensions involved in a specific task, e.g., purchasing woods for studs and rafters (linear), purchasing flooring and walling materials (square), and purchasing cement for a foundation (cubic). Be sure to point out that mixtures such as cement and mortar involve decisions about proportions of other substances, e.g., sand and gravel, thus influencing amount of cubic yards of cement purchased. Note the cement that is not ready-mix comes in bags measured by weight. The individual must then convert pounds into cubic yards based upon the various proportions in mixtures.

Clothing and Textiles

The individual:

1.   Measures and adjusts cuffs.

Functional Essence   Instructional plans should have as their functional essence the measuring and adjusting of cuffs to style, customer measurements, and customer preferences.

2.   Measures and cuts fabric.

Functional Essence   Instructional plans should have as their functional essence the measuring and cutting of fabrics as specified in patterns and work orders. Instructional activities should include a variety of measurements introducing and practicing whole numbers and fractional parts.

3.   Receives and invoices garments.

Functional Essence   Instructional plans should have as their functional essence the counting of garments received and their invoicing by style number, size, and color combinations.

4.   Assembles articles and garments for packaging.

Functional Essence   Instructional plans should have as their functional essence the assemblying and counting of articles by style number, size, and color combinations for packaging.

5.   Shortens or lengthens skirts, dresses, and coats.

Functional Essence   Instructional plans should have as their functional essence the shortening or lengthening of skirts, dresses, and coats according to work orders. Provide the individual with a variety of different measurements.

6.   Performs waistline, hipline, and bustline alterations.

Functional Essence   Instructional plans should have as their functional essence the altering of clothes according to work orders. Provide the individual with a variety of different measurements and work with diverse fabrics.

**Automotive and
Power Service**

The individual:

1. Measures worn or defective parts to see if a replacement is needed.

Functional Essence   Instructional plans should have as their functional essence the use of automotive measuring tools to see if a part needs to be replaced or is incompatible. Parts of engines and motors should be measured as part of this instructional experience.

2. Adjusts and uses a torque wrench.

Functional Essence   Instructional plans should have as their functional essence the reading of manuals to determine foot/lb or centimeter/kilogram of rotary force before using a torque wrench to replace spark plugs, bolts, and nuts. Instructional activities should emphasize the use of the measuring arc or gauge on the torque wrench to monitor force. Point out that there are torque wrenches that can be automatically set and provide the individual with experience in pre-setting this model.

3. Measures parts with a micrometer to see if replacement is needed.

Functional Essence   Instructional plans should have as their functional essence the measuring of thickness and irregularity in shape to determine whether parts need to be replaced, e.g., thickness of piston rings and shape of cylinders. As part of instructional experiences, review repair manuals for range of acceptable readings.

4. Maintains and services lubrication systems according to a specified schedule.

Functional Essence   Instructional plans should have as their functional essence the reading of service manuals to ascertain recommended maintenance of lubrication system schedules. Instructional activities should provide the individual with opportunities to decide on the time when lubrication should be carried out. Simulated and real situations should be employed when feasible.

5. Estimates amount of money needed for damage repairs.

Functional Essence   Instructional plans should have as their functional essence the use of up-to-date parts catalogs, service manuals, and company booklets and instructions as a means of estimating cost of repairs. Instructional activities must involve the location of prices, the computation of total cost including cost of labor, and verification of the estimate by a supervisor whenever appropriate. Provide the individual with experiences with various brand, year, and model information.

6. Measures refrigerant temperature and quantity to see if adjustment or replacement is needed.

Functional Essence   Instructional plans should have as their functional essence the development of skill in measuring refrigerant temperature and quantity. Provide the individual with instructional experiences in which replacement is needed and in which adjustments are necessary. Review replacement schedules that are independent of quantity on hand but rather reflect the need for fresh, chemically sound refrigerant.

The individual:

1. Operates various types of electronic calculators for business purposes.

Functional Essence Instructional plans should have as their functional essence the skillful use of the electronic calculator to carry out mathematical operations as required, e.g., the totaling of payroll deductions to arrive at the face amount of an employee's paycheck. Instructional activities should be provided involving all the operations and their combinations with whole and decimal numbers.

2. Operates a photographic duplicating machine and produces a specified number of papers and/or documents.

Functional Essence Instructional plans should have as their functional essence the setting of the dial or dials on a photographic duplicating machine to the desired number of copies. Instructional activities should also stress that the individual must examine the copy and verify by counting that he has obtained the requested number of papers or documents.

3. Operates a hand or automatically operated collating machine for specific business purposes.

Functional Essence Instructional plans should have as their functional essence the placement of papers in a specified order into a collating machine. Instructional plans should focus on the rapid, efficient, and correct collation of papers. Emphasis must be placed on inserting the papers in their proper numerical sequence.

4. Fills customer orders.

Functional Essence Instructional plans should have as their functional essence the filling of customer's orders with particular reference to the number of each item desired, the size of items, and the weight of items. Provide the individual with simulated orders that he must fill. Vary the items requested, the quantity, size, and weight to allow for maximum opportunity to practice and refine mathematical skills.

5. Prepares purchasing documents according to specified number or size.

Functional Essence Instructional plans should have as their functional essence the preparation of purchasing documents to reflect the items desired and their quantity, size, and weight as appropriate. Instructional activities should include the use of typical purchasing forms and cover the computation of sub-totals as well as the grand total.

6. Computes sales and billings for accounts receivable.

Functional Essence Instructional plans should have as their functional essence the computing of sales and billings for entry into accounts receivable. Instructional experiences should include various mathematical operations:
    a. multiplying to find the price of multiple items from the price for one;
    b. adding to obtain totals;
    c. subtracting discounts, sales percentages, and deposits; and
    d. dividing to find the price of one item when the price is given for multiple items.

7. Operates a postage meter.

Functional Essence   Instructional plans should have as their functional essence the weighing of letters or parcels for shipping and the determination of cost by reference to the rate chart. Instructional activities should deal with various weight letters and packages, various types of delivery, and varying destinations, i.e., where there is a different rate schedule.

8. Receives and checks payments in over-the-counter sales.

Functional Essence   Instructional plans should have as their functional essence the development of currency and coin-counting skills and the making of change in over-the-counter sales. Instructional activities should include a variety of amounts owed and the various combinations of currency and coins to ensure that the individual has sufficient experience and practice.

9. Distributes petty cash funds.

Functional Essence   Instructional plans should have as their functional essence the development of those skills involved in keeping a petty cash ledger. These skills include:
   a. verification of amount spent (including collection of receipts and determination of legitimacy of expenditure);
   b. counting out of funds for reimbursement;
   c. counting of change as appropriate;
   d. subtraction of cash distribution; and
   e. verification of accuracy of money left.
Activities should also emphasize keeping the money secure and replenishing it before funds are depleted.

10. Prepares a payroll.

Functional Essence   Instructional plans should have as their functional essence the development of the several skills involved in preparing a simple payroll. These skills include:
   a. confirming hours and days worked, including earned sick leave, vacation days, and paid holidays;
   b. multiplying rate of pay by hours or days as applicable;
   c. determining all deductions and totaling these; and
   d. subtracting all deductions to arrive at net pay.
Instructional activities should involve the development of a matrix or chart from which pertinent data can be transferred to the check stub.

**Agriculture and
Natural Resources**

The individual:
1. Plants annuals and transplants seedlings, potted plants, trees, and shrubs according to a schedule.

Functional Essence   Instructional plans should have as their functional essence the following of a schedule for planting perennials, annuals, and for transplanting seedlings, potted plants, trees, and shrubs. Instructional activities should emphasize the reasons for the schedule with particular reference to seasons and climate. A calendar should be referred to throughout these discussions and activities.

2. Waters plants according to a schedule.

Functional Essence   Instructional plans should have as their functional essence the development of a schedule for watering plants. Instructional activities should focus on the differing watering and sunlight needs of the various types of plants in his care. A schedule chart may be prepared by plant name as a visual reminder.

3. Selects and applies appropriate soil fertilizers according to directions.

Functional Essence   Instructional plans should have as their functional essence the scheduling of applications of soil fertilizers according to directions on packages and according to pamphlets, brochures, books, and other references that report on the nutritional needs of plants. A schedule of "feeding" should be developed that specifies time, amount, type(s) of fertilizer, and each plant under the individual's care.

4. Maintains and services hydraulic and lubricating systems according to a schedule.

Functional Essence   Instructional plans should have as their functional essence the observance of service schedules for hydraulic and lubricating systems as they appear in service manuals and factory specifications. Attention should be paid to mileage and other numerical gauges that signal the need for service.

5. Cuts and prepares pulp wood.

Functional Essence   Instructional plans should have as their functional essence the cutting of wood which is to be later used for fertilizer or pulp products. Care should be taken when using tools such as chain saws and those machines that reduce wood stock to pulp.

Distribution

The individual:
1. Uses transportation rate scales.

Functional Essence   Instructional plans should have as their functional essence the use of transportation rate scales in determining the most efficient and most economical way of shipping goods. Essential mathematical operations include the weighing of parcels and the computation of the rate by destination and carrier. Instructional activities should involve different weight parcels headed for different destinations to provide the individual with sufficient practice.

2. Counts incoming shipments.

Functional Essence   Instructional plans should have as their functional essence the development of counting skills with particular reference to the simple counting of incoming packages. Provide the individual with a variety of counting tasks.

3. Takes and maintains inventories.

Functional Essence   Instructional plans should have as their functional essence the development of tallying and computing skills involved in conducting inventories and in recording counts by type of item. Provide the individual with sufficient practice in counting. Demonstrate how to tally and count by groups.

4. Fills a stock order.

Functional Essence   Instructional plans should have as their functional essence the filling of stock orders according to size, shape, and number of items. Instructional activities should feature a variety of items, quantities, sizes, and shapes to afford the individual sufficient experience.

5. Selects size of appropriate shipping container to hold a specified number of items.

Functional Essence   Instructional plans should have as their functional essence the estimation of container size to hold a specified number of items. Practice should be given in estimating the size container for different quantities of the same item. Instructional activities should focus on collecting and packaging tasks.

6. Weighs a shipment of goods.

Functional Essence   Instructional plans should have as their functional essence the weighing of goods received when weight is a factor in cost of item or transportation charges. Experiences should be provided for different sizes and weights of packages and parcels.

7. Uses measurement and layout tools.

Functional Essence   Instructional plans should have as their functional essence the use of measurement and layout tools as an aid in developing construction and related plans. Point out that layout tools are especially designed for this and must be treated carefully.

8. Makes out sales checks.

Functional Essence   Instructional plans should have as their functional essence the making out of sales checks by copying prices from price lists, computing the costs of more than one of an item, and totaling the cost of all items less any discounts and plus any sales tax.

9. Handles cash sales transactions.

Functional Essence   Instructional plans should have as their functional essence the development of currency- and coin-counting skills and the making of change. Instructional activities should include a variety of amounts owed and the various combinations of currency and coins to ensure that the individual has sufficient experience and practice.

10. Operates a cash register.

Functional Essence   Instructional plans should have as their functional essence the development of skills in operating a cash register, namely:
   a. matching amounts on register with amounts on bills;
   b. pressing item category keys, e.g., "g" for grocery;
   c. pressing sub-total and total keys;
   d. pressing keys after counting customer's payment;
   e. reading amount of change as recorded on receipts or on the cash register itself; and
   f. counting out of change.

11. Balances cash fund and cash register.

Functional Essence   Instructional plans should have as their functional essence the verification of cash register receipts with cash funds. Instructional experiences should be provided with various amounts of cash and various totals, including ones that balance and some that are under and over.

SAMPLE INSTRUCTIONAL PLAN

Topic Area WORK-FUNCTIONAL MATHEMATICS   Date 9/23/81

Teacher L. Blodgett

Time Allotted 30-40 minutes

Individual(s) or Group Members Involved:
L. Smithson, K. Castle,
L. Swan, A. Berger, M. Bourne

Special Notes or Precautions Be sure to remind the individual to report any discrepancies in an actual check to the appropriate individual or department.

General Objective

The individual will function as a worker as independently and skillfully as possible by performing necessary mathematical operations.

Specific Objective (10)

The individual checks the net amount of his paycheck and compares it to gross pay less deductions.

Instructional Objective

After being given four problems involving the determination of net pay, the individual will correctly add all deductions and then subtract that total from the gross pay.

Materials and Equipment

Check stubs

Motivating Activity

Tell the group that you know someone who had to call the Payroll Department because he was paid the wrong amount. Show a transparency of an incorrect pay stub. Point out the error and ask individuals to verify your calculations.

Instructional Procedures

1. Begin by asking individuals to verify the calculations on several different pay stubs.
2. Use an individual's actual pay stubs for computation purposes. Review the processes of addition and subtraction and the proper use of paper and pencil to ensure accuracy.
3. Give each individual four problems to solve involving the determination of net pay.

Individualized Reinforcement and Reinforcement Schedules

Praise the individual for correct responses.

Collect the papers to check on the accuracy of the individual's computations. Record the individual's responses on the "Work: Functional Mathematics Checklist."

Follow-Up Activity/Objective

If the individual achieves the instructional objective, proceed to Specific Objective #11, "The individual fills out deposit slips correctly when depositing checks."

Instructional Resources

Blank paychecks and stubs from local businesses
Employee information bulletins and pamphlets

Observations and Comments:

chapter 7
LEISURE EXPERIENCES

Traditionally, leisure experiences have been viewed as sports related, competitive activities that are secondary to more traditional curricular areas. When programs did emphasize education for leisure, they, typically, were provided by parks and recreation agencies or by specialists working in the areas of recreation and physical education. Methodology and approaches to teaching the area of leisure have either been narrowly defined or absent from educational programs. In part, this phenomenon can be attributed to the attitude held by professionals and many parents that leisure activities are of secondary importance in planning programs of instruction.

Leisure experiences are a positive and valuable resource to people as they function on a daily basis in society. Leisure experiences facilitate learning, adapting, and adjusting during non-work hours; combat negative stress; develop physical fitness; and foster relaxation.

Leisure in a comprehensive educational context offers an innovative channel that will:

1. allow an individual to know himself in relation to others;
2. enhance the quality of his life;
3. fulfill his specific needs, capabilities, and values by selecting meaningful experiences; and
4. enable an individual to evaluate his use of time and behaviors in simple to complex situations.

This section addresses the importance of leisure experiences for individuals with learning problems. It discusses the need for reading, writing, and mathematics in the leisure domains of:

playing games;
sports and physical fitness;
camping and outdoor activities;
nature study;
hobby activities;
craft activities;
art activities; and
entertainment and cultural activities.

Throughout this section, the emphasis is on enjoyment and fitness rather than on winning and competing with others. The past emphasis on leisure experiences as skill dominated must change. Leisure is a state of mind that offers all individuals the opportunity to experience new and creative avenues for fulfilling their lives.

For most people, social encounters are primarily a direct result of participating in leisure experiences. Because of this, the integration of leisure experiences in instructional programs is essential to preparing individuals for living a good and enriching life.

Readers may wish to consult "Readings and Resources" at the end of this book for relevant information in programming for adolescents and adults as participants in leisure experiences.

GENERAL OBJECTIVES

READING   The individual will function in leisure experiences as independently and skillfully as possible by identifying words and other symbols.

WRITING   The individual will function in leisure experiences as independently and skillfully as possible by performing diverse written tasks.

MATHEMATICS   The individual will function in leisure experiences as independently and skillfully as possible by performing necessary mathematical operations.

FUNCTIONAL READING / INSTRUCTIONAL OBJECTIVES

GENERAL OBJECTIVE: The individual will function in leisure experiences as independently and skillfully as possible by identifying words and other symbols.

NOTE: In all games, sports, and other activities requiring strength, endurance, and agility, attention must be given to any physical limitations of the individual. It is suggested that the emphasis throughout be on enjoyment and fitness rather than on winning and competing with others.

PLAY AND GAMES

The individual:
1. Follows the diagrams and instruction booklets for playing and scoring high activity games and plays these games during leisure-time pursuits.

Functional Essence   Instructional plans should have as their functional essence the development of those skills necessary to follow the diagrammatic and written instructions found in instructional booklets in such games as:
   a.   Dodgeball;
   b.   Tetherball;
   c.   Four Square;
   d.   Greek Dodge;
   e.   Racing Games;
   f.   Keep Away; and
   g.   Elimination.

Experiences should be provided so that the individual will determine the procedures and rules for each of these games with as little assistance as possible. The emphasis throughout must be on encouraging the individual to choose one or more of these games for leisure activities. Emphasize the physical and mental benefits of high activity games.

2. Follows the diagrams and instruction booklets for playing and scoring low activity games and plays these games during leisure-time pursuits.

Functional Essence   Instructional plans should have as their functional essence the development of those skills necessary to follow the diagrammatic and written instructions found in instructional booklets in such games as:
   a.   Croquet;
   b.   Miniature Golf;
   c.   Frisbee;
   d.   Jumping Rope Games;
   e.   Hopscotch; and
   f.   Musical Chairs.

Experiences should be provided so that the individual will determine the procedures and rules for each of these games with as little assistance as possible. The emphasis throughout must be on encouraging the individual to choose one or more of these games for leisure activities.

3. Follows the diagrams for playing and scoring target games and plays these games during leisure-time pursuits.

Functional Essence   Instructional plans should have as their functional essence the development of those skills necessary to follow the diagrammatic and written instructions found in instructional booklets in such games as:

a.	Ring Toss;	d.	Tiddly Winks;
b.	Darts;	e.	Jarts; and
c.	Marbles;	f.	Toss-A-Dart.

Experiences should be provided so that the individual will determine the procedures and rules for each of these games with as little assistance as possible. The emphasis throughout must be on encouraging the individual to choose one or more of these games for leisure activities.

4. Follows the diagrams and instruction booklets for playing balance games and plays these games during leisure-time pursuits.

Functional Essence   Instructional plans should have as their functional essence the development of those skills necessary to follow the diagrammatic and written instructions found in instructional booklets in such games as:

a.	Pick-Up-Sticks;	e.	Tip-It;
b.	Bash;	f.	Operation;
c.	Dominoes;	g.	Jack Straws; and
d.	Twister;	h.	Blockhead.

Experiences should be provided so that the individual will determine the procedures and rules for each of these games with as little assistance as possible. The emphasis throughout must be on encouraging the individual to choose one or more of these games for leisure activities.

5. Follows the diagrams and instruction booklets for playing and scoring table games and plays these games during leisure-time pursuits.

Functional Essence   Instructional plans should have as their functional essence the development of those skills necessary to follow the diagrammatic and written instructions found in instructional booklets in such games as:

a.	Ping Pong;	e.	Table Hockey;
b.	Pool;	f.	Air Hockey; and
c.	Foos Ball;	g.	Billiards.
d.	Shuffle Board;		

Experiences should be provided so that the individual will determine the procedures and rules for each of these games with as little assistance as possible. The emphasis throughout must be on encouraging the individual to choose one or more of these games for leisure activities.

6. Follows the rules in the instruction booklets for playing and scoring card games and plays these games during leisure-time pursuits.

Functional Essence   Instructional plans should have as their functional essence the development of those skills necessary to follow the diagrammatic and written instructions found in instructional booklets in such games as:

a. Rummy;
b. Solitaire;
c. Poker;
d. Casino;
e. Pinochle;
f. Canasta;
g. Concentration;
h. Crazy Eights, Jacks, or Sevens;
i. Cribbage;
j. Fan Tan;
k. Go Fish;
l. Hearts;
m. I Doubt It;
n. Russian Bank;
o. Spite and Malice;
p. Black Jack (Twenty-One); and
q. Mille Bornes.

Experiences should be provided so that the individual will determine the procedures and rules for each of these games with as little assistance as possible. The emphasis throughout must be on encouraging the individual to choose one or more of these games for leisure activities.

7. Follows the diagrams and instruction booklets for playing games of chance and plays these games during leisure-time pursuits.

Functional Essence   Instructional plans should have as their functional essence the development of those skills necessary to follow the diagrammatic and written instructions found in instructional booklets in such games as:

a. Bingo;
b. Lotto;
c. Dice;
d. Yahtzee;
e. Double Yahtzee;
f. Roulette; and
g. Easy Money.

Experiences should be provided so that the individual will determine the procedures and rules for each of these games with as little assistance as possible. The emphasis throughout must be on encouraging the individual to choose one or more of these games for leisure activities.

8. Follows the rules found in instruction booklets for strategy games and plays these games during leisure-time pursuits.

Functional Essence   Instructional plans should have as their functional essence the development of those skills necessary to follow the diagrammatic and written instructions found in instructional booklets in such games as:

a. Checkers;
b. Chinese Checkers;
c. Sorry;
d. Parcheesi;
e. Rummy-Q;
f. Trouble;
g. Backgammon;
h. Chess;
i. Stratego;
j. Battleship;
k. Brainwaves;
l. Monopoly;
m. Whosit?;
n. Scrabble; and
o. Master Mind.

Experiences should be provided so that the individual will determine the procedures and rules for each of these games with as little assistance as possible. The emphasis throughout must be on encouraging the individual to choose one or more of these games for leisure activities.

9. Follows the rules found in instruction booklets for real-life games and plays these games during leisure-time pursuits.

Functional Essence   Instructional plans should have as their functional essence the development of those skills necessary to follow the diagrammatic and written instructions found in instructional booklets in such games as:

 a. Monopoly;
 b. Game of Life;
 c. Easy Money;
 d. Careers; and
 e. Pay Day.

Experiences should be provided so that the individual will determine the procedures and rules for each of these games with as little assistance as possible. The emphasis throughout must be on encouraging the individual to choose one or more of these games for leisure activities.

10. Follows the rules found in instruction booklets for knowledge and word games and plays these games during leisure-time pursuits.

Functional Essence Instructional plans should have as their functional essence the development of those skills necessary to follow the diagrammatic and written instructions found in instructional booklets in such games as:

a.	Twenty Questions;	g.	Game of the States;
b.	Concentration;	h.	Spill and Spell;
c.	Password;	i.	Read Around;
d.	Scrabble;	j.	Got A Minute;
e.	Word Squares;	k.	Alphabet Game; and
f.	Categories (Guggenheim);	l.	Scoring Anagrams.

Experiences should be provided so that the individual will determine the procedures and rules for each of these games with as little assistance as possible. The emphasis throughout must be on encouraging the individual to choose one or more of these games for leisure activities.

11. Identifies the cards in a standard deck of cards.

Functional Essence Instructional plans should have as their functional essence the identification of the cards in a standard deck of cards by suit and face value. Instructional activities should involve the identification of the four symbols that designate suit and the identification of numerals, letters, and pictures that signal face value. Experiences should also be provided that assist the individual in placing the cards within suits in typical rank order, i.e., 2–10, J, Q, K, and A.

12. Plays chance, strategy, real-life, and knowledge and word games that require the individual to determine moves and other actions from words printed on cards and boards.

Functional Essence Instructional plans should have as their functional essence the development of skills involved in determining the written information on game cards and boards and then following through on their directions. Game boards and game cards should be collected from the diverse games to which the individual has been and is likely to be exposed. Use these written materials for functional reading activities.

SPORTS AND PHYSICAL FITNESS

The individual:
1. Follows the written operating procedures and diagrams for operating bicycles and rides for pleasure.

Functional Essence Instructional plans should have as their functional essence the development of those skills necessary to follow the diagrammatic and written instructions for operating a bicycle. Instructional activities should emphasize bicycle safety, maintenance, and traffic regulations. Emphasis should also be placed on the physical and mental benefits of bicycle riding. Whenever possible, simple maintenance procedures should be reviewed and the individual assisted in following them. Bicycle trips should be planned with experiences provided in different locations (e.g., bicycle paths and routes, rural routes, and city streets).

2. Follows the written safety directions for skating activities (Roller and Skateboard) and participates in them either individually, with friends, or as part of a skating team.

Functional Essence

Instructional plans should have as their functional essence the development of those skills necessary to follow the safety directions for:
    a. roller skating;
    b. ice skating; and
    c. skateboarding.

Experiences should be provided so that the individual will determine the safety rules for these activities with as little assistance as possible. The emphasis throughout must be on safety and on encouraging the individual to choose one or more of these activities for leisure-time enjoyment. Emphasize the physical and mental benefits.

3. Follows the diagrams and instruction booklets for participating in water sports and engages in these activities during leisure-time pursuits.

Functional Essence

Instructional plans should have as their functional essence the development of those skills necessary to follow the diagrammatic and written instructions found in instructional booklets for such sports as:
    a. swimming;
    b. diving;
    c. snorkeling; and
    d. water polo.

Experiences should be provided so that the individual will determine the procedures and rules for these sports with as little help as possible. The emphasis throughout must be on safety and on encouraging the individual to choose one or more of these sports for leisure activities. Emphasize the physical and mental benefits of water sports.

4. Follows the diagrams and instruction booklets for participating in boating activities and engages in them during leisure-time pursuits.

Functional Essence

Instructional plans should have as their functional essence the development of those skills necessary to follow the diagrammatic and written instructions found in instructional booklets for such sports as:
    a. rowing;
    b. canoeing;
    c. motoring; and
    d. sailing.

Experiences should be provided so that the individual will determine the procedures and rules for these sports with as little help as possible. The emphasis throughout must be on safety and on encouraging the individual to choose one or more of these sports for leisure activities. Emphasize the physical and mental benefits of boating activities.

5. Follows the diagrams and instruction booklets for participating in snow sports and engages in these activities during leisure-time pursuits.

Functional Essence Instructional plans should have as their functional essence the development of those skills necessary to follow the diagrammatic and written instructions found in instructional booklets for such sports as:
   a. skiing;
   b. sledding; and
   c. tobogganing.
Experiences should be provided so that the individual will determine the procedures and rules for these sports with as little help as possible. The emphasis throughout must be on safety and on encouraging the individual to choose one or more of these sports for leisure activities. Emphasize the physical and mental benefits of snow sports.

6. Follows the diagrams and instructions in outdoor and wilderness manuals for participating in mountain sport activities and engages in these activities during leisure-time pursuits.

Functional Essence Instructional plans should have as their functional essence the development of those skills necessary to follow the diagrammatic and written instructions found in instructional booklets for such sports as:
   a. hiking;
   b. climbing; and
   c. rappeling.
Experiences should be provided so that the individual will determine the procedures and rules for these sports with as little help as possible. The emphasis throughout must be on safety and on encouraging the individual to choose one or more of these sports for leisure activities. Emphasize the physical and mental benefits of mountain sports.

7. Follows the diagrams and instructional booklets for participating in exercise and physical fitness activities and engages in these activities as part of a fitness program and during leisure-time pursuits.

Functional Essence Instructional plans should have as their functional essence the development of those skills necessary to follow the diagrammatic and written instructions found in instructional booklets for such sports as:
   a. calisthenics;   f. weight lifting;
   b. fast walking;   g. yoga;
   c. jogging;   h. karate;
   d. tumbling;   i. rope jumping; and
   e. aerobics;   j. isometrics.
Experiences should be provided so that the individual will determine the procedures and rules for these sports with as little help as possible. The emphasis throughout must be on safety and on encouraging the individual to choose one or more of these sports for leisure activities. Emphasize the physical and mental benefits of exercise and general fitness programs.

8. Follows the diagrams and instruction booklets for participating in two-person sports and engages in these activities during leisure-time pursuits.

Functional Essence Instructional plans should have as their functional essence the development of those skills necessary to follow the diagrammatic and written instructions found in instructional booklets for such sports as:
   a. badminton;   e. squash;   i. karate;
   b. hand ball;   f. table tennis;   j. golf;
   c. racquet ball; g. boxing;   k. tennis; and
   d. tetherball;   h. judo;   l. bowling.

Experiences should be provided so that the individual will determine the procedures and rules for these sports with as little help as possible. The emphasis throughout must be on safety and on encouraging the individual to choose one or more of these sports for leisure activities. Emphasize the physical and mental benefits of two-person sports.

9. Follows the diagrams and instruction booklets for participating in team sports and engages in these activities during leisure-time pursuits.

Functional Essence   Instructional plans should have as their functional essence the development of those skills necessary to follow the diagrammatic and written instructions found in instructional booklets for such sports as:

a. baseball;	f. volley ball;
b. softball;	g. soccer;
c. basketball;	h. track and field games; and
d. football;	i. bowling.
e. kickball;	

Experiences should be provided so that the individual will determine the procedures and rules for these sports with as little help as possible. The emphasis throughout must be on safety and on encouraging the individual to choose one or more of these sports for leisure activities. Emphasize the physical and mental benefits of team sports.

CAMPING AND OUTDOOR ACTIVITIES

The individual:
1. Follows fishing rules found in outdoor or wilderness manuals.

Functional Essence   Instructional plans should have as their functional essence the development of those skills involved in locating and comprehending fishing rules as outlined in outdoor and wilderness manuals. Instructional activities should include a review of typical rules as they apply to:

a. ice fishing;
b. salt-water fishing;
c. fresh-water fishing;
d. catching crabs, lobsters, and other seafood; and
e. catching live bait.

Experiences should be provided in reading, discussing, and implementing each of these fishing activities. Emphasis throughout should be on encouraging the individual to pursue one or more of these activities as appropriate to his interests, environment, and budget.

2. Follows the directions and rules for camping as they appear in booklets and manuals.

Functional Essence   Instructional plans should have as their functional essence the development of those skills involved in locating and comprehending the directions relevant to camping and camp sites as they appear in booklets and manuals. Instructional activities should involve going on a camp-out and on an overnight camping trip. These trips should provide the individual with experience in the variety of skills required for these outdoor activities. Skills to be covered include:

a. tying knots;
b. setting and extinguishing a campfire;
c. cooking;

    d.   putting up a tent or other shelter;

    e.   moving about safely;

    f.   avoiding getting lost; and

    g.   avoiding dangerous animals and plants.

Emphasis throughout should be on encouraging the individual to pursue camping and camp-out activities as appropriate to his interests, environment, and budget.

3.   Follows the directions and rules for outdoor cooking activities as they appear in booklets and manuals.

Functional Essence   Instructional plans should have as their functional essence the development of those skills involved in locating and comprehending the directions pertinent to outdoor cooking activities as they appear in booklets and manuals. Instructional activities should involve carrying out various picnics, including backyard barbeques and clambakes. These picnics and cook-outs should provide the individual with experience in:

    a.   purchasing appropriate foods and beverages;

    b.   preparing the foods and beverages;

    c.   purchasing supplies, e.g., paper plates, cups, charcoal, napkins, and plastic utensils;

    d.   packing the supplies and food;

    e.   starting and extinguishing a fire;

    f.   cleaning up and garbage disposal; and

    g.   planning and carrying out diverse recreational activities.

All activities should be presented with an emphasis on safety and the opportunities for enjoyment through outdoor social events.

4.   Follows the directions and rules for campfire activities as they appear in outdoor manuals, magazines, and pamphlets.

Functional Essence   Instructional plans should have as their functional essence the development of those skills involved in locating and comprehending the directions and rules for campfire activities as outlined in outdoor manuals, magazines and pamphlets. Instructional activities should include:

    a.   building a fireplace;

    b.   wood gathering;

    c.   chopping wood;

    d.   building and maintaining a fire; and

    e.   extinguishing a fire.

Experiences should be provided in reading, discussing, and implementing each of these activities. Emphasis throughout should be on encouraging the individual to participate in these activities as appropriate to the individual's interests and time and budgetary constraints.

5.   Follows the schematics and diagrams for various outdoor activities.

Functional Essence   Instructional plans should have as their functional essence the development of those skills involved in locating and comprehending the schematics and diagrams for various outdoor activities, including:

    a.   operating a camp lamp;

    b.   operating a camp stove;

    c.   using utensils;

    d.   tying ropes;

    e.   using a knife;

    f.   using an axe; and

    g.   using a compass.

Emphasis should be placed on the correct and safe procedures to follow in each of the above activities. Sufficient practice should be provided until the individual is functionally independent whenever practicable.

6. Follows recipes and plans for cooking meals outdoors.

Functional Essence   Instructional plans should have as their functional essence the planning of meals and the following of recipes for outdoor meals, including:
   a. picnics and barbeques;
   b. trips to park, playground, and beachlike areas;
   c. camp-outs;
   d. overnight camping; and
   e. weekend and week-long camping.
Instructional activities should concentrate on the collection of suitable recipes for these different occasions. Menus should be planned, meals prepared, and outings taken.

NATURE STUDY

The individual:
1. Identifies characteristics of foliage, plants, and animals as described in nature books and magazines and observes scenery and wildlife.

Functional Essence   Instructional plans should have as their functional essence the development of those skills involved in identifying the characteristics of foliage, plants, and animals as described in nature books. Instructional activities should concentrate on the skilled observation of scenery and of wildlife based upon the information found in pertinent nature magazines and books. Trips should be taken to parks, arboretums, wildlife and bird sanctuaries, and botanical and zoological gardens for the purpose of identifying the foliage, plants, and animals found there. Activities should include photography and other art experiences based upon natural themes.

2. Reviews information found in outdoor magazines or books and participates in exploration activities.

Functional Essence   Instructional plans should have as their functional essence the development of those skills involved in locating and interpreting information found in magazines and books and participates in:
   a. nature walks;
   b. beach combing;
   c. bird watching;
   d. rockhounding; and
   e. cave exploring.
Instructional experiences should involve all of the above activities in the attempt to develop an interest in one or more of these nature study activities. Trips involving those activities that are feasible in the individual's immediate environment should be planned. Throughout all instructional activities, safe behaviors should be encouraged and reinforced.

3. Reviews information found in "how to" books and participates in plant-care activities.

Functional Essence   Instructional plans should have as their functional essence the development of those skills involved in locating and interpreting information found in "How to Care

For" books and:
a. raises and cares for house plants;
b. raises and cares for flowers;
c. raises and cares for a garden;
d. raises and cares for a lawn; and
e. grafts.

Instructional experiences should include all of the above activities in the attempt to develop an interest in one or more of these gardening and plant-care activities.

4. Follows the rules and directions found in pet booklets and takes care of animals.

Functional Essence   Instructional plans should have as their functional essence the development of those skills involved in locating and interpreting information found in pet booklets and takes care of:
a. fish and other aquatic pets;
b. reptiles;
c. birds;
d. cats, dogs, and other small mammals; and
e. large domestic animals, e.g., horses, cows, and goats.

Instructional activities should involve the care of all these animals in the hope of developing an interest in one or more of these pet-care activities. The complete ramifications should be thoroughly explored including cost of care and the various responsibilities involved.

HOBBY ACTIVITIES

The individual:
1. Collects pictures, autographs, and other memorabilia of athletes, movie stars, and other celebrities.

Functional Essence   Instructional plans should have as their functional essence the introduction of the idea that collections of memorabilia of celebrities can be an enjoyable and potentially profitable hobby. Instructional activities should focus upon exposing the individual to the possible types of memorabilia collections, the ways of acquiring them, and the likely cost. Specialty magazines and other sources of information on this hobby should be reviewed.

2. Reviews coin, stamp, and medal catalogs and brochures and begins a collection according to his interest.

Functional Essence   Instructional plans should have as their functional essence the introduction of the idea that collections of coins, stamps, and medals can be an enjoyable and potentially profitable hobby. Instructional activities should concentrate on exposing the individual to the several types of collections, the ways of acquiring them, methods of storing them, safety considerations, and the likely costs. Specialty magazines, catalogs, and brochures should be reviewed for price, availability, conventions, and information on new editions.

3. Reviews catalogs and specialty magazines that advertise collections and participates in their collection.

Functional Essence   Instructional plans should have as their functional essence the introduction of the idea that there are a variety of collectibles, including:
a. natural objects; d. art objects;
b. models; e. antiques; and
c. dolls; f. low-cost objects, e.g., buttons and matchbook covers.

Instructional activities should be provided in collecting all of the above by reviewing catalogs and specialty magazines and sample collections whenever they are available. Reviewed also should be methods of acquisition and possible costs.

CRAFT ACTIVITIES

The individual:

1. Locates recipes describing cooking and food crafts and prepares them.

Functional Essence

Instructional plans should have as their functional essence the locating and preparing of various foods and food crafts, including:

    a. nutritional desserts;
    b. holiday foods;
    c. drinks; and
    d. dried food.

Instructional activities should concentrate on the preparation of nutritional recipes. Emphasis should be placed on the idea that food preparation, besides being a necessary function, can be a pleasurable hobby.

2. Obtains and reviews books and pamphlets for decorating activities for his home or for gift making.

Functional Essence

Instructional plans should have as their functional essence the development of decorating skills including:

    a. floral arrangements;   f. antiquing;
    b. centerpiece making;   g. string art;
    c. holiday decorations;   h. batiking; and
    d. collages and decoupage;   i. soap making.
    e. candle making;

Instructional activities should include experiences with all of the above decorating activities in the hope of developing interest in one or more of them as possible hobbies and as a way of making household decorations and of producing personal, interesting, unusual, and less expensive gifts.

3. Follows the direction booklets and pamphlets for crafts involving fibers and fabrics and makes personal items as well as gifts for others.

Functional Essence

Instructional plans should have as their functional essence the development of skills in creating crafts involving interlacing and interlocking. Typical directions should be collected for the following crafts:

    a. macramé;
    b. quilting;
    c. braiding;
    d. crocheting;
    e. knitting; and
    f. sewing.

Experiences should be provided in each of these activities in order to develop interest and skill in one or more of these areas. Whenever practical, personal items and gifts for others should be created.

4. Reviews directions in booklets and papers that are included in model and craft kits and materials and then makes personal items as well as gifts for others.

Functional Essence

Instructional plans should have as their functional essence the development of those skills involved in following the directions in booklets and papers and then creating:

    a. models;
    b. paper crafts;
    c. leather crafts;
    d. textile crafts;
    e. wood crafts; and
    f. metal crafts.

Experiences should be provided in each of these activities to develop interest and skill in one or more of these activities. Whenever practical, personal items and gifts for others should be crafted.

ARTS ACTIVITIES

The individual:

1. Obtains and reviews brochures, pamphlets, magazines, and books on graphic art activities.

Functional Essence

Instructional plans should have as their functional essence the encouragement of the individual to engage in graphic art activities through the exploration of various art media, techniques, and styles, and then the creation of art products. Instructional activities should expose the individual to:

    a. photography (still and movie);   e. block printing;
    b. silk-screening;   f. offset printing;
    c. stenciling;   g. lithographing; and
    d. etching;   h. marbeling.

Brochures, pamphlets, specialty magazines, and graphic art books should be collected and reviewed for their suggestions relevant to various art techniques, styles, and materials. Emphasis throughout graphic art exploration should be on interesting the individual in pursuing one or more art activities during his leisure time and as a means of providing the individual with an outlet for creative expression.

2. Obtains and reviews specialty magazines and books on painting and drawing activities.

Functional Essence

Instructional plans should have as their functional essence the encouragement of the individual to engage in painting and drawing activities through the exploration of various painting media and techniques and the creation of paintings and drawings. Instructional activities should expose the individual to painting and drawing in:

    a. tempera;   e. pastels;
    b. watercolor;   f. charcoal;
    c. oil;   g. crayon; and
    d. paint (acrylic and other types);   h. pencil.

Experiences should be provided in the exploration of these various types of drawing materials and their different effects. Also, exploration should include different materials that can be painted, e.g., canvas, wood, ceramics. Books and specialty magazines should be collected and reviewed for suggestions relevant to various art and drawing techniques and styles. Emphasis should be on developing an interest in pursuing painting and drawing activities during leisure time and as a means of providing the individual with an opportunity for creative expression.

3. Obtains and reviews instructional pamphlets, specialty magazines, and books on sculpture. (*See* Sample Instructional Plan.)

Functional Essence

Instructional plans should have as their functional essence the encouragement of the individual to engage in sculpture activities through the exploration of various sculpting techniques and then the creation of art products. Instructional activities should acquaint the individual with sculpting in:

a. wood;
b. soap;
c. ceramics;
d. metal;
e. fabrics;
f. string;
g. paper;
h. junk; and
i. clay.

Pamphlets, specialty magazines, and books should be obtained and reviewed for their sculpting suggestions. Emphasis throughout should be on arousing the individual's interest in pursuing one or more sculpting techniques or media during leisure time and as a means of creative expression.

4. Obtains and reviews song sheets, album covers, and books and reviews schedules and announcements for musical events.

Functional Essence Instructional plans should have as their functional essence the encouragement of the individual to engage in musical activities during his leisure hours. Instructional activities should include experiences in music appreciation, i.e., listening to musical performances on the radio, records, television, the stage, and in concert as well as performing through singing and playing musical instruments. Song sheets, album covers, and music books should be reviewed for music of interest. Records should be examined for performers and musical contents. Radio and television schedules and announcements of stage, opera, and concert performances should be examined for performances of interest. Songs should be taught and individual, group, and choral singing should be encouraged. The emphasis throughout should be on stimulating interest in musical events and in developing skills in performance so that the individual spends part of his leisure time engaged in musical activities.

5. Obtains and reviews poetry and prose selections.

Functional Essence Instructional plans should have as their functional essence the encouragement of the individual to engage in the exploration of poetry and prose writing and the creation of poetry and prose selections during his leisure hours. Instructional activities should also feature the development of an appreciation for poetry and prose through the reading of books of quality and of interest. Collect good poetry and prose selections that are well written and deal with feelings, emotions, problems, attitudes, values, and themes of interest to all people. Good poetry and prose transcend age, social, emotional, intellectual, cultural, and other barriers.

6. Obtains and reviews books and articles on plays and play production.

Functional Essence Instructional plans should have as their functional essence the encouragement of the individual to explore and create scenes and plays during leisure-time pursuits. Instructional activities should also focus on the appreciation of drama through reading about methods and techniques of play production including costuming, make-up, lighting, set design and construction, and staging. Instructional experiences should, in addition, stimulate interest in attending:

a. pantomimes;
b. story readings;
c. community theater productions;
d. repertory productions;
e. resident company productions;
f. touring company productions;
g. summer stock shows;
h. professional productions;
i. operas; and
j. dance recitals.

The emphasis throughout should be on motivating interest in dramatic productions and in developing skills in one or more aspects of play production so that the individual spends part of his leisure time engaged in exploring, creating, and appreciating the dramatic arts.

ENTERTAINMENT AND CULTURAL ACTIVITIES

The individual:

1. Reviews television guides and radio program listings.

Functional Essence

Instructional plans should have as their functional essence the encouragement of the individual to use radio and television in a more selective manner and for a variety of listening and viewing experiences. Instructional activities should include listening to and watching:

    a. newscasts;
    b. musical programming;
    c. sports events;
    d. movies and dramas;
    e. documentaries;
    f. interviews; and
    g. specials.

Television guides and radio program listings should be reviewed for names, performers, channels or station names and numbers, and times of performance. Quality programming should be given special attention as a means of encouraging more sophisticated listening and viewing skills. Because of the passive nature of television viewing, the abuse of television by individuals, the poor level of television programming, and the manipulative nature of television advertising, abundant time must be spent on exploring this medium with the aim of:

    a. encouraging more sophistication;
    b. avoiding its overuse; and
    c. preventing viewer manipulation.

Consumer education and resistance to advertising propaganda must play an essential part in programming for this objective.

2. Reviews newspapers for places and times of programs, workshops, and other events of interest.

Functional Essence

Instructional plans should have as their functional essence the encouragement of the individual to attend programs, workshops, classes, and other special events offered in his community. Experiences should be provided as appropriate to the individual's interests, living style, personality, and economic situation in attending:

    a. art galleries and museums;
    b. science, natural history, and other special museums;
    c. music and folk festivals;
    d. libraries;
    e. city/county/state fairs;
    f. parks and playgrounds;
    g. parades;
    h. botanical and zoological gardens;
    i. spectator sports;
    j. community education classes;
    k. special courses;
    l. self-improvement workshops;
    m. meetings of civic organizations;
    n. religious services; and
    o. church- or temple-sponsored activities and events.

Emphasis throughout this program should be on exploring the range of possible public and community activities and events with the purpose of interesting the individual in participating in one or more of these activities.

3. Obtains and reviews newspapers, magazines, and the *Yellow Pages* for listings and descriptions of restaurants and their locations.

Functional Essence   Instructional plans should have as their functional essence the development of those skills involved in reviewing newspapers, magazines, entertainment brochures, and the *Yellow Pages* to select restaurants for dining out. Instructional experiences should involve the perusal of these various print media to locate restaurant listings. These listings should then be used to determine:

  a. location;
  b. type(s) of food served;
  c. days and hours of operation;
  d. credit cards honored; and
  e. reservation policy.

Whenever possible, the individual should be exposed to various types of food including ethnic varieties with the purpose of expanding dining options. Special attention should be paid to nutrition, dietary restrictions and plans, and budgetary consideration, including cost of meals and travel expenses.

4. Obtains and reviews travel brochures.

Functional Essence   Instructional plans should have as their functional essence the development of those skills involved in reviewing travel brochures with the purpose of assisting the individual in making vacation and other travel plans. Instructional activities should also include experiences designed to acquaint the individual with various sources of travel information including travel agents, associations such as the AAA, Chambers of Commerce, visitors' bureaus, tourist agencies, and public libraries. The emphasis should be on expanding the individual's travel perspective and interests and on planning trips that are within his budget and help to improve physical and mental health.

SAMPLE INSTRUCTIONAL PLAN

Topic Area LEISURE EXPERIENCES-
FUNCTIONAL READING   Date ___6/2/81___

Teacher   Mr. Grossman
                                        Individual(s) or Group Members Involved:
Time Allotted __25-30 minutes__   C. Suggars, L. Pommer, D. Mark,
                                        J. Garber, V. Leslie

Special Notes or Precautions ___None___

General Objective

The individual will function in leisure experiences as independently and skillfully as possible by identifying words and other symbols.

Specific Objective (Art Activities 3)

The individual obtains and reviews instructional pamphlets, specialty magazines, and books on sculpture.

Instructional Objective

When given a recipe for making modeling clay, the individuals will prepare modeling clay using 1/2 cup meausres. They will accurately follow the directions in their sequence as found in the recipe.

Materials and Equipment

1. Modeling clay, recipe chart   5. Flour
2. Mixing bowls   6. Salt
3. Measuring cups   7. Water
4. Mixing spoons   8. Blank cards and marking pens

Motivating Activity

Show the members of the group a clay sculpture made by one of their peers. Tell them that they can make their own sculptures, but first they must make their own modeling clay.

Instructional Procedures

1. Place the following "Modeling Clay Recipe" chart on the chalkboard.
    a. Put 1/2 cup salt into a mixing bowl.
    b. Add two 1/2 cups of flour.
    c. Add water gradually stirring until the flour and salt
        are blended.
2. Review the recipe's ingredients and steps with each individual.
3. Tell them to read and follow the recipe.
4. When the mixture is ready, tell them to make a sculpture.
5. Place the completed sculptures on a display table. Ask each
    individual to place a name card on his sculpture.

Reinforce periodically with verbal praise. Comment on the sculptures on the display table.

Assessment Strategy

Observe each person as he measures and mixes the clay. Check to see whether he uses the measuring cups correctly and proceeds in the recipe's sequence of steps. Record the individual's performance on: "Leisure Experiences: Functional Reading Checklist."

Follow-Up Activity/Objective

If the individual achieves the instructional objective, proceed to an institutional experience in which the individual uses wood to create a sculpture.

Instructional Resources

Books on sculpture
Sculpture post cards from museums
Specialty magazines

Observations and Comments:

GENERAL OBJECTIVE: The individual will function in leisure experiences as independently and skillfully as possible by performing diverse written tasks.

The individual:

1. Writes down the scores obtained in various games.

Functional Essence   Instructional plans should have as their functional essence the development of skill in writing down scores as part of participation in games and sports. Instructional activities should focus on playing games and participating in sports events that require score keeping. Collect various forms and score sheets and play the games. Demonstrate how to keep score, assist the individual in keeping score, and work with the individual until he can keep score independently in a variety of games and sports.

2. Writes and/or constructs words in knowledge and word games.

Functional Essence   Instructional plans should have as their functional essence the development of writing and word construction skills as part of participating in knowledge and word games including:

a.	Scrabble;	g.	Word Yahtzee;
b.	Hangman;	h.	Mad-Libs;
c.	Categories (Guggenheim);	i.	Sentence Cube Game;
d.	Word Squares;	j.	Crossword Cubes
e.	Life;	k.	Perquackey; and
f.	Game of the States;	l.	Anagrams.

Instructional activities should involve playing all of these games and on encouraging the individual to play these games during his leisure time.

3. Uses order forms to order sports and other recreational materials and equipment.

Functional Essence   Instructional plans should have as their functional essence the development of those writing skills involved in completing an order form. Instructional activities should include the completion of sample order forms found in catalogs, newspapers, and magazines that feature recreational materials and equipment. Particular attention should be directed toward those materials and equipment for recreational activities of particular interest to the individual. Whenever the individual wishes to actually order materials and equipment, review the order form and assist him as necessary.

4. Writes or prints labels and headings for section dividers and other category and type designations in collections and albums.

Functional Essence   Instructional plans should have as their functional essence the development of those writing skills necessary to preparing labels for albums and collections. Instructional activities should emphasize the proper storing and recording of collections. The individual's actual collections should be employed to develop systems of storage and retrieval. Help the individual in printing labels and headings that separate subcategories of material.

5. Prints or writes words and sayings on arts and crafts products.

Functional Essence   Instructional plans should have as their functional essence the development of those writing skills involved in printing or writing his name, words, and sayings on various arts and crafts products including:

 a. posters;
 b. collages;
 c. paintings;
 d. charcoals and pastels;
 e. decorations;
 f. greeting cards; and
 g. creative writings.

Instructional activities should involve making those products of interest to the individual and assisting him in adding word and phrase elements.

6. Writes greeting card verses, song lyrics, and poetry.

Functional Essence Instructional plans should have as their functional essence the development of those writing skills involved in exploring the various themes, styles, and techniques of writing simple verses, poetry, and lyrics. Instructional activities should concentrate on creating written products that bring enjoyment during the creative process and in the sharing of the written product. The individual should be encouraged to read aloud those selections he wishes to share with others. Point out that a creative work makes a special gift for a friend or relative.

7. Writes scenes and plays.

Functional Essence Instructional plans should have as their functional essence the development of those writing skills involved in exploring the various techniques, styles, and themes of writing scenes and plays. Instructional activities should focus on creating written products that bring enjoyment during the creative process and in their enactment. Creative dramatics should be engaged in as a precursor experience to creative writing. Dramatic situations should be presented with characters delineated and then the individual and his peers challenged to create the scene or scenes. Later on the creative challenge is to write it down directly or to record the material and then transcribe it. Whenever reasonable, the goal should be to put on a play for the enjoyment of the individual and his peers and, perhaps, for an invited audience.

8. Writes vignettes and simple prose selections.

Functional Essence Instructional plans should have as their functional essence the development of those writing skills involved in exploring the various elements that comprise the writing of vignettes and simple prose selections. Instructional activities should focus on creating written products that bring enjoyment during the creative process and in the sharing of the written product. The individual should be encouraged to read aloud those selections he wishes to share with others. Point out that a creative work may serve as a special gift for a relative or friend.

9. Writes away for reservations.

Functional Essence Instructional plans should have as their functional essence the development of those writing skills involved in composing a business letter requesting reservations for:

 a. a campsite;
 b. a hotel or motel room;
 c. a room at a resort;
 d. a concert, dance recital, play, or opera; and
 e. a sports event.

Instructional activities should center upon the development of a general format of a letter that contains relevant information typical of reservation requests, including days and dates, arrival times, and prices.

10. Fills out a registration or check-in form at a hotel, motel, or resort. (*See* Sample Instructional Plan.)

Functional Essence   Instructional plans should have as their functional essence the development of those writing skills invovled in completing a check-in or registration form. Instructional activities should be geared toward assisting the individual in:

    a. printing his name;
    b. printing his address;
    c. printing the name of his employer;
    d. printing the year and make of his car;
    e. printing his license plate number and the state name (car registration); and
    f. signing his name.

Sample registration forms for representative hotels, motels, and resorts should be used in practice session.

STEPHEN BENJAMIN HOTEL Cambridge Springs, Pa. 16302 Phone (814) 397-2618		
Room		Advance Deposit:
	Name:	
No. Party	Address:	Folio No.
Out/Date	City/State:	Rate:
Arrive	Firm/Company:	Bill No.: 2314
	PLEASE NOTE: 7% STATE TAX ADDED ON ROOM AND MEALS	Charges:
	_____ Guest's Signature	TOTAL

Figure 61.   Sample hotel/motel registration forms.

11. Fills out luggage identification tags.

Functional Essence Instructional plans should have as their functional essence the development of skill in completing luggage indentification tags. Instructional activities should focus on:
   a. printing his name;
   b. printing his address;
   c. printing the name of his destination; and
   d. writing his flight number.
Sample luggage tags typical of those used by transportation companies should be reviewed and filled out in practice sessions. Also, identification tags that are commonly found attached to luggage should be reviewed and completed.

12. Writes down experiences and observations in a personal diary.

Functional Essence Instructional plans should have as their functional essence the encouragement of the individual to write down experiences and observations in a personal diary. Instructional experiences should highlight the possible enjoyment that may be derived from keeping a diary. Be sure to emphasize that keeping a diary is a personal decision and that if one is kept that it should be kept in a secure place to prevent others from reading private and personal material. Demonstrate how observations and experiences written in a diary may be used to write personal letters and in creative writing.

13. Writes cards and invitation letters to friends and relatives.

Functional Essence Instructional plans should have as their functional essence the development of those writing skills necessary to fill out a card or write a friendly letter of invitation to prospective guests. Instructional activities should emphasize that parties and

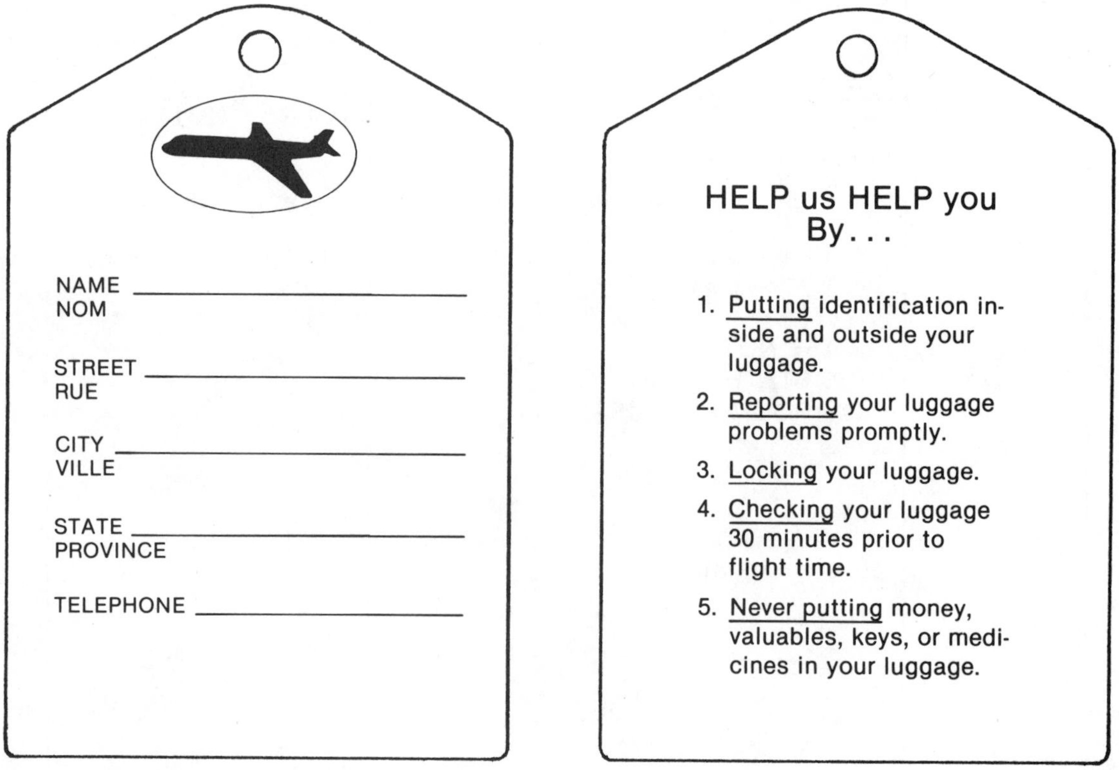

NAME _____
NOM

STREET _____
RUE

CITY _____
VILLE

STATE _____
PROVINCE

TELEPHONE _____

HELP us HELP you
By...

1. Putting identification inside and outside your luggage.

2. Reporting your luggage problems promptly.

3. Locking your luggage.

4. Checking your luggage 30 minutes prior to flight time.

5. Never putting money, valuables, keys, or medicines in your luggage.

Figure 62. Luggage identification tag.

various social gatherings such as picnics and barbecues are ways of enjoying leisure time. Point out the reciprocal nature of such events, i.e., one plans social gatherings at one's home or apartment for others who have entertained the individual in the past.

14. Writes friendly letters to friends, relatives, and pen pals.

Functional Essence Instructional plans should have as their functional essence the encouragement of the individual to pursue regular personal correspondence to friends, relatives, and pen pals. Instructional activities should assist the individual in relating interesting experiences, describing events of interest, sharing information, asking pertinent questions, and extending personal courtesies such as inquiring about the health of the individual and his family and friends. Sufficient practice should be provided until the individual is able to compose letters independently. Include practice in addressing envelopes. Be sure to point out that sending and receiving letters bring enjoyment as well as provide the individual with a means of keeping in touch with those people who are not easily communicated with by telephone or by visits.

15. Writes fan letters to celebrities.

Functional Essence Instructional plans should have as their functional essence the development of skill in writing a fan letter. In instructional activities, be sure to point out that the writing of fan letters is just one of countless ways of spending leisure time. Be careful not to encourage this activity unless the individual expresses an interest in it. If he does, assist him in writing letters that express admiration while exhibiting personal restraint and good taste. Remind the individual to keep answers and photographs received as part of a collection.

16. Writes business letters requesting information from recreation agencies.

Functional Essence Instructional plans should have as their functional essence the development of skills in writing a business letter with special reference to seeking information concerning recreational possibilities. Instructional activities should feature the development of a suitable letter format and a review of pertinent agencies that can supply information such as recreation department, park departments, and travel organizations and agents.

17. Writes down and files favored recipes.

Functional Essence Instructional plans should have as their functional essence the development of those writing skills involved in copying recipes from newspapers, magazines, books, and package labels and in writing down recipes dictated by others. Instructional experiences should focus on both of these different skills. Also, attention should be paid to developing a filing system of favorite, nutritious, and economical recipes to be used in meal planning and preparation. Include the planning of foods and beverages for parties and other social gatherings.

18. Writes down and files the procedures for arts and crafts projects.

Functional Essence Instructional plans should have as their functional essence the development of those writing skills involved in copying the procedures for carrying out arts and crafts activities found in newspapers, specialty and other magazines and books. Attention should be directed toward developing a filing system of successful, interesting, and inexpensive arts and crafts projects. Whenever an arts and crafts project is completed and the individual enjoys the process and product, encourage him to record the procedures and file it away for future use as a leisure time activity and to make objects for use in his own home or to give to others.

SAMPLE INSTRUCTIONAL PLAN

Topic Area   LEISURE EXPERIENCES-
             FUNCTIONAL WRITING   Date _____ 4/16/82 _____

Teacher _____ Ms. Erdman _____

                                  Individual(s) or Group Members Involved:
Time Allotted _____ 25-35 minutes _____   S. Smith, A. Blechman,
                                  L. Miller, M. Johnson, C. Wong

Special Notes or Precautions _____ None _____

General Objective

     The individual will function in leisure experiences as independently and skillfully as possible by performing diverse written tasks.

Specific Objective (10)

     The individual fills out a registration or check-in form at a hotel, motel, or resort.

Instructional Objective

     When given a hotel, motel, or resort check-in or registration form, the individual will provide all relevant information correctly by:
       a. printing his name;
       b. printing his address;
       c. printing the name of his employer;
       d. printing the year and make of his car;
       e. printing his license plate number and the state of registration; and
       f. signing his name.

Materials and Equipment

    1. Sample registration forms for representative hotels, motels, and resorts.
    2. Slides and post cards of representative hotels, motels, and resorts.
    3. Car registration forms (simulated)

Motivating Activity

    Show the group post cards and slides of representative hotels, motels, and resorts. Discuss their location, rates, and other pertinent factors. Explain that when someone stays at one of these places he must register. At this point, show a chart of a sample registration form.

Instructional Procedures

    1. Review the key words on the chart.
    2. Provide the members of the group with facsimiles of the chart to be individually completed. Provide individuals who do not have cars with simulated registrations.

3. Once the individuals have had sufficient practice, provide them with copies of actual forms. Each person should receive a registration form and an information packet from a different hotel, motel, or resort.
4. Ask them to fill these forms out and provide assistance as needed.

Individualized Reinforcement and Reinforcement Schedules

Praise all individuals for correctly completing activity. Add additional praise for C. Wong.

Assessment Strategy

Collect the individual's form and check to determine the accuracy of the written information he has furnished. Record the individual's performance on "Leisure Experience: Functional Writing Checklist."

Follow-Up Activity/Objective

If the individual achieves the instructional objective, proceed to Specific Objective #11, i.e., "The individual fills out luggage identification tags."

Instructional Resources

Brochures from hotels, motels, and resorts

Observations and Comments:

FUNCTIONAL MATHEMATICS / INSTRUCTIONAL OBJECTIVES

GENERAL OBJECTIVE: The individual will function in leisure experiences as independently and skillfully as possible by performing necessary mathematical operations.

The individual:

1. Records and tallies scores obtained in games and then determines the winner and order of finish.

Functional Essence

Instructional plans should have as their functional essence the development of those computational skills involved in tallying scores of games and sports events. Instructional activities should provide the individual with experiences in playing various games in an effort to encourage the playing of one or more of these games during leisure time and to develop competency in computing scores so that he can be an active and informed participant in one or more of these games from start to finish.

2. Identifies the face value of cards and plays his hand on that basis.

Functional Essence

Instructional plans should have as their functional essence the determination of the value of a card hand based on the face value of the individual cards in that hand. Instructional activities should include experiences in playing a wide range of card games including:

a.	Rummy;	i.	Cribbage;
b.	Solitaire;	j.	Fan Tan;
c.	Poker;	k.	Go Fish;
d.	Casino;	l.	Hearts;
e.	Pinochle;	m.	I Doubt It;
f.	Canasta;	n.	Russian Bank;
g.	Concentration;	o.	Spite and Malice; and
h.	Crazy Eights, Jacks, or Sevens;	p.	Black Jack or Twenty-One.

In some of these games, face value determination involves placing cards in value sequences and/or matching cards of the same value. The ultimate goal is for the individual to play one or more card games for pleasure. While playing skill is developed, attention must be paid to warning the individual of problems arising from using cards and other games to gamble.

3. Uses play money in transactions in games involving business and finance.

Functional Essence

Instructional plans should have as their functional essence the development of skills involved in the handling of play money in real-life games such as:

    a. Monopoly;
    b. Life;
    c. Easy Money; and
    d. Pay Day.

Instructional activities should involve playing these games and others and in handling the counting of money and the making of change involving various denominations of paper currency.

4. Totals the amount rolled on dice in games where player order and/or amount of spaces moved are determined by the throws of the dice. (*See* Sample Instructional Plan.)

Functional Essence

Instructional plans should have as their functional essence the computation of the value of thrown dice. Instructional activities should involve the playing of board games, games of chance, strategy games, and other games where the roll of the dice determines:

a. player order;
b. number of spaces to be moved;
c. partial scores; and
d. winners and losers.

The emphasis throughout should be on helping the individual to become a skilled participant in one or more games in which dice are used.

5. Determines time elapsed in activities involving speed or time periods.

Functional Essence   Instructional plans should have as their functional essence the development of those time-telling skills involved in determining the amount of time elapsed from start to finish of recreational activities involving time periods such as football and basketball and speed of participants, e.g., races. Instructional activities should be designed to acquaint the individual with all those games and sports where time elapsed is critical. The individual should be given the opportunity to serve as time keeper. Records of timed performances should be reviewed and time elements discussed from the perspective of the spectator of sports and of televised events.

6. Computes team averages and individual player averages of team members.

Functional Essence   Instructional plans should have as their functional essence the computation of player and team averages. Instructional activities should involve the individual in the calculation of percentages as well as the comparison of the percentages of different players and teams. The determination of player statistics should be done for all individual and team sports for various positions as applicable. Special attention should be given to the individual's own averages as he participates in athletic events, e.g., golf, bowling, baseball, and swimming.

7. Determines the amount of food needed for outings.

Functional Essence   Instructional plans should have as their functional essence the calculations of amount of food needed based upon the expected number of persons at picnics, barbeques, and other outings where food will be served. Instructional activities should include the collection of recipes and their multiplication by set amounts for greater number of eaters. Also, experiences should be provided in which a set number or weight of a food item is hypothesized for each participant and the total quantity or weight of the food calculated, e.g., two frankfurters and ¼ lb. of potato salad per person.

8. Counts the amount of fish and seafood caught.

Functional Essence   Instructional plans should have as their functional essence the simple counting of the number of fish and seafood caught. Instructional activities should include counting by parts of dozens and dozens as well as simple counting. Whenever possible, actual catches should be counted.

9. Measures the size and weight of fish and seafood caught.

Functional Essence   Instructional plans should have as their functional essence the measurement of fish and seafood caught. Instructional activities should involve weighing and measuring the length of these fish and seafood. Whenever possible, actual catches should be weighed on scales and measured with tape measures and rulers.

10. Counts the number of rocks, shells, and other natural objects collected.

Functional Essence Instructional plans should have as their functional essence the simple counting of natural objects in a personal collection. Instructional experiences should involve actual counting of rocks, shells, and other natural objects in the individual's collection. When there is no individual collection, use a collection of one of his peers or associates. If none are available, simulated experiences may be provided.

11. Counts the number of items in his collection by individual units and by sub-categories or types.

Functional Essence Instructional plans should have as their functional essence the simple counting of objects in a collection both by individual units and by sub-categories or types, e.g., the number of postcards and the number of postcards from Spain. Instructional experiences should involve these two aspects in examining the individual's collection. When there is no individual collection, use a collection of one of his peers or associates. Simulated experiences may also be provided.

12. Measures the growth patterns of pets.

Functional Essence Instructional plans should have as their functional essence the measurement of pet growth through the use of scales, tape measures, and rulers. Instructional activities should be provided using the individual's pet. A chart should be developed so that the individual can record and chart the pet's weight, height, and length changes. In the absence of a pet, a group pet should be obtained and the measuring and charting processes rotated.

13. Determines the cost of feeding and caring for pets.

Functional Essence Instructional plans should have as their functional essence the calculation of the cost of feeding and caring for a pet. Instructional activities should focus first on identifying various types of pets and then estimating the cost of feeding and caring for each pet. Remember to consider changes in the estimates depending on the type of pet, the size of pet, and the age of the pet. Review brochures, books, and pamphlets relevant to pet care for information. Be sure to include unexpected costs such as illness. When the individual owns a pet, record the weekly or monthly expenses for three or more periods and average the expenses for a budget. Then periodically change this budgeted estimate as the pet gets larger and older. When considering the purchase of a pet, assist the individual in deciding whether his budget can be stretched to accommodate the cost.

14. Determines the cost of participating in various recreational activities.

Functional Essence Instructional plans should have as their functional essence the calculation of the cost of various recreational activities. These recreational events should be placed in categories according to the relative cost. Begin with those events that do not involve an admission cost and calculate the indirect costs such as travel expenses and special food and beverages. Instructional experiences should then continue on to those activities in which admission is charged. In these cases, indirect costs should also be computed and added to the admission cost. Then, the focus should shift to identifying recreational events of interest to the individual and determining the impact on the individual's budget. Recreational costs must be a subitem on the individual's budget.

15. Determines the cost of acquiring models, stamps, dolls, and other collectibles.

Functional Essence Instructional plans should have as their functional essence the calculation of the cost of acquiring models, stamps, dolls, and other collectibles. Instructional activities should focus on obtaining pamphlets, brochures, specialty magazines, books, and advertisements that describe the items that are available and prices or estimated prices. From these various cataloging of items and prices, ask the individual to draw up a hypothetical shopping list. Compute the cost of this list. The individual, if he is interested in starting a collection, should be required to demonstrate that his budget can support the gradual acquisition of a collection.

16. Prepares food and engages in other food crafts.

Functional Essence   Instructional plans should have as their functional essence the calculation of the cost of preparing food for social gatherings and outings as well as the cost of creating food crafts. Instructional activities should provide the individual with abundant experiences in computing the cost of converting the recipes for food and beverages for numbers of guests. Also, experiences should be provided in estimating the cost of producing a variety of food crafts. Emphasis throughout should be on determining individual interest and whether food items can fit into the individual's budget for recreational and entertainment purposes.

17. Purchases supplies needed for various arts and crafts activities.

Functional Essence   Instructional plans should have as their functional essence the calculation of the cost of purchasing supplies needed to carry out various arts and crafts projects. Instructional activities should concentrate on identifying projects whose processes and products are likely to interest the individual. Experiences should be provided in computing the cost of materials for these projects and the individual instructed to determine whether they meet budgeted amounts for recreational activities. When a crafts product is to be used for a gift, indicate that the cost should be counted under a more appropriate category such as gifts and entertainment or miscellaneous expenses.

18. Measures out various substances to engage in various arts and crafts projects.

Functional Essence   Instructional plans should have as their functional essence the use of various measuring spoons, measuring cups, and small scales to measure out ingredients for arts and crafts projects. Projects involving processes and products that are of interest to the individual should be engaged in with emphasis placed on relative exactness of measurement and on the cost of these projects as they relate to budgeted amounts for recreation and other expenses. The goal in all leisure activities continues to be toward developing interest in one or more arts and crafts processes as possible recreational endeavors.

19. Estimates the cost of a meal or snack at a cafeteria or restaurant before ordering.

Functional Essence   Instructional plans should have as their functional essence the estimation of the cost of a snack or meal at a cafeteria or restaurant based on the estimate arrived through calculating rounded-off prices that appear on menus. Collect sample menus from the various restaurants in the community and provide the individual with instructional experiences in giving the individual a budgeted amount for a snack or meal and then observing him as he selects a meal whose costs (including tax and tip) are within the amount he has on hand. Sufficient experience should be provided in ordering from different menus and with different beginning amounts. After sufficient experience, actual trips to restaurants and cafeterias should be scheduled.

20. Determines the cost of newspapers, magazines, and books.

Functional Essence   Instructional plans should have as their functional essence the calculation of the cost of newspapers, magazines, and books. Instructional experiences should include the review of available newspapers in the individual's community to establish a newspaper that appeals to the individual. Once this selection is made, assist the individual in computing the cost of the newspaper on a weekly basis including Sunday editions. Then proceed to an exploration of magazines available in the community to establish whether there are one or more magazines of interest to the individual. Compute the cost of buying the magazine at newsstand prices and at subscription prices. Determine whether the individual can purchase the magazine or magazines of interest according to budget projections. Repeat the above activities for paperback and other books, depending on the reading skills and interest as well as the individual's budget.

21. Determines the cost of automobile trips.

Functional Essence   Instructional plans should have as their functional essence the calculation of the cost of automobile trips including short as well as longer trips. Instructional activities should include the determination of the total costs including:
   a. tune-up;
   b. gas;
   c. oil;
   d. tolls;
   e. insurance; and
   f. depreciation.
Hypothetical trips should be planned originating from the individual's home or apartment. These trips should be scheduled to places of interest to the individual, and then the relative costs should be computed. Later, actual trips should be planned and the costs computed. Include, when applicable, the cost of accommodations, taxes, tips, and meals in the total cost.

22. Determines the cost of train, bus, boat, and airplane trips.

Functional Essence   Instructional plans should have as their functional essence the calculation of the cost of transportation via train, bus, boat, or airplane. Hypothetical trips should be planned to various destinations using one or more of the above means of transportation. Determining factors should include availability of time, travel connections, costs, and the value of the American dollar when considering travel to foreign countries. Include a discussion of discount and group rates as well as low season rates. Contact travel agencies where no fee is charged to assist the individual in planning and making reservations and in confirming various plans. Emphasis throughout must be on determining whether the individual can afford to take the trip.

SAMPLE INSTRUCTIONAL PLAN

Topic Area LEISURE EXPERIENCES-
FUNCTIONAL MATHEMATICS   Date ___3/16/82___

Teacher ___Mr. Petit___

Time Allotted ___50-60 minutes___

Individual(s) or Group Members Involved:
M. Mouton, J. Stark,
K. Balladino, L. Abrams

Special Notes or Precautions ___None___

General Objective

The individual will function in leisure experiences as independently and skillfully as possible by performing necessary mathematical operations.

Specific Objective (4)

The individual totals the amount rolled on dice in games where player order and/or amount of spaces moved are determined by the throws of the dice.

Instructional Objective

During a game of "Monopoly," the individual will identify player order and number of spaces he and other players should move according to the roll of the dice. He will do so with 100% accuracy.

Materials and Equipment

A monopoly set

Motivating Activity

Deal out the play money amounts to each player as specified in Monopoly game instructions. As you are passing out the money, explain the game or review the rules as appropriate.

Instructional Procedures

1. Roll the dice and total the amount of the roll.
2. Show the group members the various possible combinations.
3. Ask each one to roll the dice several times and then to announce his score.
4. After sufficient practice, roll the dice to determine player order. Ask the individual with the highest roll to announce that he is first. Proceed in this way until everyone identifies his position. Practice several times in preparation for the actual game. Be sure to include the resolution of ties, i.e., roll again. (This skill involves the application of the idea that 3 + 5 and 4 + 4 both belong to the eight family.)
5. After sufficient practice, roll the dice to determine number of spaces to be moved. Ask each individual to announce the number

of spaces he can move according to the roll of the dice.

6. After sufficient simulation, proceed to playing the game.

Individualized Reinforcement and Reinforcement Schedules

During the playing of the game praise the individuals for correctly following the rules. For L. Abrams praise continually in the beginning.

Assessment Strategy

Listen to each individual's responses relevant to player order and spaces to be moved. Observe the individual as he plays "Monopoly." Record each individual's performance on "Leisure Experiences: Functional Mathematics Checklist."

Follow-Up Activity/Objective

If the individual achieves the instructional objective, proceed to Specific Objective #5, i.e., "The individual determines time elapsed in activities involving speed or time periods.

Instructional Resources

Monopoly Rule Booklet

Observations and Comments:

chapter 8
SUGGESTED READINGS AND RESOURCES

The information presented in this section provides the reader with additional teaching content in the area of functional academics. A variety of instructional kits, filmstrips, workbooks, and other media that have been successfully used with adolescents and adults with learning problems are highlighted. Select readings in vocational, consumer, and leisure education have also been integrated into this resource section and should prove helpful to practitioners requiring functional academic information in these areas.

The majority of resources that follow are directly applicable to both handicapped and nonhandicapped individuals. Many of them, however, will have to be modified or adapted according to individual learning needs.

A special attempt has also been made to provide information that addresses current teaching methodology and strategies in the basic areas of reading, writing, and mathematics.

It is highly recommended that a sample of this information be reviewed before one develops a functional academic program.

THE HOME

Braga, L., and J. Braga. 1975. Learning and Growing: A Guide to Child Development. Prentice-Hall, Englewood Cliffs, N.J.

Brosnahan, J. P., and B. W. Milne. 1978. A Calendar of Home/School Activities. Goodyear Publishing Co., Santa Monica, Calif.

Brown, V. (Ed.). 1976. On reviewing cookbooks: From kitchen to classroom. J. Learn. Disabil. 9:63–68.

Bryan, T. 1976. Learning disabled children's comprehension of non-verbal communication. J. Learn. Disabil. 10:501–506.

Casella, R. L. 1979. T.V. time. Instructor 89:80.

Cassidy, J., and C. Vukelich. 1978. Survival reading for parents and kids: A parent education program. Read. Teach. 31:638–641.

Chain, S. P. 1977. Maryland Children's Guide. Urban Affairs Publishing Co., Baltimore.

Dale, M. E. 1979. Do you get it? Helping students understand humor. Teach. Excep. Children 11:105.

Davis, D. E. 1977. My Friends and Me. A Program to Promote the Personal and Social Development of Young Children. Circle Pines, American Guidance Service, Minn.

Dinkmeyer, D. 1970, 1973. Developing Understanding of Self and Others (DUSO). Programs to Promote Children's Social and Emotional Development. Circle Pines, American Guidance Service, Minn.

Dupont, H., and C. Dupo. 1979. Transition. A Program to Help Students Through the Difficult Passage From Childhood to Middle Adolescence. Circle Pines, American Guidance Service, Minn.

Dupont, H., S. O. Gardner, and D. S. Brody. 1974. Toward Affective Development (TAD): An Activity-Centered Program Designed to Stimulate Psychological and Affective Development. Circle Pines, American Guidance Service, Minn.

Edge, D., et al. 1979. Parent involvement: A consumer perspective; in the home and community. Educ. & Train. Ment. Retard. 14:143–144.

Fishco, D. T. 1977. Follett Coping Skills Series. Follett

Publishing Company, Chicago, Ill.

Hanley, P. E. 1979. Handmade games for home and school. Day Care and Early Educ. 7:38–40.

Hood, B. I., and B. F. Brown. 1979. Students with epilepsy: Guidelines for vocational counseling.

Knapczyk, D., and J. Hoppi. 1975. Development of co-operative and competitive play responses in developmentally disabled children. Am. J. Ment. Defic. 80:245–255.

Koschnick, K., and S. Ludwig (Eds.). 1975. The World of Work. New Readers Press, Syracuse, N.Y.

Lerner, M., and A. Palladian. 1977. Early Career Books. Lerner Publications, Minneapolis, Minn.

Let's Play to Grow. 1980. Joseph P. Kennedy, Jr., Foundation, Washington, D.C.

Lucier, D., and J. Lucier. 1980. Experience in everyday economics. Arith. Teach. 27:38–41.

Lupin, Mimi. 1979. Peace, Harmony, Awareness: A Relaxation Program for Children. Teaching Resources Corporation, Boston.

Ploutz, P. F. 1975. Rip-Off. Educational Games, Athens, Ohio.

Pyrczak, F. 1977. Readability of directions on potentially hazardous household products. Read. Improv. 14:77–81.

SRA Guidance Staff. 1975. SRA Job Family Series. Science Research Associates, Chicago, Ill.

Scarry, R. 1976–77. What Do People Do All Day? Random House, New York.

Schwarzrock, S. 1979. Contemporary Concerns of Youth: Materials for Discussion, Problem Solving Personal and Social Development in Grades 7–12. Circle Pines, American Guidance Service, Minn.

Shultheis, P., R. Paine, A. Morgan-Brown, S. Smith, and R. Hanson. 1980. Household Mathematics. Media Materials, Baltimore.

Siperstein, G. N., and J. Gottlieb. 1977. Physical appearance and academic performance as factors affecting children's attitudes toward handicapped peers. Am. J. Ment. Defic. 5:455–462.

Smith, K. 1977. Cultivate the habit of reading newspapers intelligently. Quill and Scroll 52:16–17.

Sucher, F. 1979. Home-grown approach to boosting reading skills. Early Years 9:58–59.

Weyant, M. E. 1979. Science/math fair for kids/dads. Day Care and Early Educ. 7:26–28.

Wheeler, J., A. Ford, J. Nietupski, and L. Brown. 1979. Teaching adolescent moderately/severely handicapped students to use food classification skills and calculator-related subtraction skills to shop in supermarkets. In: L. Brown, M. Falvey, D. Baumgart, I. Pumpian, J. Schroeder, and L. Gruenwald (Eds.), Strategies for Teaching Chronological Age-Appropriate Skills to Adolescent and Young Adult Severely Handicapped Students. (Vol. 9.) Madison School System, Madison, Wis.

THE SCHOOL

Abbott, R. E. 1976. The newspaper as a teaching tool. Pointer 20:52–55.

Aiken, L. 1977. Mathematics as a creative language. Arith. Teach. 24:251–255.

Ainsworth, B. 1980. Functional Reading Filmstrip Series. Media Materials, Baltimore.

Anderson, M., N. J. Boren, W. H. Caniglia, and E. Krohn. 1980. The Apple Tree Language Program: A Patterned Program of Linguistic Expansion Through Reinforced Experience and Evaluations. Dormac, Oreg.

Arithmetic Skill Text for Daily Living. 1977. Special Service Supply, Huntington, N.Y.

Armstrong, J. R., and H. Schmidt. 1972. Simple materials for teaching early number concepts to trainable level mentally retarded pupils. Arith. Teach. 19:149–153.

Artzt, A. 1979. Student teams in mathematics class. Math. Teach. 72:505–508.

Balow, B., D. Fuchs, and M. Kasbohm. 1978. Teaching non-readers to read: An evaluation of the effectiveness of the Minneapolis Public Schools Basic Skill Centers. J. Learn. Disabil. 11:351–354.

Bartel, N. 1975. Problems in arithmetic achievement. In: D. Hammill and N. Bartel (Eds.), Teaching Children with Learning and Behavior Problems. Allyn and Bacon, Boston.

Basic Handwriting Series. 1978. Continental Press, Englishtown, Pa.

Beal, L., and R. E. Potter. 1979. The use of objects and pictures as language stimuli: Influence on response complexity. J. Childhood Communic. Disorders 3:47–58.

Beattie, I. D. 1979. Children's strategies for solving subtraction-fact combinations. Arith. Teach. 27: 14–15.

Behrmann, P. 1975. The four r's: Reading, 'riting, 'rithmetic and respect. J. Learn. Disabil. 8:555–556.

Belina, V. S. 1975. Planning for Your Own Apartment. Fearon-Pitman Publishers, Belmont, Calif.

Bell & Howell and the Editors of Fearon-Pitman. 1976. Master It! With the Language Master. Fearon-Pitman Publishers, Belmont, Calif.

Bender, M., P. Valletutti, and R. Bender. 1976. Functional Academics for the Mildly and Moderately Handicapped. Teaching the Moderately and Severly Handicapped (vol. 3). University Park Press, Baltimore.

Blackwell, J. 1976. When 2 + 2 ain't 4. Lang. Arts 53:

422–424.

Blanchard, D., and L. McClellan. 1978. Grammar Games for Early Primary Grades. Arrowhead Publishing, Tampa, Fla.

Blanchard, D., and L. McClellan. 1978. Math Games for Grades 1–3. Arrowhead Publishing, Tampa, Fla.

Broome, K., and C. L. Wambold. 1977. Teaching basic math facts to EMR children through tracting and learning center activities. Educ. & Train. Ment. Retard. 12:120–124.

Brown, L., and L. Perlmutter. 1971. Teaching functional reading to trainable level retarded students. Educ. & Train. Ment. Retard. 6:74–83.

Burke, D. 1980. Systematic Sentence Builder. Modern Education Corporation, Okla.

Burke, D., and K. Burke. 1980. Sensory-Motor Writing Program. Modern Education Corporation, Okla.

Burns, J., and D. Swan. 1980. Reading Without Books: A Remedial Program for Learning Sight Words, Using Newspapers, Magazines and Product Labels. Fearon-Pitman Publishers, Belmont, Calif.

Burns, M. 1980. Thinking is a math skill, too. Learning 8:39–41.

Bush, L. P. 1979. Placeholders: Formula vs. form; geometric shapes instead of letters. Math. Teach. 72:517–518.

Buyers Guide 1980. Sources of information for equipment and teaching aids. Voc. Ed. 55:61–77.

Canfield, J., and H. C. Wells. 1976. 100 Ways to Enhance Self-Concept in the Classroom. Prentice-Hall, Englewood Cliffs, N.J.

Cassidy, J., and V. Sharkey. 1977. Rithmetic reading. Teacher 94:50–54.

Cassidy, J., and P. Walzl. 1977. Developing survival reading competencies. Teach. Excep. Children 11:20–21.

Cheasebro, M. 1979. Math for profit. Am. Educ. 15:22–27.

Clark, A., S. Boyd, and S. MacCrae. 1975. A classroom program teaching disadvantaged youths to write biographic information. J. Appl. Behav. Anal. 8(1):67–76.

Copeland, R. W. 1974. How Children Learn Mathematics. Macmillan, New York.

Copes, L. 1979. Is there life after mathematics? Am. Math. Monthly 86:383–386.

Cox, L. 1975. Diagnosing and remediating systematic errors in addition and subtraction computations. Arith. Teach. 22:151–157.

Crutcher, C. E., and Hofmeister, A. M. 1975. Effective use of objectives and monitoring. Teach. Excep. Children 7:78–80.

Davis, C., A. Hirshoren, and J. T. Hunt. 1974. Classified ads as reading material for the educable retarded. Excep. Children 41:45–47.

DeBruin, J. E., and T. C. Gibney. 1979. Solving everyday problems using mathematics and science process skills. School Sci. & Math. 79:613–617.

Dede, R. 1979. Mapping with math. Instructor 89:124.

Degler, L. S. 1978. Using the newspaper to develop reading comprehension skills. J. Read. 21:339–342.

DeHouske, E. J. 1979. Original writing: A therapeutic tool in working with disturbed adolescents. Teach. Excep. Children 11:66–70.

Developing Writing Skills. 1980. Media Materials, Baltimore.

DeVito, A. 1979. Scope and directions of basic skills activities. School Sci. & Math. 79:627–630.

Dominie, M., and L. Brown. 1977. Teaching severely handicapped students reading skills requiring printed answers to who, what, and where questions. Educ. & Train. Ment. Retard. 12:324–331.

Dunlap, W. P. 1976. Measuring mathematical attitudes of EMR children. Educ. & Train. Ment. Retard. 11:212–217.

Dunlap, W. P., et al. 1979. Determining learning disabilities in mathematics. Acad. Ther. 15:81–85.

Dunlap, W., and A. House. 1976. Why Johnny can't compute. J. Learn. Disabil. 9:210–214.

Fadiman, C., and J. Howard. 1979. Empty Pages: A Search for Writing Competence in School and Society. Fearon-Pitman Publishers, Belmont, Calif.

Federal Register. August 23, 1977. Part II, Implementation of Part B of the Education for All Handicapped Children Act. U.S. Office of Education, HEW, Washington, D.C.

Fennell, Francis. 1980. Multiplication and Division Filmstrip Series. Media Materials, Baltimore.

Feshbach, S., H. Adelman, and W. Fuller. 1977. Prediction of reading and academic problems. J. Educ. Psychol. 69:299–308.

Foster, G. 1979. Movement and math. J. Phys. Educ. 77:21.

Frank, A. R. 1978. Teaching money skills with a number line. Teach. Excep. Children 10(2):46–48.

Froese, V. 1976. Functional reading levels: From graded word lists. Alberta J. Educ. Res. 22:325–329.

Fry, E. 1979. Typing Course for Children. Dreier Educational Systems, Highland Park, N.J.

Gantt, Walter N. 1977. Learning modules: Individualizing the reading methods course. Read. World 16(4):305–311.

Gardner, D. C., and M. A. Kurtz. 1979. Teaching technical vocabulary to handicapped students. Read. Improv. 16:252–257.

Greenburg, Joanne C. 1980. Sight Vocabulary Series. Media Materials, Baltimore.

Greitzer, S. L. 1979. Eighth U.S.A. Mathematical Olympiad. Math. Teach. 72:658–659.

Greitzer, S. L. 1979. Twentieth International Mathematical Olympiad. Am. Math. Monthly 86:747–749.

Gustason, G., D. Pfeitzing, and E. Zawolkow. 1975. Signing Exact English. Modern Signs Press, Silver Spring, Md.

Hamill, A. D'O., and G. F. Bober. 1976. Typing in Plain English: Text-Workbook and Teacher's Manual; Reading Level, Grade 6.0; Interest Level, Grades 6–12. Fearon-Pitman Publishers, Belmont, Calif.

Hamm, R. P. 1975. Metric Language: Rhythmic Reading. Belwin Mills, Melville, New York.

Hanson, Robert. 1980. Fraction Filmstrip Series. Media Materials, Baltimore.

Hernandez, N. G. 1979. Word problem skits for the deaf. Arith. Teach. 27:14–16.

Hoffman, J. C. 1979. Bridging a gap. Arith. Teach. 27:18–19.

Hoffman, R. 1979. Mathematics you can touch; Mathematics Laboratory at the University of Denver. Learning 8:46–48.

Hollingsworth, Shirley. 1976. The Background of Educators' Interest in Learning Modules: Why Modules? Paper presented at the Annual Meeting of the International Reading Association in Anaheim, Calif. (ERIC Document Reproduction Service no. ED 123 626.)

Idea Bonanza; Math. 1979. Learning 8:24–27.

Individualized Mathematics: Metric Drill and Practice Kit. 1975. Random House, Westminster, Md.

Johnson, D. C. 1979. Teaching estimation and reasonableness of results. Arith. Teach. 27:34–35.

Jones, W. 1980. Using Measurement Series. Media Materials, Baltimore.

Kahn, H. F. 1979. Needed: An alternative for mathematics textbooks. School Sci. and Math. 79:473–476.

Kennedy, L. 1975. Guiding Children to Mathematical Discovery. 2nd Ed. Wadsworth, Belmont, Calif.

Kiraly, J., Jr., and A. Morishima. 1974. Developing mathematical skills by applying Piaget's Theory. Educ. & Train. Ment. Retard. 9:62–65.

Kokaska, S. M. 1975. A notation system in arithmetic skills. Educ. & Train. Ment. Retard. 10:96–101.

Kostel, F. 1979. Number line, one more time. Math. Teach. 72:428.

Krockover, G. H. 1979. Solving everyday problems by applying science and mathematics principles. School Sci. & Math. 79:607–612.

Lerner, S. 1976. Aspects of teaching long division to a group of exceptional children. J. Learn. Disabil. 6:151–156.

Lowe, M. L., and A. J. Cuvo. 1976. Teaching coin summation to the mentally retarded. J. Appl. Behav. Anal. 9:483–489.

Lundstrom, L. J., and R. A. Nelson. 1978. Sight Singing Flash Cards. Chorister's Guild, Dallas, Tex.

Mager, R. F. 1975. Preparing Instructional Objectives. Fearon Publishers, Belmont, Calif.

Mahmoud, C. C., E. E. Gickling, and C. H. Hargis. 1975. The effectiveness of T.V. in teaching sight words to students with learning disabilities. J. Learn. Disabil. 8:37–40.

Mallet, J., and M. Bartch. 1979. Menagerie math. Instructor 89:132–133.

Manipulative Place Value Kit. 1975. Great Ideas, Houppauge, N.Y.

Math Kit—Addition. 1978. Benefit Press, Westchester, Ill.

Mathematics: texts and supplements (cont.). 1979. Curric. Rev. 18:130–139, 221–230.

Mattleman, M. S., H. E. Blake. 1977. Study skills: Prescriptions for survival. Lang. Arts 54:925–927.

McCarty, G. 1979. Display calculators bring a new dimension to teaching. Audiovis. Instruc. 72:448–449.

McGettigan, J. F. 1972. The development of number as logical constructions. Educ. & Train. Ment. Retard. 7:183–188.

Mendoza, M. A., W. J. Holt, and D. A. Jackson. 1978. Circles and tape: An easy, teacher implemented way to teach fundamental writing skills. Teach. Excep. Children 10(4):48–51.

Miller, C. 1979. Accelerated mathematics program for the gifted and talented middle school students. Gifted Child Q. 23:608–610.

Nelson, D. W. 1979. Time-out math. Instructor 89:161.

Nelson, J. T., J. B. Troup, M. L. Thuriow, P. H. Krus, and J. E. Turnure. 1975. An assessment of the effectiveness of the Money, Measurement and Time Program for TMR students. ERIC Document Reproduction Service. (no. ED 115 045) University of Minnesota, Minneapolis.

Nelson, R. S. 1979. Multiplication games that every child can play. Arith. Teach. 27:34–35.

Nichols, S. 1977. Number concepts for school beginners. Is it possible? Arith. Teach. 24:275–282.

Ogletree, E. J., and V. Ujlaki. 1976. A motoric approach to teaching multiplication to the mentally retarded child. Educ. & Train. Ment. Retard. 11:129–134.

O'Such, T., and L. T. Hirst. 1979. Using musical television commercials to teach reading. Teach. Excep. Children 11(4):80–83.

Quandt, I. V. 1977. Teaching Reading: A Human Process. Rand McNally Publishing Co., Chicago, Ill.

Radeka, N. 1975. Manual multiplication—a handy way of multiplying. Educ. & Train. Ment. Retard. 10:102.

Rappaport, D. 1976. Mathematics—for whom? Arith. Teach. 23:343–345.

Ravanelli, R. 1980. Don't get caught; danger adds excitement to drill. Learning 8:47.

Reynolds, M., and J. Birch. 1977. Teaching Exceptional Children in All America's Schools. The Council for Exceptional Children, Reston, Va.

Robinson, M. L. 1979. Linear measure for those shorter than a meter. School Sci. & Math. 79:513–516.

Ross, A. D. 1976. Psychological Aspects of Learning Disabilities and Reading Disorders. McGraw-Hill, New York.

SRA Lunchbox—Manuscript Handwriting. 1977. SRA, Chicago, Ill.

Saunders, H. 1980. When are we ever gonna have to use this? Math. Teach. 73:7–16.

Sawyer, T. 1977. Why speech will not totally replace writing. Coll. Compos. & Commun. 28:43–48.

Scalzitti, J. 1979. Mathematics on tour. Arith. Teach. 27:44.

Sherrill, J. M. 1979. Subtraction: Decomposition versus equal addends. Arith. Teach. 27:16–17.

Short, J. R., and B. Dickerson. 1979. The Newspaper: An Alternative Textbook. Fearon-Pitman Publishers, Belmont, Calif.

Shuman, R. B. 1975. Of course he can read—he's in high school. J. Read. 19:36–41.

Soverly, R., et al. 1975. The newspaper as a tool for teaching kids to read. Phi Delta Kappan 57:260–261.

Speilberg, F. 1979. How some teachers teach writing: By reviewing grammar in math. Today's Educ. 68:40.

Spitze, H. T. 1979. Teaching home economics for today and tomorrow. Forecast Home Econ. 24:75.

Sternberg, L. 1977. Essential Math and Language Skills. Hubbard, Northbrook, Ill.

Stoutamire, Virginia, and Ken Kyre. 1975. The Uniformity-Flexibility Gap in Curriculum Development: An Experiment with Promise. (ERIC Document Reproduction Service no. ED 103 057.)

Sykes, E. L. 1976. Arithmetic Activities Handbook: An Individualized and Group Approach to Teaching the Basic Skills. Parker Publishing, New York.

Thiessen, D. 1979. Measurement activities using the metric system. Arith. Teach. 27:36–37.

Thompson, D. G. 1977. Writing Long-Term and Short-Term Objectives. Research Press Co., Champaign, Ill.

Trembley, P., and H. Luke. 1977. A model for a remedial mathematics program. Arith. Teach. 24:140–144.

Utz, W. R. 1979. Blind students in the mathematical classroom. Am. Math. Monthly 86:491–494.

Vacca, R. T. 1975. The development of a functional reading strategy: Implications for content area instruction. J. Educ. Res. 69:108–112.

Visual Aids and Learning Materials. 1979. Forecast Home Econ. 25:7–38.

Walker, Bonnie L. 1980. Written Expression Series. Media Materials, Baltimore.

Wasdovich, D. H. 1979. Polygons, spirals and shells: interview. Math. Teach. 72:409–412.

Wesson, J. B. 1979. Graphs and charts: An important topic for the middle grades. School Sci. & Math. 79:592–596.

Woodward, E., and T. Hamel. 1979. Calculator lessons involving population, inflation, and energy. Math. Teach. 72:450–457.

Woolfe, M. T. 1980. Math/reading skills connection. Teacher 97:76.

Wyatt, K. E., and W. L. Sengstock. 1975. Meters, liters, and grams: The metric system and its implications for curriculum for exceptional children. Teach. Excep. Children 8(2):58–60.

Young, E., and L. V. Rodenborn. 1976. Improving communication skills in vocational courses. J. Read. 19:373–377.

THE COMMUNITY

Ainsworth, B., and R. Abbott. 1980. Reading Map Series. Media Materials, Baltimore.

Ainsworth, B., and D. Trautman. 1980. Survival Reading at Home Series. Media Materials, Baltimore.

Aninger, M., and K. Bolinsky. 1977. Levels of independent functioning of retarded adults in apartments. Ment. Retard. 15(4):12–13.

Baird, A. S., and D. Goldie. 1979. Activities and experiences develop spatial and sensory understanding. Teach. Excep. Children 11:116–119.

Barnard, J. D., E. R. Christophersen, and M. M. Wolf. 1977. Teaching children appropriate shopping behavior through parent training in the supermarket setting. J. Appl. Behav. Anal. 10:49–59.

Belina, V. S. 1975. Planning Your Own Apartment: Text-Workbook and Teachers' Guide; Reading Level, 3.0; Interest Level, Grades 7–12/ABE. Fearon-Pitman Publishers, Belmont, Calif.

Bender, M., P. Valletutti, and R. Bender. 1976. Communication, Socialization, Safety, and Leisure Time Skills. Teaching the Moderately and Severely Handicapped, vol. 2. University Park Press, Baltimore.

Birenbaum, A., and M. A. Re. 1979. Resettling mentally retarded adults in the community—almost 4 years later. Am. J. Ment. Defic. 83:323–329.

Bordwell, M. 1975. A community involvement program for the trainable adolescent. Teach. Excep. Children 7:110–114.

Butler, E. W., and A. T. Bjaanes. 1978. Activities and the use of time by retarded persons in community care facilities. In: G. P. Sacket (Ed.), Theory and Applications in Mental Retardation. Observing Behavior, vol. 1. University Park Press, Baltimore.

Canario, J. 1980. The Put-Down Pro and Other Plays: Getting Along with Friends. A Set of Workbooks Designed for Secondary Students to Develop Language Arts and Socialization Skills, Book 1B. Janus Book Publishers, Calif.

Cassidy, J., and T. Shanahan. 1979. Survival skills: Some considerations. J. Read. 23:136–140.

Certo, N., R. Schwartz, and L. Brown. 1975. Community transportation: Teaching severely handicapped students to ride a public bus system. In: L. Brown, T. Crowner, W. Williams, and R. York (Eds.), Madison's Alternative to Zero Exclusion: A Book of Readings (vol. 5). Madison Public School System, Madison, Wis.

Conley, E. L. 1975. Shopping for the best price; game. Forecast Home Econ. 21:F20.

Crnic, K. A., and H. A. Pym. 1979. Training mentally retarded adults in independent living skills. Ment. Retard. 17:13–16.

Dorfman, J. 1975. Consumer Survival Kit. Praeger, New York.

Doyle, Edward. 1980. Skills for Daily Living Series. Media Materials, Baltimore.

Dreith, R., and A. Kreps. 1975. Community Living Skills Guide—Wardrobe II: Selection and Buying of Clothing. Metropolitan State College, The College for Living, Denver, Colo.

Elliott, P. C. 1979. Money changer's bingo. Arith. Teach. 27:50–51.

Fairchild, E., and L. Neal. 1975. Common-Unity in the Community—A Forward Looking Program of Recreation and Leisure Services for the Handicapped. University of Oregon, Center of Leisure Studies, Eugene.

Fetterman, E. 1975. Consumer education using community resources. Forecast Home Econ. 20:FA-20.

Findelstein, M., et al. 1977. Living in a Consumer's World. Globe Book Company, New York.

Flexer, R., and K. Boyd. 1976. Teaching Money Skills to the Mentally Retarded Person: A Manual of Procedures. Texas Tech University, Research and Training Center, Lubbock.

Garman, E. T. 1979. Developing your own simulation games in consumer education. Clearing House 52: 322–325.

Gathany, T. A. 1979. Involving students in problem solving. Math. Teach. 72:617–622.

George, R. 1978. The New Consumer Survival Kit: adapted from the series produced by the Maryland Center for Public Broadcasting. Little, Brown, Boston.

Geunther, J. E., and R. L. Hohn. 1976. Self-paced use of a consumer education learning package. Psychol. in the Schools 13:191–194.

Goldstein, Herbert. 1977. Merrill's Social Learning Curriculum. Charles E. Merrill, Columbus, Ohio.

Guthrie, J. 1979. Research: Functional reading: One or many. J. Read. 22:648–650.

Halpern, A. S. 1975. Measuring social and prevocation awareness in mildly retarded adolescents. Am. J. Ment. Defic. 80(1):81–89.

Hecht, A. T. 1979. Environmental problem solving. Arith. Teach. 27:42–43.

Hersen, M., and R. M. Eisler. 1976. Social skills training. In: W. E. Craighead, A. Kazdin, and M. J. Mahoney (Eds.), Behavior Modification: Principles, Issues and Applications. Houghton Mifflin, Boston.

James, E., and C. Barkin. 1977. Managing Your Money. Children's Press, Chicago, Ill.

James, E., and C. Barkin. 1977. Understanding Money. Children's Press, Chicago, Ill.

Jew, W., and R. Tong. 1976. Job Interview Kit. Janus Book Publishers, Hayward, Calif.

Jones, W., and R. Hanson. 1980. Consumer Mathematics Series. Media Materials, Baltimore.

Kelley, P. 1977. Building Safe Driving Skills, Revised Ed.: Text, Workbook, Chapter Tests and Teachers' Guide; Reading Level, Grade 3.0; Interest Level, Grades 7–12/ABE. Fearon-Pitman Publishers, Belmont, Calif.

Knox, Carolyn. 1980. Using the Telephone Directory. Media Materials, Baltimore.

Kokaska, C., and A. Schmidt. 1976. Preparing students for the job market. Educ. & Train. Ment. Retard. 11:80–82.

Kreps, A., and J. Black. 1975. Community Living Skills Guide—Money Management II (Checkbooks, Budgets, and Survival Math). Metropolitan State College, The College for Living, Denver, Colo.

Kundel, S. E. 1979. Metric instruction for the adult consumer. Lifelong Learning: The Adult Years 3: 10–13.

Langrehr, F. W., and J. B. Mason. Spring 1978. Influence of formal instruction in consumer education academic units on attitudes toward the marketplace: A case study of Illinois students. J. Econ. Educ. 9:133–134.

Larkin, E. F., and G. L. Grotta. 1977. The newspaper as a source of consumer information for young adults. J. Advert. 6:5–10.

Layton, J. 1930. Reading Signs for Survival Series. Media Materials, Baltimore.

Levy, L., R. Feldman, and S. Simpson. 1976. The Consumer in the Marketplace; Interest Level, Grades 7–12. Fearon-Pitman Publishers, Belmont, Calif.

Livingstone, A. 1977. Janus Job Interview Guide. Janus Book Publishers, Hayward, Calif.

Lobb, C. 1977. Exploring Careers Through Part-Time and Summer Employment. Richards Rosen Press, New York.

Ludwig, S. 1977. Be Informed on Buying a House. New Readers Press, Syracuse, New York.

Ludwig, S. 1977. Be Informed on Renting a Place to Live. New Readers Press, Syracuse, New York.

McDevitt, S. C., M. P. Smith, D. W. Schmidt, and M. Rosen. 1978. The deinstitutionalized citizen: Adjustment and quality of life. Ment. Retard. 16:22–24.

McGee, D. W. 1979. Using the telephone directory as a learning tool. Teach. Excep. Children 12:34–36.

McMullen, D. A. 1975. Teaching protection words. Teach. Except. Children 7:74–77.

Newspaper Reading. 1977. Gary Lawson, Elk Grove, Calif.

Nietupski, R., N. Certo, I. Pumpian, and K. Belmore. 1976. Supermarket shopping: Teaching severely handicapped students to generate shopping lists and make purchases functionally linked with meal preparation. In: L. Brown, N. Certo, K. Belmore, and T. Crowner (Eds.), Papers and Programs Related to Public School Services for Secondary Age Severely Handicapped Students (vol. 6, part I). Madison Metropolitan School District, Madison, Wis.

Orr, G. J. 1977. Money management in life situations. Educ. & Train. Ment. Retard. 12:65–68.

Perske, R., and J. Marquis. 1973. Learning to live in an apartment: Retarded adults from institutions and dedicated citizens. Ment. Retard. 11(5):18–19.

Programmed Math for Daily Living. 1978. TQ Publishers, Corpus Christi, Tex.

Rader, W. D. 1978. Improving critical reading through consumer education. Soc. Educ. 42:18–20.

Reis, R. 1977. A curriculum for real life reading skills. J. Read. 21:208–211.

Roderman, W. H. 1979. Getting Around Cities and Towns: A Janus Survival Guide. Janus Book Publishers, Hayward, Calif.

Roderman, W. H. 1978. Reading and Following Directions: A Janus Survival Guide. Janus Book Publishers, Hayward, Calif.

Rupley, W. H., and P. B. Gwinn. Reading in the real word. Read. World 18:117–122.

Scheerenberger, R. C., and D. Felsenthal. 1977. Community settings for MR persons: Satisfaction and activities. Ment. Retard. 15(4):3–7.

Shultheis, P., R. Paine, A. Morgan-Brown, S. Smith, and R. Hanson. 1980. Shopping Mathematics. Media Materials, Baltimore.

Smithsonian Institution. 1977. Museums and Handicapped Students—Guidelines for Educators. Smithsonian Institution, Washington, D.C.

Stewart, M. D. 1977. Survey of community employer attitudes toward hiring the handicapped. Ment. Retard. 15:30–31.

Thompson, A. G. 1979. Estimating and approximating. School Sci. & Math. 79:575–580.

Tiller, C. 1978. An Activities of Daily Living Curriculum for Handicapped Adults. Magic Valley Rehabilitation Services, Twin Falls, Idaho.

Walzl, P., and J. Cassidy. 1978. Developing survival reading competencies. Teach. Excep. Children 11:20–22.

Watson, N., and A. Kreps. 1975. Community Living Skills Guide—Leisure Time for Adults. Metropolitan State College, The College for Living, Denver, Colo.

Wehman, P. 1975. Toward a social skills curriculum for developmentally disabled clients in vocational settings. Rehabil. Lit. 3(11):342–348.

Worpole, K. 1975. The gates: Writing within the community. Children's Lit. Educ. 17:766–787.

Young, R. 1979. Down-home math. School and Community 65:16–17.

CONSUMER SKILLS

Barrera, F. J., and S. R. Schroeder. 1976. Effects of price manipulations on consumer behavior in a sheltered workshop token economy. Am. J. Ment. Defic. 81:172–180.

Bellamy, T., and K. Buttars. 1975. Teaching trainable level retarded students to count money: Toward personal independence through academic instruction. Educ. & Train. Ment. Retard. 10:18–26.

Blum, M. L. 1977. Psychology and Consumer Affairs. Harper and Row, New York.

Brown, F. S. 1977. Managing Your Money. J. Weston Walch, Portland, Oreg.

Bruni, J. V., and H. Silverman. 1976. Introducing consumer education; activities with money. Arith. Teach. 23:324–331.

Certo, N., and B. Swetlik. 1976. Making purchases: A functional money use program for severely handicapped students. In: L. Brown, et al. (Eds.), Madison's Alternative to Zero Exclusion: Papers and Programs Related to Public School Services for Secondary Age Severely Handicapped Students. Madison Public School System, Madison, Wis.

Cuvo, A. J., and M. L. Lowe. 1976. Teaching coin summation to the mentally retarded. J. Appl. Behav. Anal. 9:483–489.

Dull, E. 1980. Could we split the rent? Instructor 89: 102–103.

Grotta, G. L., et al. 1975. How readers perceive and use a small daily newspaper. Journalism Q. 52:711–715.

Hill, C. R. 1976. Trademarks and Brand Management: Selected Annotations. United States Trademark Association, New York.

Huffman, S. 1979. Get What You Pay For. Pal Life Competency Program, Xerox Education Publications, Middletown, Conn.

Jew, W., and C. Tandy. 1977. Using the Want Ads: A Janus Survival Guide. Janus Book Publishers, Hayward, Calif.

Knox, Carolyn. 1980. Paying Your Bills. Media Materials, Baltimore.

Koller, E. Z., and T. J. Mulhern. 1977. Use of a pocket calculator to train arithmetic skills with trainable adolescents. Educ. & Train. Ment. Retard. 12:332–335.

Lazerick, B. E. 1979. Making money is motivating. Teacher 97:98–101.

Ludwig, S. 1976. Be Informed on Personal Credit. New Readers Press, Syracuse, New York.

Ludwig, S. (Ed.). 1976. Be Informed on Taxes. New Readers Press, Syracuse, New York.

Maurizi, A. 1978. Prices and Consumer Information. American Enterprise Institute for Public Policy Research, Washington, D.C.

Mayer, K. R. 1980. Teach students to become better postal consumers. Bus. Educ. Forum 34:21–22.

Maynes, E. S. 1976. Decision-Making for Consumers. MacMillan, New York.

McGough, E. 1975. Dollars and Sense. Morrow, New York.

Morton, J. S., and R. R. Rezny. 1978. Consumer Action. Houghton Mifflin, Boston.

Moving Up in Money. 1976. DLM Co., Niles, Ill.

Opsata, M. 1980. Consumer awareness. Instructor 89: 154–156.

Price, R. G., C. Hall, and W. Blockhus. 1978. Business and You As A Consumer, Worker, and Citizen. McGraw-Hill, New York.

Pyrczak, F. 1978. Knowledge of abbreviations used in classified advertisements on employment opportunities. J. Read. 21:493–497.

Richey, J. 1980. Banking Language: A Survival Vocabulary. Janus Book Publishers, Hayward, Calif.

Richey, J. 1979. Clothing Language: A Survival Vocabulary. Janus Book Publishers, Hayward, Calif.

Richey, J. 1980. Credit Language: A Survival Vocabulary. Janus Book Publishers, Hayward, Calif.

Richey, J. 1978. Drugstore Language: A Survival Vocabulary. Janus Book Publishers, Hayward, Calif.

Richey, J. 1978. Job Application Language: A Survival Vocabulary. Janus Book Publishers, Hayward, Calif.

Richey, J. 1978. Restaurant Language: A Survival Vocabulary. Janus Book Publishers, Hayward, Calif.

Richey, J. 1978. Supermarket Language: A Survival Vocabulary. Janus Book Publishers, Hayward, Calif.

Rosenberg, R. R., and J. Risser. 1979. Consumer Math and You. McGraw-Hill, New York.

Roth, E. B. July 1978. Consumer education. Am. Educ. 14:30–31.

Saake, T. F. 1977. Business and Consumer Mathematics. Addison-Wesley, Menlo Park, Calif.

Salzman, S. A., and C. D. Miller. 1978. Mathematics for Business in a Consumer Age. Scott, Foresman and Co., Glenview, Ill.

Scheidell, J. M. 1978. Advertising, Prices, and Consumer Reaction: A Dynamic Analysis. American Enterprise Institute for Public Policy Research, Washington, D.C.

Schmelzel, C. R. 1975. Garage sale; game. Forecast Home Econ. 21:F18–19.

Shapiro, J. 1977. Dollars and Sense. Scholastic Book Services, New York.

Shultheis, P., R. Paine, A. Morgan-Brown, S. Smith, and R. Hanson. 1980. Mathematics for Banking. Media Materials, Baltimore.

Stables, W. A. 1979. Consumer economics and consumer protection. J. Bus. Educ. 54:351–352.

Thompson, L. L. 1978. Consumer Mathematics. Glencoe Publishing, Encino, Calif.

Thurlow, M. L., J. E. Turnure, A. M. Taylos, P. H. Krus, R. Howe, and J. B. Troup. 1975. An assessment of the effectiveness of the Money, Measurement and Time Program for EMR children. University of Minnesota, Minneapolis, Minn. (ERIC Document Reproduction Service no. ED 115-043.)

Warner, B. 1979. How I teach boys and girls; science at the supermarket. Forecast Home Econ. 24:50–51.

Weeks, D. 1977. Be Informed on Banking. New Readers Press, Syracuse, N.Y.

Weeks, D. 1978. Be Informed on Personal Insurance. New Readers Press, Syracuse, N.Y.

Wheeler, J., A. Ford, J. Nietupski, R. Loomis, and L. Brown. 1980. Teaching moderately and severely handicapped adolescents to shop in supermarkets using pocket calculators. Educ. & Train. Ment. Retard. 15:105–111.

Wolf, H. A. 1977. Managing Your Money. Allyn and Bacon, Boston.

WORK

Ackerman, A. S., M. Baygell, and M. Fishel. 1979. It Happened on the Job. Globe Book Co., New York.

Ammerman, G. R. 1975. Your Future in Food Technology Careers. Richard Rosen Press, New York.

Ancona, G. 1976. And What Do You Do? E. P. Dutton and Co., New York.

Anema, D. 1978. Don't Get Fired! 13 Ways to Hold Your Job. Janus Book Publishers, Hayward, Calif.

Anema, D. 1979. Get Hired! 13 Ways to Get a Job. Janus Book Publishers, Hayward, Calif.

Baker, E. 1976. I Want To Be An Auto Mechanic. Children's Press, Chicago.

Baker, E. 1976. I Want To Be A Draftsman. Children's Press, Chicago.

Baker, E. 1976. I Want To Be A Gymnast. Children's Press, Chicago.

Baker, E. 1976. I Want To Be A Postal Clerk. Children's Press, Chicago.

Baker, E. 1975. I Want To Be A Printer. Children's Press, Chicago.

Baker, E. 1975. I Want To Be A Telephone Operator. Children's Press, Chicago.

Baker, J. 1975. They're banking on career orientation. Bus. Educ. Forum 30:11.

Baker, J. F. 1979. Career Ed custom-made for kids. School and Community 66:8–9.

Becker, R. L. 1975. Manual: Reading-Free Vocational Interest Inventory. American Association on Mental Deficiency, Washington, D.C.

Becker, R. L., A. Z. Soforenko, and Q. Widener. 1979. Career education for trainable mentally retarded youth. Educ. & Train. Ment. Retard. 14:101–105.

Belmore, K., and L. Brown. 1976. A job skill inventory strategy for use in a public school vocational training program for severely handicapped potential workers. In: L. Brown, N. Certo, K. Belmore, and T. Crowner (Eds.), Papers and Programs Related to Public School Service for Secondary Age Severely Handicapped Students (vol. 6, part 1.), Madison Metropolitan School District, Madison, Wis.

Bender, M. 1978. Teaching through imitation: Industrial education for the moderately and severely retarded. Educ. & Train. Ment. Retard. 13:9–15.

Berger, M. 1977. Industry at Work. Franklin Watts, New York.

Berndt, W., and D. Pritchard. 1975. The National Guidance Handbook: A Guide to Vocational Education Programs. Science Research Associates, Chicago, Ill.

Black, T. J. 1976. Where do I go from here? The involvement of vocational rehabilitation and occupational education with the learning disabled in North Carolina. Rehabil. Lit. 37:168–171.

Blau, M., et al. 1976. Adventures in the World of Work. Random House, New York.

Blumberg, R. 1976. Fire Fighters. Franklin Watts, New York.

Boland, S. K. 1977. Materials and resources for the career development of retarded individuals. Educ. & Train. Ment. Retard. 12:163–164.

Booth, A. L. 1978. Careers in Politics for the New Woman. Franklin Watts, New York.

Bostwick, B. E. 1977. Finding the Job You've Always Wanted. John Wiley & Sons, New York.

Boynton, R. E. 1976. Your Future in Banking. Richard Rosen Press, New York.

Brolin, D. E. 1977. Career development: A national priority. Educ. & Train. Ment. Retard. 12:154–156.

Brolin, D. E. 1976. Vocational Preparation of Retarded Citizens. Charles E. Merrill Publishing Co., Columbus, Ohio.

Brolin, D. E., and N. C. Gysbers. 1979. Career education for persons with handicaps. Personnel and Guidance J. 58:258–262.

Brolin, D. E., and Kobaska. 1979. Career Education for Handicapped Children and Youth. Charles E. Merrill Publishing Co., Columbus, Ohio.

Buffer, J. J. 1979. Industrial arts and consumer education. Man/Society/Technology 39:28–29.

Burger, G. 1978. Program Model for Projects with Industry. Chicago Jewish Vocational Service, Chicago, Ill.

Cady, J. L. 1975. Pretend you are—an author. Teach. Excep. Children 8(1):26–30.

Canario, J. 1980. The Big Hassle and Other Plays: Getting Along with Authority. A Set of Workbooks Designed for Secondary Students to Develop Language Arts and Socialization Skills. Book 1A. Janus Book Publishers, Hayward, Calif.

Career Education; Texts and supplements (cont.) 1979. Curric. Rev. 18:186–203.

Carlson, B. W., and D. R. Ginglend. 1977. Ready to Work: The Development of Occupational Skills, Attitudes, and Behaviors with Retarded Persons. Abington Press, Nashville, Tenn.

Cawood, L. T. (Ed.). 1975. Work-Oriented Rehabilitation Dictionary and Synonyms. Northwest Association of Rehabilitation Industries, Seattle, Wash.

Cegelka, P. T. 1977. Exemplary projects and programs for the career development of retarded individuals. Educ. & Train. Ment. Retard. 12:16–163.

Christ, H. I. 1979. The World of Careers. Globe Book Co., New York.

Christen, C. A. 1975. Career Education and Home Economics. Houghton Mifflin Co., Boston.

Clennon, S. 1975. Training special students for employment. Teach. Excep. Children 7:106–107.

Clow, J. E. 1980. How are career, consumer, and economic education related? Educ. Leadership 37: 518–522.

Cohen, C., and J. Drugo. 1976. Utilization of the OVIS with an EMR population. Voc. Eval. & Work Adj. Bull. 9(1):22–25.

Columbo, J. C., T. J. Gershan, and L. Sarandoulias. 1978. Guidelines for Employment Orientation Programs—Special Needs Students. Vocational Technical Curriculum Laboratory, Rutgers University, New Brunswick.

Conley, J., and W. Wernick. 1976. Interview Strategies for Career Development. Argus Communications, Niles, Ill.

Cook, J. L. 1980. Technical math in the auto shop. School Shop 39:31.

Cook, M. J. 1980. Solving Life Problems in Occupational Knowledge. McGraw-Hill, New York.

Cormany, R. B. 1975. A careers unit for the junior high EMR student. Educ. & Train. Ment. Retard. 10:151–154.

Cosgrave, G. 1978. Career Planning Series. University of Toronto/Teachers College Press, New York.

Dahl, P. 1978. Mainstreaming Guidebook for Vocational Educators—Teaching the Handicapped. Olympus Publishing Co., Salt Lake City, Utah.

D'Alonzo, B. J. 1977. Trends and issues in career education for the mentally retarded. Educ. & Train. Ment. Retard. 12:156–158.

David, S., and M. Ward. 1978. Vocational education of handicapped students: A guide for policy development. The Council for Exceptional Children, Reston, Va.

Dowdell, D., and J. Dowdell. 1975. Careers in Horticultural Sciences. Julian Messner, New York.

Doyle, R. V. 1975. Your Career in Interior Design. Julian Messner, New York.

Durst, S. B., and W. H. Stern. 1976. Your Future in Real Estate. Richard Rosen Press, New York.

Educational Materials and Equipment. 1978. Careers in Science. Educational Materials and Equipment, New York.

Fair, G. W., and A. R. Sullivan. 1980. Career opportunities for culturally diverse handicapped youth. Excep. Children 46:626–631.

Fenton, D. X. 1977. Ms. Architect. Westminster Press, Philadelphia, Pa.

Fiarotta, N., and P. Fiarotta. 1977. Be What You Want To Be! Workman Publishing Co., New York.

Fuller, J. W., and T. O. Whealon. 1979. Career Education: A Lifelong Process. Nelson-Hall, Chicago, Ill.

Gaynor, P. 1975. Introduction to Vocations for Educable Mentally Retarded. Curriculum Laboratory, Department of Vocational-Technical Education, Rutgers University, New Brunswick.

Gess, D., and R. C. Miles. 1975. Careers: A Supplemental Reading Program, Levels A, B, C. Harcourt, Brace & Jovanowich, New York.

Goldberg, H. R., and B. Greenberger. 1977. The Job Ahead: A Career Reading Series. Science Research Associates, Chicago, Ill.

Greenebaum, L. G. 1976. Looking Forward to a Career in Electronics. Dillon Press, Minneapolis, Minn.

Greif, E. C. 1979. Store Tack: An Introduction to Retail Merchandising; Reading Level, Secondary; Interest Level, Grades 7–12. Fearon-Pitman Publishers, Belmont, Calif.

Gysbers, N. C., and L. L. West. 1975. Career Education: Its Implications for the Educable Retarded (working paper no. 3). University of Missouri, Columbia.

Halacy, D. S. 1975. Survival in the World of Work. Scribner's, New York.

Harrison, W. C. 1977. Here is Your Career: Auto Mechanic. G. P. Putnam's Sons, New York.

Hawes, G. R., M. Hawes, and C. Fleming. 1977. Careers Today: A Guide to Good Jobs Without a Degree. Taplinger Publishing Co., New York.

Holloway, J. A., and J. T. Naper. 1975. Introducing Career Concepts: Series I and Series II. Science Research Associates, Chicago, Ill.

Hopkins, L. B. 1980. Help wanted! Jobs for tomorrow. Lang. Arts 57:66–69.

Hoppock, R. 1976. Occupational Information. McGraw-Hill Book Company, New York.

Horton, L. 1975. Art Careers: A Concise Guide. Franklin Watts, New York.

Horton, L., et al. 1976. Career Concise Guides. Franklin Watts, New York.

Hoyt, K. B. 1975. Career Education: Contributions Evolving to a Concept. Olympus, Salt Lake City, Utah.

Hutchinson, H. D. 1975. Horizons: Readings and Communication Activities for Voc-Tech Students. Benziger, Bruce and Glencoe, Beverly Hills, Calif.

Jew, W., and R. Tong. 1976. Janus Job Planner. Janus Book Publishers, Hayward, Calif.

Job Experience Kits. Science Research Associates, Chicago, Ill. 60611.

Kahn, C., W. Jew, and R. Tong. 1980. My Job Application File: Workbook and Teacher's Manual. Janus Book Publishers, Hayward, Calif.

Karger, D. W. 1978. How to Choose a Career. Franklin Watts, New York.

Karlin, M. S. 1975. Solving Your Career Mystery. Richards Rosen Press, New York.

Kemp, J. E. 1977. Instructional Design. Fearon-Pitman

Publishers, Belmont, Calif.

Knox, Carolyn. 1980. Getting A Job. Media Materials, Baltimore.

Kosmakos, M., and L. A. Decker. 1977. A group vocational project for LD students. Acad. Ther. 13:87–90.

Lake, T. (Ed.) n.d. Career Education: Exemplary Programs for the Handicapped. The Council for Exceptional Children, Reston, Va.

Leggett, C. L. 1978. Special education and career education: A call for a new partnership. Educ. & Train. Ment. Retard. 13:430–431.

Liebers, A. 1975. You Can Be A Mechanic. Lothrop, Lee and Shephard, New York.

Lutz, R. J., and L. A. Phelps. 1977. Career Exploration and Preparation for the Special Needs Learner. Allyn and Bacon, Boston.

McGonagle, B., and M. McGonagle. 1975. Careers in Aviation in the Sky and on the Ground. Lothrop, Lee and Shepard, New York.

Millard, R., et al. 1975. Careers in the Earth Sciences. Julian Messner, New York.

Mori, A. 1979. Vocational education and special education: A new partnership in career education. J. Career Educ. 6:55–59.

Morrison, P. C. 1978. The Business Office. McGraw-Hill, New York.

Moynahan, Terry. 1980. Vocational education and the handicapped. Today's Educ. 2:47–49.

National Center of Research in Vocational Education. 1977. Professional Teacher Education Module Series: Develop A Unit of Instruction. Ohio State University, Columbus.

National Textbook Co. 1977–79. Career Horizons. National Textbook Co., Skokie, Ill.

Newsweek. 1977. Earning A Living: A Realistic Guide to Working. Newsweek Multimedia, Pleasantville.

Newton, D. E. 1977. Activities for Exploring Health Careers. J. Weston Walch, Portland, Oreg.

Newton, D. E. 1977. Spirit Master Activities for Exploring Careers in Sports and Recreation. J. Weston Walch, Portland, Oreg.

Nolan, E. J. 1979. Strategies for implementing career awareness. School Couns. 26:350–353.

Occupations (Deluxe Inlay Puzzles). Judy Co., Minneapolis, Minn.

Olympus Research Corporation. 1975. An assessment of vocational education programs for the handicapped under Part B of the 1968 Amendments to the Vocational Education Act. Olympus Research Corporation, Salt Lake City, Utah.

Parker, B., and D. Buchkoski. 1978. Vocational Exploration Curriculum. St. Paul Technical Vocational Institute, Program for Deaf Students, St. Paul, Minn.

Parker, D. H., S. W. Parker, and W. H. Fryback. 1975. Decision Making for Career Development: A Role Playing Program. Science Research Associates, Chicago, Ill.

Pearson, R. E. 1977. Building Maintenance Course of Study Outline. Vocational-Technical Curriculum Laboratory, Rutgers University, New Brunswick.

Perlman, L. 1978. Job Placement Study. National Industries for the Severely Handicapped, Washington, D.C.

Peterson, M. P. 1976. Job Lab I and II. Houghton Mifflin, Boston.

Phelps, H. A. 1976. Competency-based inservice education for secondary school personnel serving special needs students in vocational education. A formative field test evaluation. University of Illinois, Urbana, Ill. (Final Report, HEW Project No. 498AH-500481.)

President's Committee on Employment of the Handicapped. 1976. Affirmative Action to Employ the Handicapped: A Pocket Guide. President's Committee on Employment of the Handicapped. Washington, D.C.

Psychological Corporation. 1976, 1977. Industrial Reading Test (IRT): A Test of Reading Ability Designed with Trainees for Technical or Vocational Training Programs, Grades 9–12 and Adult. Psychological Corporation, New York.

Rice, R. 1978–79. Activities for Exploring Careers. J. Weston Walch, Portland, Oreg.

Richardson, S. A. 1978. Careers of mentally retarded young persons: Services, jobs, and interpersonal relations. Am. J. Ment. Defic. 82:349–358.

Schalock, R. 1976. Competitive Employment Screening Test and Manual. Mid-Nebraska Mental Retardation Services, Hastings, Neb.

Schmidt, W. I., and B. F. Dykeman. 1979. Testing the effectiveness of a career education program for potential dropouts. Education 99:287–290.

Schweich, P. D. 1975. The development of choices: An educational approach to employment. Acad. Ther. 10: 277–283.

Sewell, W. H., and R. M. Hauser. 1975. Education, Occupation and Earnings. Academic Press, New York.

Shultheis, P., R. Paine, A. Morgan-Brown, S. Smith, and R. Hanson. 1980. Career Mathematics. Media Materials, Baltimore.

Stodden, R. A., A. Robert, J. Casale, and E. S. Schwartz. 1977. Work evaluation and the mentally retarded: Review and recommendations. Ment. Retard. 15:25–27.

Stodden, R. A., R. N. Ianacone, and A. L. Lazar. 1979. Occupational interests and mentally retarded people: Review and recommendations. Ment. Retard.

17:294–298.

TMR Pre-Vocational Training Kit. 1978. Occupational Education. Mafex Associates, Johnstown, Pa.

Tesolowski, D. G. 1979. Job Readiness Training Curriculum. Stout Vocational Rehabilitation Institute, University of Wisconsin, Stout, Menomonie.

Thornton, L. J. 1979. Reading sensitivity in post-secondary occupational education. Lifelong Learning: The Adult Years 3:12–15.

Todd, R. D., and K. R. Todd. 1975. Aim for a Job Working with Your Hands. Richards Rosen Press, New York.

Vacca, R. T. 1978. The reading-career education connection. Read. Horiz. 18:138–141.

Van Etten, C., and B. Watson. 1977. Career education materials for the learning disabled. J. Learn. Disabil. 10:264–270.

Vogelsang, J. 1978. Find the Career That's Right for You! Hart Publishing, New York.

Walker, Bonnie. 1980. Getting A Job Series. Media Materials, Baltimore.

Walker, Bonnie. 1980. On The Job Skills Filmstrip Series. Media Materials, Baltimore.

Walker, Bonnie L., and Barbara Wainer. 1980. Work-Related Skills Series. Media Materials, Baltimore.

Washburn, W. Y. 1975. Where to go in voc-ed, for secondary LD students. Acad. Ther. 11(1):31–35.

Weisenstein, G. R. 1977. Vocational education's contribution in the career development of retarded individuals. Educ. & Train. Ment. Retard. 12:158–160.

Weisenstein, G. R. 1976. Vocational education for exceptional persons: Have educators let it drop through a crack in their services continuum? Thresholds Sec. Educ. 2:16.

Weisenstein, G. R. 1975. Using a pictorial job training manual in an occupational training program for high school EMR students. Educ. & Train. Ment. Retard. 10:30–35.

LEISURE EXPERIENCES

AAHPER. 1975. Leisure Today. Selected Readings. AAHPER, Washington, D.C.

AAHPERD. 1976. Education for leisure. J. Phys. Educ. & Rec. AAHPERD, Washington, D.C.

Ackerman, J. V. 1979. Developmental Physical Activity: An Individualized Approach. Hawkins and Associates, Washington, D.C.

Amary, I. 1975. Creative Recreation for the Mentally Retarded. Charles C Thomas, Springfield, Ill.

Appell, L. S. 1979. Enhancing learning and enriching lives: Arts in the education of handicapped children. Teach. Excep. Children 11:74–76.

Arlin, M., and G. Roth. 1978. Pupils' use of time while reading comics and books. Am. Educ. Res. J. 15:

201–216.

Brannan, S. 1977. A special education viewpoint: Consultation in the public schools. In: J. Goldstein (Ed.), Consultation: Enhancing Leisure Service Delivery to Handicapped Children and Youth. National Recreation and Park Association, Arlington, Va.

Brannan, S. 1979. Project Explore: Expanding Programs and Learning in Outdoor Recreation/Education for the Handicapped. Hawkins and Associates, Washington, D.C.

Brannan, S. 1975. Trends and issues in leisure education for the handicapped. In: E. Fairchild and L. Neal (Eds.), Common-Unity in the Community—A Forward Looking Program of Recreation and Leisure Services for the Handicapped. University of Oregon, Center of Leisure Studies, Eugene.

Byers, E. S. 1979. Wilderness camping as a therapy for emotionally disturbed children: A critical review. Excep. Children 45:628–635.

Byrnes, M. M. 1980. Basic skills bingo. Teacher 97: 77.

Choate, R., R. Berg, L. Kjelson, and E. Troth. 1976. Music for Early Childhood. American Book Co., New York.

Cormany, R. B. 1974. Outdoor education for the retarded child. Educ. & Train. Ment. Retard. 9:66–69.

Curtis, R. E. 1976. Your Future in Music. Richard Rosen Press, New York.

Evans, J., and J. E. Moore. 1979. Art Moves the Basics Along. Vehicle Units. Evan-Moor Corp., Hollywood, Calif.

Fait, G., and G. Fait. 1976. Physical Education for the Elementary School Child. W. B. Saunders, Philadelphia, Pa.

Favell, J., and P. Cannon. 1977. An evaluation of entertainment materials for severely retarded persons. Am. J. Ment. Defic. 81:357–362.

Fenton, B., and D. X. Fenton. 1978. Tourism and Hospitality. Westminster Press, Philadelphia, Pa.

Funk, D. 1980. Guidelines for Planning Travel for the Physically Handicapped: A Handbook for Travel Agents, Tour Wholesalers, and Recreation/Travel Personnel. Hawkins and Associates, Washington, D.C.

Gair, S. 1976. The GMVR Program, Receptive, Expressive Learning Through Art. (mimeo). Dr. Sondra B. Gair, 5134 Wissioning Road, Washington, D.C.

Goldstein, J. 1977. Consultation: Enhancing Leisure Service Delivery to Handicapped Children and Youth. National Recreation and Park Association, Arlington, Va.

Graham, R. M. 1975. Music for the Exceptional Child. Music Educator's National Conference, Reston,

Va.

Hall, J. T., N. H. Sweeny, and J. H. Esser. 1976. Until the Whistle Blows: A Collection of Games, Dances, and Activities for the Four-to-Eight Year Olds. Goodyear Publishing Co., Santa Monica, Calif.

Hallenbeck, Phyllis N. 1976. Remediation with comic strips. J. Learn. Disabil. 9:11–15.

Hawkins, D. 1976. A Systems Model for Developing a Leisure Education Program for Handicapped Children and Youth. Leisure Information Service, Washington, D.C.

Hedberg, Sally. 1980. Outdoor education can help the handicapped. Today's Educ. 2:54–56.

Hirst, L. T., and T. O'Such. 1979. Using musical television commercials to teach reading. Teach. Excep. Children 11:80–81.

Joswiak, K. 1979. Leisure Counseling Program Materials for the Developmentally Disabled. Hawkins and Associates, Washington, D.C.

Labanowich, S., N. Andrews, and J. N. Pollock. 1978. Recreation for the Homebound Aging. Hawkins and Associates, Washington, D.C.

Laus, M. D. 1977. Travel Instruction for the Handicapped. Charles C Thomas, Springfield, Ill.

Lavine, R. 1980. Personal Computers Serving People —A Guide to Human Service Applications in the Fields of Education, Rehabilitation, Creative Art, Recreation and Leisure. Hawkins and Associates, Washington, D.C.

MacWilliam, L. J. 1977. Travel and community experience for multiply handicapped students. Teach. Excep. Children 9:49–51.

Marion, R. 1979. Leisure time activities for trainable mentally retarded adolescents. Teach. Excep. Children 11(4):154–158.

Marlowe, M. 1980. Games analysis: Designing games for handicapped children. Teach. Excep. Children 12:48–51.

McCrory, R. 1979. Art. Good Apple, Carthage, Ill.

McKechnie, G. E. 1979. Manual for the Leisure Activities Blank. Consulting Psychology Press, Palo Alto, Calif.

Mosby, C. V., and T. M. Shea. 1977. Camping for Special Children. Author, St. Louis, Mo.

Nathanson, D. W., A. Cynamon, and K. Lehman. 1975. Miami snow poets: Creative writing for exceptional children. Teach. Excep. Children 8(3):87–92.

Nesbitt, J. A. 1978. Educating the Handicapped Child for Leisure Fulfillment. Recreation Education Program, The University of Iowa, Iowa City.

Orlick, T. 1978. Winning Through Cooperation: Competitive Insanity—Cooperative Alternatives. Hawkins and Associates, Washington, D.C.

Overs, R., et al. 1977. Avocational Counseling Manual: A Complete Guide to Leisure Guidance. Hawkins and Associates, Washington, D.C.

Pangrazi, R. P. 1975. Dynamic Physical Education for Elementary School Children. Burgess, Minneapolis, Minn.

Reber, J., and C. Huyck. 1976. Art Survival Guide for the Elementary Teacher. Fearon-Pitman Publishers, Belmont, Calif.

Rousseau, D. M. 1978. Relationship of work to nonwork. J. Appl. Psychol. 63:513–517.

Shields, E. W. 1979. Intramurals: An avenue for developing leisure values. J. Phys. Educ. & Recr. 50:75–77.

Shultheis, P., R. Paine, A. Morgan-Brown, S. Smith, and R. Hanson. 1980. Traveler's Mathematics. Media Materials, Baltimore.

Special Olympics, 1980. Sports Skills Instructional Program. Special Olympics, Washington, D.C.

Thiagarajan, S. 1976. Designing instructional games for handicapped learner. Focus on Exceptional Children 7.

Tolman, M. N. 1979. Multiplication football. Arith. Teach. 27:36.

Triebel, J., and M. Manning. 1976. I Think I Can Learn to Cook or I Can Cook to Think and Learn. Academic Therapy Publications, San Rafael, Calif.

Verhoven, P., and J. Goldstein. 1976. Leisure Activity Participation and Handicapped Populations: An Assessment of Research Needs. National Recreation and Park Association, Arlington, Va.

Vinton, D., et al. 1978. Camping and Environmental Education for Handicapped Children and Youth. Hawkins and Associates, Washington, D.C.

Wehman, P. 1976. A leisure time activities curriculum for the developmentally disabled. Educ. & Train. Ment. Retard. 11:309–313.

Wehman, P. 1978. Effects of different environmental conditions on leisure time activity of the severely and profoundly handicapped. J. Spec. Educ. 12:183–193.

Wehman, P. 1977. Helping The Mentally Retarded Acquire Play Skills: A Behavioral Approach. Charles C Thomas, Springfield, Ill.

Wehman, P. 1979. Teaching table games to severely retarded children. Ment. Retard. 17:150–151.

Wheeler, P. 1980. The Sports Skills Instructional Program. Special Olympics, Washington, D.C.

Wittenmyer, J., M. Parisi, and M. Kurth. 1976. A Guide to Leisure-Time Activity Programs for Developmentally Disabled Adults. Wisconsin Association for Retarded Citizens, Madison.

Woodward, E. 1980. Mathematics lesson for super bowl week. School Sci. & Math. 80:65–68.

Yvon, B., et al. 1980. Stalking math on the nature trail.

Early Years 10:40–41.

Zeyen, D., R. Lancaster, and L. Odum. 1977. Leisure Education Advancement Project: Curriculum K-12 and Teachers, Curriculum Manual. National Recreation and Park Association, Arlington, Va.

INDEX

Buildings—*continued*
in, 80
stores and business location
in, 78
temperature determined from
signs on, 85
time determined from clock
on, 85
Bulletin board, reviewing at
work, 166
Bus
cost of trip, 252
for going to work, 161
stops, 80
Business
hours of, 78
location of, 94
in office building, 78
by sign, 77–78
time needed to arrive at, 94–95
see also Work
Business letters, 245
Business occupations, *see* Work

Cafeteria
cost of meals in, 251
location of at work, 165
meals ordered from, 76
meals paid for at, 92
Calculator, 55, 57
directions for operating, 175
operating at work, 198, 216
for simple computations,
69–70
Calendar, 20
determining days of work
with, 160
notations written on, 43
school, 59
using, 45
Calisthenics, 229
on charts and posters, 57–58
see also Physical fitness;
Sports
Campfire, 231
Camping, 230–232
campfire, 231
cooking, 231
fishing, 230, 249
meals, 232
food required for, 249
Card games
card identification, 227
face value of cards, 248
playing and scoring, 225–226
Cards, *see* Credit cards
Cars
cost of trip in, 252
jobs related to, *see* Work
odometer, 95
parking meter operation, 83,
93
parking signs, 82, 92
road maps, 81–82

scale, 95
safe driving, 162
symbols within, 81, 84
traffic signs, 81, 95
Catalogs
office material ordered from,
195
placing orders in, 126–127
services from, 112–113
Catalog store orders, 89
Chance games, playing and
scoring, 226, 227
Charitable contributions, review
of, 122
Checking account, *see* Banks
Circuit breakers, 32
Cleaning products
bathroom, 28
kitchen, 18–19, 44–45
Clock
on buildings, 85
setting alarm, 24, 45, 204
see also Time
Clothes dryer, 30–31
Clothing
buying, 139–141
consumer skills for, 107–108
jobs related to, *see* Work
labeled for work, 184
needed for work, 160
tailor altering, 141–142
washing and dry cleaning, 24,
25, 141
coin-operated, 142
Coffee, preparation, 13–14
Coin collections, 233
Coins, *see* Currency/coin usage
Collections, *see* Hobbies
Combination lock
for apartment storage room,
33
for school locker, 54
unlocking, 67
Communication media, *see*
Work
Community, 73
mathematics in, 74, 92
address sequences, 94
apartment number, 94
mail schedules, 92
meals at restaurants paid
for, 92
odd and even street number-
ing, 94
odometer and map scale, 95
parking meter, 93
parking signs, 92
sample instructional plan,
96–97
taxi fare, 93
telephone usage, 92
time needed for arrival at
bank, business or store,
94–95
traffic signs, 95

transit schedules, 94
vending machine, 92
reading in, 74
apartment number location,
77
brochures and flyers, 85, 89
building or house location,
77
bus identification of, 80
business and store hours,
78
business and store location,
78
bus stops, 80
car operation, 81–83, 84
clocks on buildings, 85
elevators, 83
entrances and exits, 78
fire exits, 78
mail schedule, 74–75
meals from menu, 76
newspapers, 84
parking meters, 83
parking signs, 82
personal card location, 85
postage, 74
posters and notices, 85
public building demeanor,
80
public restrooms, 74
road maps, 81–82
sample instructional plan,
86–87
shelter area location, 80
street location and identification, 77
street map, 80
taxi fare, 83
telephones, 74
temperature determination,
85
transit maps, 81, 82
transit schedules, 81, 83
vending machines, 76
warning signs, 78, 79
services in, *see* Services, in
home and community
writing in, 74, 88
appointments, 88
forms, 88
notebook maintenance, 88
sample instructional plan,
90–91
surveys and petitions, 88
telephone directory, 88
Compensation, for work, 166,
205, 206
Congratulatory cards, to fellow
workers, 185
Construction, *see* Work
Consumer skills, 99
mathematics for, 100, 135
clothing, 139–142
drugs and medicine,
138–139